The battle for a culture always .... a .... for hearts and minds, and the fight for hearts and minds is always a fight for words, especially the power of defining words. In this important book, Scott Allen has provided an essential handbook for our most significant cultural conflict: the words that matter most, how they are being redefined, and the definitions we must fight for.

John Stonestreet
President of Colson Center and host of *Breakpoint*

Ten Words is an eye-opening book. Words such as *love, justice, human, freedom,* and *sex* no longer mean what they used to. Allen is right that words have power. If we want to disciple the next generation of young Christians and wisely engage our culture, we need to clearly understand the reasons behind these shifts in meaning and be discerning in our use of words. This book will help you do just that.

Sean McDowell, PhD
Professor at Talbot School of Theology, author or editor of over twenty books, and a popular YouTuber.

Words matter. Successful revolutions begin by rewriting the dictionary to radically alter how people think about core concepts such as truth, justice, and humanity. Scott Allen's fascinating exploration of ten essential words shows how this battle over words works and how to reclaim their biblically based meanings to bring restoration and flourishing. This is an excellent book for anyone who wants to think more clearly—and biblically—about how we use language.

Jeff Myers, PhD
President, Summit Ministries

Scott Allen's book hands us the key to reclaiming our culture and nation. True words give life, vision, and purpose to families and nations, but enemies of the gospel hijack words to destroy us. Our weakness is their greater power. Revival requires Christians to speak words with true, biblical definitions. Only God's truth is true love.

Kelly Monroe Kullberg
Founder of the Veritas Forum and author of *Finding God at Harvard.*
General Secretary, American Association of Evangelicals (AAE)

I thoroughly enjoyed this book. I immediately understood its utmost importance, and I think you will, too. The power of words to shape us and to shape culture is so simple and yet so profound an idea. I thank God that Scott wrote this book. It is a blessing, truly. His mastery of the subject and the certainty of his thesis (just read the last paragraph of the introduction!), combined with the simple clarity of his writing, makes this book both readable and urgent. If you want to know why America is rapidly becoming unrecognizable, this book makes it obvious. The stakes could not be higher, especially for our children and our children's children. A book like this concerns the cultural battles ahead and the ones that are raging right now. Read it and be equipped to take the stand we all must take.

Jon Benzinger
Lead Pastor, Redeemer Bible Church (Gilbert, Arizona), President, Redeemer Seminary, and Founder of *HelpingPastors.org*

As the secular, postmodern world continues to demand the right to redefine its own reality and truth, Scott Allen's book serves as a timely reminder for Christians. It underscores the urgent need for an intentional, authentic Christian philosophy of first principles. Allen's book is a Declaration of Intellectual Independence from a world that doesn't share even the most basic principles of right, justice, or truth with Christian believers. Christians must not be content to permit the world to define the truth for them but must seek it at the font: the cornerstone, the solid rock, Jesus Christ. Allen begins a long-overdue conversation among Christians about whether we will finally begin to take responsibility for our worldview or abandon thought to the secular world. I recommend that Christians interested in taking responsibility for their fundamental worldview begin by reading and considering Allen's book as the beginning of what must become a broad, fruitful conversation among Christians about the roots of our intellectual and social lives.

Dr. Benjamin L. Mabry
Lincoln Memorial University

One of the most critical battles our society is currently facing is the war over language. Whoever controls language establishes culture. By combining a social and cultural understanding with a missional theology of discipling nations, Scott Allen addresses the importance of language in this timely and highly relevant book. Allen reveals the Scripture's importance in forming Western culture. This book is about his refusal to embrace the modern redefinition of critical words and to recover their true biblical meaning. It carries the power to truly help people and impact culture.

Teófilo Hayashi
Senior Pastor of Zion Church (Sao Paulo, Brazil); Leader and Founder of the Dunamis Movement; and Co-leader of The Send

Scott Allen's resources have been a staple in my ministry for years. I've used them to train pastors, parents, grandparents, and the board members of some of the world's largest evangelical ministries. Scott has written a timely book that every Christian needs to read. Secularists are guilty of linguistic theft. They steal biblical words, redefine them to mean something different, and then use those words to shape our beliefs into secular views and values. This book will help you and those you love develop biblical clarity about ten important topics and remain deeply rooted in God's Word. Highly recommended.

Dr. Josh Mulvihill
Executive Director, Renewanation
Author of *Biblical Worldview*

The redefinition of critical biblical terms is one of the most important emerging fields of defending the Faith. Scott Allen makes an important contribution to that effort by writing a highly accessible book I hope many Christians will read and share with others.

Krista Bontrager
Vice President of Educational Programs and Biblical Integrity at the Center for Biblical Unity and Co-author of *Walking in Unity*

In a historic moment of embedded relativism, Scott Allen is joining a growing prophetic army of truth soldiers pushing back with both antidotes and warnings about the cost relativism has already demanded from us. Having chosen ten significant words to defend their historical meaning, Scott proceeds to give us all an excellent primer on biblical worldview as an essential housing within which these ten words must dwell. He pulls plenty of quotes from today's cultural experts on related subjects to add to the depth of his observations. Scott has done his homework in this book, and it deserves a "must read" label. Thank you, Scott!

Dennis Peacocke
Founder GoStrategic

In every generation, Christians are called to contend for the truth of the gospel. This truth is always communicated in language. Unfortunately, many Christians today are confused by the redefinition and distortion of uniquely Christian words and concepts. As a local church pastor, I cannot emphasize enough how helpful this book is. Scott gives a clear and structured explanation of the changing landscape of language and morality in our culture today and points us, by contrast, to the unchanging truth of God's Word. *Ten Words* is a must-read for any Christian in the West today. This book is a simple, clear, and timely work that helps Christians separate truth from error when morality and language are being redefined in our culture.

Blaine Braden
Lead Pastor, Eastmont Church (Bend, Oregon)

As much as ideas have consequences, language is the vehicle for perceived meaning. When words are redefined—whether knowingly or unknowingly—confusion ensues. Many of our day's great confusions and debates can be traced back to the varied meanings of shared words. Scott affirms what we often take for granted in this thoughtful and systematic work. Whoever controls the language and its meaning controls the culture. This is a wake-up call to return to the true meanings of words and understand their value and impact on the culture.

Katherine Gallagher
CEO of GoStrategic

10 WORDS
TO HEAL OUR
BROKEN WORLD

10 WORDS
TO HEAL OUR
BROKEN WORLD

MARRIAGE
JUSTICE
SEX
FREEDOM
HUMAN
AUTHORITY
LOVE
TRUTH
BEAUTY
FAITH

RESTORING THE MEANING OF
OUR MOST IMPORTANT WORDS

SCOTT DAVID ALLEN

credo
house publishers

Published in the United States of America by Credo House Publishers,
a division of Credo Communications, LLC, Grand Rapids, Michigan
credohousepublishers.com

Unless otherwise noted, Scripture quotations are from the Holy Bible, New International Version®, NIV® Copyright ©1973, 1978, 1984, 2011 by Biblica, Inc.®. Used by permission. All rights reserved worldwide.

ISBN: 978-1-62586-286-0

Cover and interior design by Frank Gutbrod
Editing by Donna Huisjen and Stan Guthrie

Printed in the United States of America
First edition

In reconstructing a society in collapse,
the first priority is to restore the proper meaning of words.

CONFUCIUS

The words of the Lord are flawless,
like silver purified in a crucible,
like gold refined seven times.

PSALM 12:6

	True Meaning	Redefined to Mean
Truth	That which accords with, or corresponds with, objective reality.	(1) An internal, personal, and subjective sense of reality that exists only in the mind. (2) A social construct created to advantage the dominant group.
Human	Pertaining to man (male and female), mankind, humans are physical and spiritual beings, created by God in His image, with intrinsic dignity, incalculable worth, and unalienable rights to life and liberty. Humans are created for an intimate relationship with their Creator, as well as relationships with one another. God created humans to wisely steward and govern the created world, and they are accountable to Him for how they carry out this task.	(1) A form of animal life, the product of a purposeless process of material evolution; a biological machine. (2) A radically autonomous, willing creature. An independent, self-determining agent. (3) A socially and historically determined being, a representative of a particular culture or identity group.
Sex	(1) The God-created male-female division. (2) Sexual intercourse between a man and a woman; a comprehensive one-flesh union of heart, mind, spirit, and body, often issuing in the gift of children. Sexual intercourse is a gift from God exclusively for the uniting of husband and wife in marriage.	(1) Synonymous with gender, a social construct; a person's subjective sense of their sexual identity, without regard to biology or anatomy. (2) The ultimate source of personal identity and meaning. (3) Any form of recreational sexual activity done to give pleasure.
Marriage	A God-ordained, comprehensive, exclusive, and permanent union that brings a man and a woman together as husband and wife, to be father and mother to any children their union brings into being. It is based on the anthropological truth that men and women are different and complementary, the biological fact that reproduction depends on a man and a woman, and the social reality that children need both a mother and a father.[1]	A legally recognized, romantic caregiving relationship between consenting adults who intend to live together as sexual and domestic partners.
Freedom	The capacity to self-govern; to act according to one's choices within God's created order and under His moral law.	The power or right to act, speak or think as one wants without hindrance or restraint.

Authority	The power or right to issue commands, rules, or laws and to ensure they are carried out. Human authority is delegated from God, the supreme authority, and is accountable to Him. When properly exercised, authority creates conditions in which people thrive by providing wise leadership in a context of ordered liberty. Jesus, our model for authority in practice, sacrificially serves those under authority for their good.	An arbitrary, self-serving, and often harsh and oppressive use of power and control. A concentration of power in human government or rule that is unaccountable to God, constitutional limits, or the people under authority.
Justice	Conformity to God's moral standard as revealed in the Ten Commandments and the Royal Law: "love your neighbor as yourself." (1) Living in right relationship with God and others; giving people their due as image-bearers of God. (2) Impartially rendering judgment, righting wrongs, and meting out punishment for lawbreaking. A task reserved for God and God-ordained authorities including parents in the home, elders in the church, teachers in the school, and civil authorities in the state.	Deconstructing traditional systems and structures deemed to be oppressive, and redistributing power and resources from oppressors to their victims in the pursuit of equality of outcome.
Faith	To assent to the weight of evidence; to trust in the truthfulness and reliability of something or someone based on a careful search of available evidence and personal experience.	Affirming the truthfulness of something without regard to evidence, or even despite a lack of evidence.
Beauty	A combination of qualities present in a thing or person, both externally and internally, that gives joy and deep satisfaction. Beauty can move us deeply and fill us with awe and wonder. Because God is its ultimate source, beauty has an objective reality that transcends personal tastes.	A combination of aesthetic qualities that appeal to one's personal, subjective senses or tastes. Beauty is entirely a matter of personal preference and individual expression.
Love	(1) A source of pleasure, joy, or delight. (2) A strong affection, often accompanied by romantic feelings and sexual attraction. (3) To value, cherish, or treasure. (4) Fidelity and devotion. Faithful commitment. (5) To seek the good of another, to give for his or her benefit, even at a significant personal cost.	(1) A source of pleasure, joy, or delight. (2) A strong affection, often accompanied by romantic feelings and sexual attraction.

CONTENTS

FOREWORD

If you are concerned about the events unfolding in our world today, this book is a must-read. Western elites, in tandem with the woke mob, have effectively transformed the landscape of our culture here in the United States and throughout the Western world from that of flourishing, pluralistic democracies to relativistic, feelings-driven tyrannies. But, you might wonder, how did they do this? In short, they did this through the redefining of words.

I, Darrow Miller, am a co-founder of the Disciple Nations Alliance. I'm also an author and teacher. In my youth I was mentored by Francis Schaeffer in Switzerland, and I have worked for fifty years to help the poor and hungry. I've lived at the unlikely intersection of worldview and development for most of my life. I have seen firsthand the power of language to build culture and the power of culture to build families, communities, and nations.

I recruited and trained Scott Allen to work overseas as a cross-cultural missionary in Japan forty years ago. Scott has become a good friend and co-worker at the Disciple Nations Alliance. He is compassionate, thoughtful, analytical, and passionate about ideas. We share an interest in the power of words to shape a culture and a nation. In addition to being an excellent administrator, Scott is a gifted writer who has authored or co-authored several books.

Scott's interest in words started decades ago and has culminated in this book. Scott understands that words serve as containers for ideas and that ideas have consequences.

Christian worldview teacher Dennis Peacocke says,

Whoever controls the language controls the culture. Words have incredible power because they set the agendas

1

of whole nations. The words we use describe a situation or problem and frame how we approach it. They actually trigger a series of emotional and conceptual releases within us that capture our minds and inhibit our ability to view reality from another perspective. It's not bullets that ultimately win wars; it's words. A bullet won't make you die for someone, but the right word lodged within you will make you fearless.

When we think of words in terms of bullets, we realize that enemies of the gospel have effectively disarmed the church. The church today, often ignorant of the biblical definitions of words, learns from our dominant postmodern culture how to define essential words like *human*, *sex*, *marriage*, and *justice*.

Scott has seen the expansion and power of this tactic and now offers you the antidote: the recovery of truth through the recovery of God's definitions of words.

In this book Scott quotes historian Thomas Cahill's book *The Gift of the Jews* to illustrate where the language of freedom and opportunity came from. Cahill writes:

> The Jews gave us a whole new vocabulary. . . . Most of our best words, in fact—new, adventure, surprise, unique, individual, person, vocation; time, history, future, freedom, progress, spirit; faith, hope, justice [and I would add love, compassion, human dignity, and human rights]—are the gifts of the Jews.

The Jews gave us this language through the Bible. In *Ten Words to Heal Our Broken World: Restoring the True Meaning of our Most Important Words*, Scott contrasts the historic, biblical meanings of essential words with today's current, redefined meanings to show how these critical word that have shaped the West have been consciously changed and manipulated to conform to the atheistic, materialistic, and postmodern worldview of our age.

If you are watching the world shake under your feet and our culture decline before your eyes and want to understand why this is happening, you must understand the power of words.

May we, as the church, understand our heritage and the language of freedom. May we recover the lost tools of culture-building as we recover the words that can heal our land. In these chaotic times, may we build cultures founded on the Rock of Jesus through the power of His Word.

Darrow L. Miller
Phoenix, Arizona
August 2024

INTRODUCTION

"Through your offspring, all nations on earth will be blessed" (Genesis 12:3; 22:18). So promised God to Abraham, the forefather of Israel, and of the church (Galatians 3:7–9). The great, unchanging plan of God through the ages is to work through His people, the offspring of Abraham, to bless the nations He loves.

God saved His people for a purpose—to be a light to the nations and work for the good of our neighbors. To be part of creating cultures that are free, just, and compassionate. To be salt that preserves all that is good, true, and beautiful from dissolution and decline.

We know that sharing the gospel is central to this task, as we invite our neighbors into a personal relationship with their Creator through faith in Jesus Christ. The gospel is the starting point of renewal and transformation, personally and culturally. But there is much more work to do. Cultures thrive in the rich soil of truth, and the biblical definitions of words and language lead us into truth.

Words are incredibly powerful. "In the beginning was the Word, and the Word was with God, and the Word was God," begins the Gospel of John. The Word spoke the universe into being. It's no overstatement to say that we live in a word-based universe.

God created us in His image with the capacity to use words and language to create culture. "Culture lives by language," wrote Catholic historian Robert Lewis Wilken, "and the sentiments, thoughts, and feelings of a Christian culture are formed and carried by the language of the Scriptures."

In his masterful book *The Gifts of the Jews,*[2] historian Thomas Cahill tells us that four thousand years ago Abram (later Abraham) heard the voice of God and followed that voice in faith. As he turned from worshiping pagan idols to the One True God, his understanding of the world was transformed. Subsequently, his vocabulary changed, and so did the world's. He writes:

> The Jews gave us a whole new vocabulary, a whole new Temple of the Spirit, an inner landscape of ideas and feelings that had never been known before . . . We can hardly get up in the morning or cross the street without being Jewish. We dream Jewish dreams and hope Jewish hopes. Most of our best words, in fact—new, adventure, surprise, unique, individual, person, vocation; time, history, future, freedom, progress, spirit; faith, hope, justice [and I would add love, compassion, human dignity, and human rights]—are the gifts of the Jews.

I love the title, *The Gifts of the Jews*, because it correctly describes these words as "gifts." Indeed, they are very precious gifts God gave as He spoke through the Holy Scriptures, which He entrusted to the Jewish nation and the church for the whole world's good.

These words and concepts created what Cahill described as "an inner landscape of ideas and feelings that had never been known before." In other words, they created a new mental space that enabled people and nations to prosper and flourish.

Do we see these words as priceless gifts from God? Not given *to* us, but given *through* us, to the world? We should.

Most of us take words for granted. We spend our days using them, not thinking deeply about their meanings, or where their definitions came from. We assume the words we use have always existed, or have similar meanings in other cultures. Not true. As Cahill says, most of our "best" words came into our language through the Bible.

For native English speakers, this transformation happened more than four hundred years ago, through the heroic and sacrificial work of Christian Englishmen such as John Wycliffe (c. 1328–1384) and William Tyndale (c. 1494–1536), who first translated the Bible into the English language.

With this, native English speakers were able to read and reflect on biblical words and definitions for the first time. Entirely new ideas, such as the biblical concepts of justice, freedom, compassion, and human dignity, began to expand and transform the minds of ordinary Englishmen, leading to profound transformations in their cultures—in politics, education, and law.

The same thing happened in France, Spain, Germany, and Holland when the Bible was translated into their native tongues, and this same process has been repeated all over the world through the hard work of Christian missionaries and Bible translators. It continues today.

Previous generations of Christian missionaries not only translated the Bible into native languages, but they taught indigenous peoples to read, so they could access the Bible directly. They set up schools and universities to institutionalize biblical definitions in education, government, law, and civil society. In this way, they transformed the world. They discipled nations.

This happened in my own country, the United States. Our nation's early institutions were built on the solid foundation of true, biblical definitions. One of our great Founding Fathers, Noah Webster, made this his life's mission. Webster is "the father of American education." He compiled the American Dictionary of the English Language in 1828, recognizing that a nation of free people required a dictionary built "from the Bible up."

His dictionary contained more biblical definitions than any other reference volume before or since. Notwithstanding the blight of slavery and other sins, this biblical legacy produced one of the freest, most prosperous, generous, and humane nations in human history—a legacy we are tragically throwing away in my lifetime. Today, in the United States and throughout the Western world, our "cultural elites" have discarded Webster's 1828 Dictionary and are busily redefining words at breakneck speed. We are abandoning God and going our own way—and with a change in worship comes a shift in language and culture.

This redefinition of words has created tremendous tension and confusion. Communication becomes fraught. We use the same words but seemingly different dictionaries. We look sideways at one another and think (with a nod to Inigo Montoya in *The Princess Bride*), "You keep using that word. I do not think it means what you think it means."

I've had the privilege of traveling to scores of nations during my career, first with the international development organization Food for the Hungry, and then with the organization I now lead, the Disciple Nations Alliance. I've seen the importance and power of words and language in human development and poverty alleviation.

One of my colleagues, Arturo, for example, worked with the Pokomchi, a Mayan people in the highlands of Guatemala—one of the poorest groups in that nation. The Pokomchi are subsistence farmers, and corn is their staple. Yet Arturo noticed that every year at harvest, rats would eat as much as half of the crop. Arturo wondered why they didn't protect the crop from the rats. They replied, "Rats have always eaten the crop this way. It was like this for our grandfathers, and our fathers, and will be this way for our children as well."

Missionaries had come to the Pokomchi villages, and some of the tribe were followers of Jesus. Churches had been planted. Many missionary organizations would consider this group "reached" and move on to the next frontier. Yet they remained in abject poverty with one of the highest infant mortality rates in the Western Hemisphere.

If the Bible had been translated into their native tongue, they were unable to read it, so for them, it remained a closed book. Arturo began to question them about their local language and learned that they had no word in their language for "dominion." For them, the idea that human beings were to rule or have dominion over the animal kingdom was completely alien. Instead, it was the opposite. What we call "nature" was more powerful than they were. So powerful, in their minds, that they were largely helpless in the face of it, and this shaped the way they thought about something as simple as rats eating their corn crop.

So Arturo began to teach them from the Bible, starting in Genesis, chapter one. He taught them that God had created them in His image. He is the great King over all, and because we are made in His image, we too are created to rule over His creation. Arturo then asked the Pokomchi: Who has dominion over the corn crop at harvest? You, or the rats?

Arturo could see the lights go on, and a whole new idea—a new mental space that never existed before—came into their minds. They answered, "The rats."

"Is this what God wants?" Arturo responded.

"No."

"So what are you going to do about it?"

With that simple question, a remarkable transformation happened in the village. The farmers developed simple corn cribs that protected their crop from the rats, and the food supply doubled. Infant mortality rates plummeted, and the Pokomchi farmers began to innovate in completely new ways. One word, *dominion*—human authority over creation—transformed an impoverished village.

This story, and similar ones, changed my entire perspective on how to help impoverished peoples and communities to rise out of poverty. The key wasn't transfers of money or technology. It would have been so easy for a Western development organization or short-term church group from North America to build corn cribs for them, but how effective would this be if the Pokomchi didn't have a word or concept of dominion?

In the West, we take words and ideas like "dominion" for granted. We were born and raised to think that we should have authority over plants and animals, and not vice versa. We assume that everyone thinks this way, but they don't.

The concept of dominion came into the world through the Bible. So did many other ideas, such as the supreme dignity and worth of all human beings regardless of their sex, ethnicity, or social status, or words and ideas such as freedom and equal justice under the law. Words such as mercy, compassion, or love, understood as sacrificial service for the benefit of another, even at great personal cost, and even if that love is not reciprocated.

All of these words and ideas came into the world through the Bible.

The key to human development is found in the Bible and in the power of biblical words. Of course, those words need to be accessible in indigenous languages; the people must be taught to read and understand them, and those words and ideas must root themselves into their cultural institutions, particularly their educational practices and systems.

This holistic understanding used to be at the very heart of Christian missions, but no more. Today, the goal for most Christian missionaries is to proclaim the gospel of salvation through faith in Jesus Christ and to gather new converts into churches. And while there remains a robust vision to see the Bible translated into native languages, there is far less interest in literacy, and almost no interest in establishing schools or universities where biblical words can be learned deeply in order to begin shaping cultures and nations.

The relatively new idea in Christian missions is that Jesus is returning soon, so we need to prioritize gospel proclamation to get people saved out of this fallen world, which is destined for destruction. Efforts to change cultures or shape nations through literacy, schools, or other forms of what some call "cultural engagement" are seen as either a secondary priority or even a complete waste of time—a distraction from the highest priority.

But just because Christians no longer have a vision beyond spiritual conversion and filling seats in local churches doesn't mean that other people don't have a vision to transform the culture by leveraging the power of words.

As my friend and mentor Darrow Miller has taught me, if you want to change culture, you must begin by changing language. The enemies of the gospel understand this very well. Someone is going to shape the culture. Someone is going to define words and embed those words into the systems and institutions at the foundations of a culture. If not Christians with true, biblical definitions that lead to freedom and human flourishing, then non-Christians with false redefinitions that destroy nations will do it.

This destruction has been happening in Western nations for the past century. Christians have largely given up on their primary calling to be salt and light by defending true definitions in the public square. Instead, we've been content to limit our faith to evangelism, attending Sunday morning worship services, and personal piety.

The church's failure to carry out her mission doesn't only harm our nations; it harms the church as well. We give our systems of education over to non-Christians and send our children through those same systems. Twelve years later, we are surprised when our children have fully absorbed the false, redefinition of many words and are no longer able to articulate true biblical definitions. Again, quoting my friend Darrow, "If the church fails to disciple the nation, the nation will disciple the church." This is where we find ourselves today, with secular postmodern culture shaping the church, and not the other way around.

As a consequence, the church loses her power as she jettisons biblical truth and tries to regain her societal role through an endless quest for relevance. This quest leads, in fact, to the church falling into deeper and deeper and deeper holes of irrelevance. The downward progression looks something like this:

- The church tries to speak relevantly to the culture;
- The church adopts the language of the culture;
- The church makes accommodation to the culture;
- The church is held captive by the culture.

Yet this is not just a disturbing sociological process. We must remember that our enemy isn't flesh and blood but is composed of "spiritual forces of evil in the heavenly realms" (Ephesians 6:12). Satan uses the redefinition of words to advance his counterfeit kingdom. His tactic is parasitic. He latches onto words given by God and redefines them—empties them of their God-given meaning, and ultimately destroys the very words and their meanings.

We see this tactic in his challenge to the words of God given to Adam and Eve in the Garden of Eden (Genesis 3:1–7). "Did God truly say . . . ?" Satan casts doubt on God's words, causing confusion that leads to rebellion and, ultimately, destruction.

Here's how this works today. Look up "marriage" in Webster's 1828 Dictionary, and you'll find this definition:

The act of uniting a man and woman for life; wedlock; the legal union of man and woman for life. Marriage is a contract both civil and religious by which parties engage to live together in mutual affection and fidelity, till death shall separate them. Marriage was instituted by God himself for the purpose of preventing the promiscuous intercourse of the sexes, for promoting domestic felicity, and for securing the maintenance and education of children.

Now look at the definition embedded in Microsoft's popular word-processing software "Word." It defines marriage as:

> A legally recognized relationship, established by a civil or religious ceremony, between two people who intend to live together as sexual and domestic partners.

Marriage, as it has been understood for millennia, is being intentionally redefined out of existence—in our lifetimes. Think of the enormously destructive cultural repercussions that the change in definition in just one word will bring about. As John Milton said, "When language in common use in any country becomes irregular and depraved, it is followed by their ruin and degradation."[2]

As I write this, efforts are well underway to redefine marriage even further by replacing "two people" with "any group," and this will almost assuredly happen, for if God doesn't define words like marriage, then the most powerful among us will. Unmoored from God, definitions change like shifting sands, and words lose all meaning.

This change in definition wasn't accidental. There was (and is) a defined, carefully executed strategy to bring it about. Behind this effort are spiritual forces of evil in the heavenly realms, intent on destroying all that God created and declared to be good, true, and beautiful.

When the United States Supreme Court enshrined this new definition of marriage as the law of the land in its *Obergefell v. Hodges* 2015 ruling, the redefinition had already been written into the dictionaries. In reflecting on this ruling, John Stonestreet of the Colson Center says:

> The absurdity of these rulings is mindboggling until you understand the ideas driving them. [We find] a clue from the self-absorbed ramblings of *Alice in Wonderland*'s Humpty Dumpty, who said, "When I use a word, it means just what I choose it to mean—neither more nor less."

For Humpty, co-opting the meaning of words makes perfect sense, because his goal is not to communicate Truth, but to become the master. The recent court rulings—and many cultural disruptions over the past decades—are really about who will be master . . . .

There's a long history detailing the manipulation of language for social control. George Orwell described the process well in his book *1984*. The language was forever being altered, "to make all other modes of thought impossible. . . ." This was done partly by the invention of new words, but chiefly by eliminating undesirable words and stripping such words as remained of unorthodox meanings. . . .

He continues:

But this isn't something only of science fiction. When Communists took over mainland China, they perpetrated a "Cultural Revolution" that disrupted family bonds, discouraged religious devotion, and dismantled the Chinese language. Simplified characters replaced five thousand years of meaning and culture.

Now, we have it here. Words like "husband" and "wife" are discriminatory, confining marriage to two people is hateful, and "religious freedom" is bigotry. And many in our society wish to make words mean just what they want them to mean.[3]

Some of the most important words in the English language—not only marriage, but words such as freedom, love, justice, sex, human, truth, and the others highlighted in this book have been redefined in a deliberate effort to advance non-biblical ideologies.

But contra postmodern deconstructionism, words are not empty vessels to be filled with whatever meaning we wish. These are God-spoken words, and to redefine them is an act of rebellion against the Creator.

I wrote this book for two main reasons. The first is my growing alarm at how rapidly many "load-bearing" words in our culture are being redefined and all the destructive consequences that will inevitably follow.

Compounding this alarm is an ever-growing awareness of how many brothers and sisters in Christ have unwittingly absorbed and adopted these redefined meanings. This ignorance of true definitions is not only a disaster for the church but for the nations the church exists to serve. Pastor Kevin DeYoung said it well:

> [Christians] are people of the Word—worshipers of the
> Word incarnate and believers in the importance of faith-
> invigorating and faith-defending words in creeds and
> confessions. Of all people, Christians should care about
> definitions.[4]

Our formation in Christlikeness must be grounded in the proper, biblical meaning of words. If we are to experience a revival in the church and a reformation of culture, it won't happen without recovering a biblical lexicon. We must heed Robert Lewis Wilken's dire warning: "We cannot be the Church if we lose our vocabulary and the conceptual framework that makes us Christian."[5]

The second reason I wrote the book, is that our mission at the Disciple Nations Alliance is to help the church recover its true mission to bless and disciple the nations. We are not content to stand by passively while the enemies of Jesus have their way in destroying nations by redefining biblical worlds.

We Christians long to see our neighbors and their families, communities, and nations flourish. We long to see nations struggling with corruption become more just. To see nations struggling with poverty become more prosperous. We are convinced this will not happen unless the dominant culture of any nation develops a biblical vocabulary and a moral and mental ecology that comports with reality.

This book can start the process by helping the church reclaim the true meaning of ten significant words that have been dramatically redefined today. Each chapter will explore a different word, following the same outline.

- We'll explore the true, God-given meaning of these words as revealed in Scripture and lived out by the church for over two thousand years.
- We'll look at how these words led directly to building free, humane, and just cultures.
- We'll then reveal how each word has been redefined and how the new meanings lead to profoundly harmful and destructive cultural changes.
- We'll conclude each chapter by exploring practical ways Christians can be salt and light by preserving and acting upon the true meanings in our daily lives.

Why these ten words? Because they are so foundational—so basic. How they are defined and understood will do more to shape a life, a family, or an entire nation, for good or ill, than almost anything else.

My motivation isn't to win a culture war but to be faithful to the calling to love our neighbors and bless our nations. I agree with the ancient Chinese philosopher Confucius, who sagely wrote, "In reconstructing a society in collapse, the first priority is to restore the proper meaning of words."

There is a true meaning for the ten words covered in this book (as well as many others). These actual definitions come from God through His Word, the Bible.[6] These true, biblical definitions are not merely valid for Christians. They are true for everyone—Christian and non-Christian alike.

Christians, as much as anyone else, need to know these true definitions and build our lives on them. This is where it starts. In our own lives, in our families, and in our places of work. From there, we need to work to conserve and defend these true definitions in the public square. We need to do what we can to see that they are institutionalized in our various social systems. Again, they are true not just for us, but for everyone. Unless our society is built on the foundation of truth, it will inevitably be built on the foundation of falsehood, and we will reap the terrible consequences.

While I trust that this book will be helpful to brothers and sisters in Christ all over the world, I have a particular concern for what is happening in the United States and other Western nations. Over the past two hundred years, they have undergone a profound shift in core worldview assumptions from biblical theism to secular materialism, to the now-emerging postmodern neo-paganism.

As the tectonic plates of culture shift in the West (and around the world), societal pressure mounts against the church. The dominant culture in the West has moved from post-Christian to anti-Christian almost overnight, and with that shift, the pressure to discard Biblical definitions grows stronger with each passing day.

Increasingly, policies and laws are being established to compel speech and action based on false redefinitions. Adhering to biblical definitions more and more results in cultural stigma and sometimes legal penalties. It even can necessitate civil disobedience.

Will the committed Christian remnant in Europe and North America withstand the pressure? Ultimately, this question will be answered by each of us, and it will primarily come down to this: Whose dictionary do we trust?

Rosaria Butterfield was doing everything she could to advance the new cultural redefinitions. She was an atheist, having rejected her Catholic childhood and what she perceived to be the superstitions and illogic of the historic Christian faith. For years, she had lived in monogamous lesbian relationships and even coauthored Syracuse University's first successful domestic partnership policy while working there as a professor of English and women's studies. At the time of her conversion, she was working on a book exposing the religious right from a lesbian feminist point of view. She approached the Bible and the biblical meaning of words and language with an agenda to tear them down. Rosaria believed the Bible to be dangerous and irrational.[7]

However, God used the gracious hospitality and genuine love of a Christian who came into Rosaria's life to break through her defenses. Over time, Rosaria began to question her worldview. Here's how she describes the change:

> This was the first of my many betrayals against the LGBT community: *whose dictionary did I trust?* The one used by the community that I helped create or the one that reflected the God who created me?[8]

That's the question. How about you? Whose dictionary do you trust?

Like the great Noah Webster before us, I hope that this book, in some small way, will contribute to a revival of the church and a reformation of culture. May it open your eyes to the power, beauty, and truthfulness of biblical words—and motivate you to faithfully steward, preserve, and pass these words and meanings down to future generations.

God has called us for such a time as this. Let us be salt and light by telling the truth about sex, marriage, love, freedom, justice, and truth itself. My prayer is that you will allow these true meanings to inform every area of your life and through you, to make an impact in your neighborhood, in your place of work, and in the broader culture for the glory of God and the good of our nations.

Scott D. Allen
Bend, Oregon
July 2024

CHAPTER 1

TRUTH

For this purpose I was born and for this purpose I have come into the world—to bear witness to the truth. Everyone who is of the truth listens to my voice.

JOHN 18:37, ESV

TRUTH
That which accords with factual, objective reality.

TRUTH REDEFINED
(1) An internal, personal, and subjective sense of reality that exists only in the mind. (2) A social construct created to advantage the dominant group.[1]

During the 2018 Golden Globes, billionaire entertainer and television mogul Oprah Winfrey's powerful acceptance speech stirred the audience attuned to the proliferating accounts of sexual abuse in the media. It even prompted speculation that Winfrey might one day run for president.[2]

"What I know for sure is that speaking your truth is the most powerful tool we all have," Winfrey said at one point, "and I'm especially proud and inspired by all the women who have felt strong enough and empowered enough to speak up and share their personal stories."[3]

Later, she added, "For too long women have not been heard or believed if they dared to speak their truth to the power of those men. But their time is up."

Winfrey's repeated formulation "your truth" perked up some ears. Byron Tau of *The Wall Street Journal* tweeted, "Oprah employed a phrase that I've noticed a lot of other [celebrities] using these days: 'your truth' instead of 'the truth.' Why that phrasing?" He suggested that the phrasing "your truth" undermines the possibility of agreed-upon facts in favor of privatized, separate versions of reality.[4]

"What is truth?" The question famously posed by Pontius Pilate to Jesus during His inquisition (see John 18:28–40) continues to ring down through the ages, right into the present. Some, like Winfrey, speak of "your truth" or "my truth." They speak of truth as a personal, private belief. To be authentic, or "true to yourself," is a supreme value. But Tau puts his finger on the problem with this redefined understanding of truth. It "undermines the possibility of agreed-upon facts." In this new, cultural definition of truth, facts disappear—indeed, *truth* disappears! According to the noted Prussian philosopher Fredrick Nietzsche, "There are no facts, only interpretations."[5]

But there *are* facts! Truth isn't merely what you or I believe. It has a real, objective meaning. We live in a real world that exists wholly apart from our beliefs about it. You may, for example, believe you can step off your roof and be supported by thin air. That may be "your truth," but is it *the* truth? Put it to the test, and you'll quickly discover that gravity exists whether you believe it or not. Because we live in a real, objective universe, knowing the truth is of utmost importance. Indeed, you likely wouldn't survive a single day, let alone flourish, apart from a knowledge of facts that correspond to reality—apart from truth.

TRUTH DEFINED

In answer to Pilate's question, truth is that which corresponds with reality. It really is that simple. Truth accurately describes reality—what actually exists, or actually happened. It is synonymous with *fact*. Thomas Aquinas defined truth similarly, saying, "A judgment is said to be true when it conforms to the external reality."[6] Antonyms of truth are illusion, falsehood, fiction, fantasy and delusion. To confuse an illusion for reality is to be mistaken. To be detached from reality is to be delusional. To say that something is true (or false), when you know it isn't, is to deceive, or to lie. "Truth exists, whether we like it or not," said Charles Chaput, the Roman Catholic Archbishop of Philadelphia. "We don't create the truth; we find it, and we have no power to change it to our tastes."[7]

> ## TRUTH
> That which accords with, or corresponds with, objective reality.

We need a knowledge of reality to survive. It is a basic human need, like air or water. Because our well-being depends on the truth, we instinctively become angry or upset when we are deceived. Truth is necessary for healthy relationships. Someone who speaks truthfully is described as honest or trustworthy. We rightly esteem such people, because they are reliable, and relationships can only grow in the fertile soil of trust.

THE REALITY OF THE WORLD AROUND US

Truth requires fixed points of reference that exist apart from our ideas, thoughts, and beliefs. The most obvious fixed point is the world around us. The computer I'm typing on, the desk I'm working at, the chair I'm sitting in, my fingers, hands, body, and mind. The egg I had for breakfast. The sky, trees, stars, and galaxies. The cells, atoms, and electrons. These things exist whether I believe in them or not. We study the physical world through science, and, as such, science is a quest for truth, a discovery of what actually exists, or what is real.

But is there a reality that exists beyond the physical world? A reality as basic, but more ultimate? The physical world itself points to the answer. We notice that the world is not random or chaotic, but orderly. From our vantage point here on Earth, the sun rises and sets in a regular pattern. The seasons change. Seeds grow into plants and bear fruit with regularity. From the motion of the planets to the inner workings of the cell, we see order and design, not randomness or chaos. Neither science nor mathematics would be possible without an orderly universe that operates according to fixed laws. Where did these so-called natural laws come from? How can this order and design be explained?

We also see purpose. "Eyes are for seeing, ears are for hearing, fins are for swimming, and wings are for flying," says author Nancy Pearcey. "Each part of an organ is exquisitely adapted to the others, and all interact in a coordinated, goal-directed fashion to achieve the purpose of the whole. This kind of integrated structure is the hallmark of design—plan, will, intention."[8] How do we explain this purpose in the physical world?

Besides purpose, we also encounter complex information. In the cell's nucleus—its command-and-control center—is the DNA molecule. Its double-helix structure stores an immense amount of information. According to Pearcey, "Geneticists talk about DNA as a 'database' that stores 'libraries' of genetic information. They analyze the way RNA—Ribonucleic acid—'translates' the four-letter language of the nucleotides into the twenty-letter language of proteins."[9]

Complex information doesn't arise by chance. That would be like believing that a pile of letters on a table could somehow arrange themselves into the Gettysburg Address purely by accident, given enough time. There is only one known source of complex, specified information, and that is a mind. But whose mind? Not ours. We discovered the DNA molecule. We didn't create it.

ULTIMATE REALITY

Every effect must have a sufficient cause. The design and purposefulness of the natural world point to a transcendent, intelligent, purposeful designer. The existence of complex information necessitates an author—a great Word behind all words.

This is the point that the apostle Paul makes in his letter to the Romans: "since the creation of the world God's invisible qualities— his eternal power and divine nature—have been clearly seen, *being understood from what has been made*" (Romans 1:20, italics added).

The physical world isn't a cosmic accident; it is a *creation*, and it points to a Creator in a way that is "clearly seen," or as America's founding fathers put it, "self-evident." The alternative is to posit that the design, order, laws, purpose, and complex information in nature somehow arose by chance. Paul says that this amounts to a willful "suppressing" of the truth (Romans 1:18). Psalm 19:1 reinforces the same theme: The heavens declare the glory of God; the skies proclaim the work of his hands. When we discover something about the natural world, we learn something about its Creator.

Science is the process we use to make these discoveries, and science itself rests on two foundational assumptions, without which, science collapses, and truth becomes meaningless.

- An intelligible universe, which is orderly, predictable, and governed by laws;
- Human beings who are set apart from the rest of the physical world in their capacity to think critically about it and discern what is true from what isn't.

In all of history, only one worldview provides a sufficient explanation for these assumptions. It was no accident that modern science was birthed from a biblical worldview, and, with it, a belief in the existence of truth that can be discovered. Some of the scientific pioneers who believed in God were Copernicus in astronomy, Bacon in establishing the scientific method, Kepler in mathematics and astronomy, Pascal in mathematics and physics, Newton in physics, and many more.[10]

The Bible begins with these words: "In the beginning, God created the heavens and earth" (Genesis 1:1). The God revealed in the Bible isn't like other gods. He isn't an impersonal cosmic force, or a grand "theory of everything." He isn't an "it" but a "He"—a personal God. He isn't the product of human imagination, a fantasy, or a fairytale. He isn't unpredictable, deceitful, and capricious like pagan gods. He can't be bribed or manipulated. Only the eternal, unchanging Creator of the universe provides a solid, reliable, fixed point of reference for reality. He is "the same yesterday, today, and forever" (Hebrews 13:8). His Word "stands fixed in the heavens" (Psalm 119:89). He is utterly truthful. "It is impossible for God to lie" (Hebrews 6:18). Both God's truthfulness and the veracity of His Word come together in this verse:

> God is not man, that he should lie,
>   or a son of man, that he should change his mind.
> Has he said, and will he not do it?
>   Or has he spoken, and will he not fulfill it?
> (Numbers 23:19, ESV)

In the Hebrew Scriptures, the word for truth is transliterated as *emeth*, a noun or adverb meaning firmness, stability, or reliability.[11] God is the firm, fixed, solid foundation for truth. He is the Great Truth behind all truth. The material world was created by Him and is dependent on Him. Apart from Him, truth has no meaning. It vanishes in a morass of subjectivism and relativism. The late BBC journalist Malcolm Muggeridge put it this way: "The essential feature and necessity of life is to know reality, which means knowing God."[12]

THE TRUTH REVEALED

God has revealed Himself to us through His creation, but also through His words. He spoke to Abraham, Isaac, and Jacob. He spoke to Moses and revealed Himself through the prophets. He revealed moral truth on Mount Sinai in the form of the Ten Commandments, which He wrote by His own hand. These truths stand as a fixed moral point for all peoples, at all times.

"As the church fathers put it, God's revelation comes to us in 'two books'—the book of God's Word (the Bible), and the book of God's world (creation)."[13] We can add to this a third "book," the book of human reason and the internal witness of conscience, or "the law written on the heart" (Romans 2:15). We search out the truth through the careful study of God's creation using the tools and methods of science, as well as the careful study of God's written Word through the principles of sound hermeneutics and with the indispensable illumination of the Holy Spirit.

God wants us to know the truth, and to live in it. Happily, He has given each of us the capacity to know the truth—our reasoning and logical minds. We can apply reason and logic, asking questions and seeking answers, to draw out the truths of the Bible and creation. This quest for the truth is a fundamental aspect of our human nature and part of our glory as image-bearers of God (Genesis 1:27).

As we read the Bible, we must keep in mind that it isn't a book of mythology. While it contains wisdom writings, prophecy, and poetry, it is fundamentally a book of *history*. It claims to describe actual events. The Gospel writers—Matthew, Mark, Luke, and John—present Jesus as a real man, not a mythological figure like Zeus. They claim to be eyewitnesses.

"We did not follow cleverly devised myths when we made known to you the power and coming of our Lord Jesus Christ," wrote the apostle Peter, "but we were eyewitnesses of his majesty" (2 Peter 1:16, ESV). History, like creation, is another fixed point that anchors truth. I was born on October 16, 1964, in Roseburg, Oregon. That is now "written in stone." It is a fact that can't be undone. This is true of events in the recent past—a few minutes or seconds ago—as well as events in the distant past. Rightly understood, the study of history is a quest for truth.

The truthfulness and reliability of the Bible as a historical record can be evaluated with the same tools and techniques any historian uses to determine the authenticity, accuracy, and reliability of any historical text. When assessed carefully alongside other ancient writings, the Bible stands alone for its historical reliability.[14]

Through this Bible, we come to understand who we are—what it means to be human, how we ought to live, and what our purpose is. We come to understand what is good, true, and beautiful. We also learn the true meanings of words defined by God in the Holy Scriptures—words such as love, justice, marriage, and, yes, truth. Words spoken by God have true, objective meanings. We redefine them at our peril.

TRUTH AND LIES

Through the Bible we also learn why evil exists. Reality is both physical and spiritual. The spiritual realm is the domain of God, but also of angels. The most powerful of these angelic beings, Satan, rebelled against God before the creation of the world. To modern ears, talk of angels and demons sounds crazy. Many people see reality as entirely physical, as matter in motion. While the spiritual realm may be derided as a fantasy, it is as real as the chair on which you sit. This unseen realm exists all around us.

According to the Bible, Satan advances his rebellion against God mainly through deception. Also known as the devil (meaning "slanderer"), he first appears (in disguise) in the Bible immediately after the account of creation in Genesis 1–2. Adam and Eve, our first human ancestors, see the devil in the form of a serpent. His first act, not surprisingly, is a deception:

> Now the serpent was more crafty than any of the wild animals the Lord God had made. He said to the woman, "Did God really say, 'You must not eat from any tree in the garden'?"

The woman said to the serpent, "We may eat fruit from the trees in the garden, but God did say, 'You must not eat fruit from the tree that is in the middle of the garden, and you must not touch it, or you will die.'"

"You will not certainly die," the serpent said to the woman". (Genesis 3:1–4)

Adam and Eve believed his lie. In so doing, they followed Satan's anti-God rebellion, and fallen humanity has been rebelling ever since. This explains our propensity to lie, deceive, or shade the truth. We commit these offenses, at least in part, out of fear that we might be known as we truly are—as sinners. Like Adam and Eve, we hide from God and from others by lying—by making ourselves out to be something we are not.

God, the source of all life, of all that is good and beautiful, cannot lie. Satan, by contrast, continually lies. His deceptions are behind all of the world's evil, brokenness, chaos, and heartbreak. "[Satan] comes only to steal and kill and destroy," says Jesus in John 10:10. "He was a murderer from the beginning, and does not stand in the truth, because there is no truth in him. When he lies, he speaks out of his own character, for he is a liar and the father of lies" (John 8:44, ESV).

THE TRUTH BECAME FLESH

God, because of His great love for His creation—and for each of us—didn't abandon us to our evil captor. Instead, He did something entirely unexpected. He came to rescue us.

History is a narrative of this unfolding rescue mission. At the very center of this story—and the center of human history—stands the incarnation. Some two thousand years ago, the Creator of all things entered time and space in human form. When we were lost in a fog of lies and deception, He came to reveal truth. He said ". . . for this reason I was born, and for this reason I came into the world, to testify to the truth. Everyone on the side of truth listens to me" (John 18:37).

But He did more than simply reveal truth. In an act of pure grace, in love Jesus laid down His life for us. Paul described Jesus in these immortal words: "God was pleased to have all his fullness dwell in him, and through him to reconcile to himself all things, whether things on earth or things in heaven, by making peace through his blood, shed on the cross" (Colossians 1:19–20). Christian apologist Gregory Koukl describes the incarnation this way:

> Even though the Son never ceased being God, still he surrendered his divine rights. He laid them aside. He let them go. Like a king who—out of love—removed his crown, set aside his scepter, took off his royal robes, donned the garb of a common beggar, and lived among the poorest of his subjects. Never ceasing to be king, he got low, so low he willingly died the death of a despised criminal—all to serve [and save] his own.[15]

In Jesus, ultimate reality became flesh and dwelt among us. Ultimate truth isn't a philosophical abstraction or metaphysical necessity. It is a *person*—Jesus Christ. In Him, love and truth, justice and compassion were manifest. In fact, we cannot discuss truth without discussing love. Love and truth cannot be separated. They are most fully defined and manifest only as they relate to each other.

The New Testament word for truth is *aletheia*, meaning "to be revealed." The Greek word from which this noun is derived is *lanthano*, which means "to lie hid." The Greeks (not unlike today's postmodernists) thought that truth was hidden. But according to the Bible, truth is now revealed in Christ. To express this, the writers of Scripture added the negative participle *a* to *lanthano* to get the word *aletheia*. That which was hidden is now revealed.

Jesus was a man like no other. He made claims no other man has made—not Buddha, Muhammad, or Confucius. He claimed not merely to speak the truth, but to *be* the truth. "I am the way and the truth and the life. No one comes to the Father except through me" (John 14:6).

Could these claims be true? If not, then Jesus was a liar, a madman, or a demon. C. S. Lewis famously said, given His stupendous claims, that the one thing we know for sure is that Jesus was not merely a great teacher of morals and ethics.

> You must make your choice. Either this man was, and is, the Son of God, or else a madman or something worse. You can shut him up for a fool, you can spit at him and kill him as a demon or you can fall at his feet and call him Lord and God, but let us not come with any patronizing nonsense about his being a great human teacher. He has not left that open to us. He did not intend to.[16]

A TRUTH CULTURE

Ideas have consequences. What a people believes about truth will be reflected in the culture it creates—in its values, norms, laws, and institutions. Psalm 115:8 tells us that we become like the God, or gods, we worship. A culture that is built on the truth about truth will flourish. Here's why.

A commitment to truth-telling is necessary for healthy relationships and a society's basic functioning. Try to imagine a society—a marriage, family, business, organization, or nation—in which everyone lied, all the time. Nobody could be trusted. Things would fall apart quickly. We forget just how important honesty is. A culture that worships a God who is good, who is utterly trustworthy, who cannot lie, will be a culture that highly values honesty in everyday relationships. It will enjoy high levels of trust in its institutions.

A quick look at the Transparency International Corruption Perception Index reveals that, with the exception of Singapore, the countries with the lowest corruption were born out of a Judeo-Christian framework. The ones with the most corruption lacked this framework.[17]

Truth is essential for justice. Justice is based on finding the truth of what actually happened. The reliability and veracity of witnesses, and the willingness of judges and juries to search out the truth, are the foundations of justice. In the Bible, giving false witness is a grave injustice and a violation of one of the Ten Commandments.

Justice depends upon an ultimate source for what is right and wrong. Justice requires a law higher than manmade laws—laws to which even kings and prime ministers are accountable. There is a reason that an image of the Ten Commandments exists at the apex of the United States Supreme Court building. Without the moral truths of the Ten Commandments, there is no justice, only the arbitrary assertion of power. Justice is inextricably linked to truth. "When truth dies, justice is buried with it."[18]

Western universities, too, were founded on the pursuit of truth. Harvard University, which is the first institution of higher education in the United States, was founded in 1636 in the Massachusetts Bay Colony. The university was named after its first benefactor, a young minister named John Harvard of Charlestown, who in 1638 left his library and half his estate to the institution. The school's motto has been *Veritas*, the Latin word for "truth." [19, 20]

At the founding of another prominent American university, the University of Virginia, Thomas Jefferson said, "This institution will be based on the illimitable freedom of the human mind. For here we are not afraid to follow truth where it may lead, nor to tolerate error so long as reason is free to combat it."[21]

Without a commitment to truth, there would be no university. Nor would there be modern science, nor journalism, nor the study of history. There would be no liberal democracy, for without truth, government becomes an exercise in raw power. Freedom and truth, like justice and truth, are inextricably linked. It is no exaggeration to say that without a commitment to truth as revealed, objective, and knowable, there would be no such thing as civilization.

Without some knowledge of the truth about the natural world, or about history, or about the One who created this world and who authors history, we cannot survive, much less thrive. Without truth, everything devolves into chaos or tyranny. Professor Sinan Aral at the Massachusetts Institute of Technology got it exactly right: "Some notion of truth is central to the proper functioning of nearly every realm of human endeavor. If we allow the world to be consumed by falsity, we are inviting catastrophe."[22] Tragically, that is exactly what we are inviting in this "post-truth" moment.

TRUTH REDEFINED

When people speak about truth today, they are not thinking about something that is real, objective, or external. Rather, in their minds, truth is internal, personal, and subjective. Today, à la Oprah Winfrey[23], we speak of "my truth" or "your truth," but not *the* truth. Today, truth isn't something you discover. It's something you create. Ken Myers of Mars Hill Audio[24] says "the reigning belief of modern culture is that each individual is the sovereign maker of meaning." He continues: "Where premodern cultures assumed a Creator . . . who established cosmic order to which human societies and individuals must conform, modern culture denies the existence of such an order and encourages each individual to assert his or her own order."[25]

TRUTH REDEFINED
An internal, personal, and subjective sense of reality that exists only in the mind.

In 1987, the University of Chicago's Allan Bloom wrote in his bestseller *The Closing of the American Mind*: "There is one thing a professor can be absolutely certain of. Almost every student entering the university believes, or says he believes, that truth is relative."[26] That was over three decades ago, and Bloom was talking about students *entering* the university. Today, these students are running our government and our leading institutions. Whether truth is relative to the individual or to the "identity group," relativism reigns. In the words of Pope Benedict XVI, we are constructing "a dictatorship of relativism."[27]

REDUCING TRUTH TO MATTER

In fifteenth century Europe, as modern science began to blossom, great mysteries of the universe started to yield their secrets, one by one. Alongside the excitement of discovery, an ancient pride began to grow in the hearts of many Enlightenment philosophers: Through science and human reason, alone, we will come to know everything. We no longer need to appeal to a supernatural realm— to God, angels, or demons to explain the workings of the universe, as people did during the former "Dark Ages."

The famous theoretical physicist Stephen Hawking captured this kind of hubris when he said, "Before we understood science, it was natural to believe that God created the universe, but now science offers a more convincing explanation."[28] According to Hawking and other like-minded intellectuals, all of reality must have an exclusively natural, not supernatural, explanation. This is the worldview of materialism, naturalism, or scientism. It reduces reality to matter, to *physical* forces, and says we can gain knowledge of truth only through a scientific study of the material world. This worldview was popularized by thinkers such as Francis Bacon, David Hume, and, most significantly, Charles Darwin. It is most at home in university science departments, particularly in physics and biology.

But our culture paid a high price when it adopted this view of reality. God, and the entire spiritual realm, had to be abandoned as a pre-scientific fantasy. But when God was removed, meaning, purpose, the human spirit, human agency, love, and creativity—not to mention an objective standard for morality and reality—went with Him. Will Provine, a Cornell historian of evolutionary biology, sums up the implications of materialism this way: "There is no life after death; no ultimate foundation for ethics; no ultimate meaning for life; no free will."[29]

Materialism fractured truth. Some have described this as the "fact/value divide,"[30] and it has profoundly shaped our thinking about truth today. Only those things that can be known through science are deemed true, real, or factual. These things, and *only* these things, are publicly authoritative, serving as the bases for public policy, law, and education. Things that science cannot study— spiritual reality, God, morals, and ethics—are deemed matters of "value" and private belief.

"Values"
Spirit, religion, meaning, purpose, ethics, morality
Private beliefs, not publicly authoritative
Unreal, fantasy

"Facts"
Phenomena known through science
Publicly authoritative
Real, true

According to this view, the material universe is the sole foundation for truth, not God and the Bible. Theology, the study of God in Scripture, once the "queen of the sciences," has been almost entirely eliminated as an academic discipline in most Western universities. Meanwhile, science has been elevated as the exclusive source of knowledge about publicly authoritative truth. Let's call this what it is: scientism. According to historian T. J. Jackson Lears, scientism is the "faith" that "science has discovered (or is about to discover) all the important truths about human life." Or, as Hawking put it: "The scientific account is complete. Theology is unnecessary."[31]

Note the bold claim here. It isn't that God or spiritual reality *might* exist, or that moral truths *might* exist. No, if science cannot study such matters, they are deemed to be unreal. According to the new arbiters of truth, they may be matters of personal taste, preference, or "value," but they cannot be sources of publicly authoritative truth. Yet this claim, ironically, is *non-scientific*. It is a philosophical assertion—that truth can be reduced to matter.

Myers explains the consequences of the fact/value divide for Christian involvement in public life:

> If Christians want to participate in public life, they are told they must abide by the rules of "public reason." These rules insist that all truth claims about ultimate reality be left at home, that public debate can only be conducted by avoiding metaphysical claims. Of course, the assumption that social life can be ordered without reference to ultimate principles is based on certain tacit beliefs about reason, human nature, and the goals of society that are not neutral. When the umpires are actually members on one of the teams, it's necessary to declare that the game is rigged. . . . Refusing the rules of engagement drawn up by [materialists] is in fact the most generous, truthful, and loving service we can offer our neighbors. After all, the cultural chaos that grieves us harms them even more.[32]

The problem is that materialism is pure reductionism. It only accounts for the *material* aspect of reality. Yes, we can gain a knowledge of truth through science and a careful study of creation, but because reality is both physical *and* spiritual, and because spiritual reality precedes physical reality,[33] science can give us only a partial understanding of truth. Because human beings are both physical and spiritual, materialism will never support our deep-seated human need for meaning, purpose, freedom, love, beauty, and creativity.

Nor can it reliably help us to distinguish good and evil. These are all nonphysical realities. As a result, materialism isn't livable. Even strict materialists irrationally, for them, live as if these nonphysical things are real—because they are!

REDUCING TRUTH TO MIND

A countervailing worldview arose almost immediately in reaction to materialism—one that inverted it. Rather than reducing reality to matter, it reduced it to *mind*. This worldview came to be known as idealism, romanticism, existentialism, or, in our day, postmodernism. Its prominent champions were Kant, Hegel, Nietzsche, Marx, Foucault, and Derrida. Today, according to the University of Toronto's Jordan Peterson, postmodernism "absolutely dominates the humanities and increasingly the social sciences in the universities."[34] Its influence has now rippled outward from the university and into the broader culture, and is now the dominant paradigm shaping Western thought and values.

Postmodernism does away with any notion of universal, objective truth. Materialism rejected God, the Bible, and spiritual reality as sources of objective truth, yet it retained the material universe as a fixed point of reference for truth. Postmodernism does away with that also. Under this system, even history isn't a fixed reference point. It asserts that no fixed points exist. Everything is relative, either to the individual, or to the "identity group" or culture.

There are no publicly authoritative facts or truths that transcend groups or cultures. There are only perspectives or interpretations—your truth, or my truth, but no longer *the* truth.

This same relativism applies to words and language. To the postmodernist, there are no objectively true or false understandings of any word or text, be it the Bible or the US Constitution. There are only perspectives and interpretations. We are now "free" to give whatever meaning we choose to any text, or to any word. Where materialism fractured the truth, postmodernism blows it apart completely.

As Nancy Pearcey explains, "Truth has been redefined as a social construction, so that every community has its own view of truth, based on its experience and perspective, which cannot be judged by anyone outside the community." She describes postmodernism's core assertion this way: "Primary reality is not matter but mind. . . . Instead of deifying matter, [postmodernism] deifies the mind . . . the mind itself [is] granted godlike creative power."[35] This worldview is perfectly captured in this boast from American social theorist Jeremy Rifkin:

> We no longer feel ourselves to be guests in someone else's home and therefore obliged to make our behavior conform with a set of preexisting cosmic rules. It is our creation now. We make the rules. We establish the parameters of reality. We create the world, and because we do, we no longer feel beholden to outside forces. We no longer have to justify our behavior, for we are now the architects of the universe. We are responsible for nothing outside ourselves, for we are the kingdom, the power, and the glory for ever and ever.[36]

So what does postmodernism look like in the real (if we may use that term!) world? Recently, an interviewer with the Family

Policy Institute of Washington ventured onto the campus of the University of Washington in Seattle. He was there to ask students some questions. The subsequent video, posted on YouTube, has received more than 5.4 million views.

The interviewer, a white male who appears to be in his thirties, asked one student: "If I told you I was a woman, what would your response be?" Student: "Good for you." Second student: "I don't have a problem with it." Interviewer: "If I told you I was Chinese; how would you respond?" Student: "I might be a little surprised, but I'd say 'good for you.'" Interviewer: "What if I told you I was 6'5" tall? Student: "I would say that so long as you are not hindering society and you're not causing harm to other people, I feel like that should be an okay thing." Interviewer: "Would you tell me I'm wrong?" Student: "I don't feel like that's my place . . . to say someone is wrong or to draw lines or boundaries." The interviewer ends the video by saying, "It shouldn't be hard to tell a 5'9" white guy that he's not a 6'5" Chinese woman, but clearly it is. Why? What does that say about our culture?"[37]

Clearly, these students have absorbed, either consciously or unconsciously, the core assumptions of postmodernism. You can be whoever (or whatever) you want. You make the rules. You establish the parameters of reality. If you are a 5'9" white male but *feel* that your "authentic" identity is a 6'5" Chinese woman, well, that can be *your* truth, and no one can say otherwise. The objective facts of your biology, ethnicity, or physical height don't matter.

There are no fixed points of reference. No boundaries. As essayist John Zmirak explains,

> We have embarked on a strange and perilous project: to transform ourselves into entirely new creatures, not bound by the rules of mortal, biological life or by the God who created us. We have no gender but what we choose, no morals but those we embrace, no debt that

we owe to the future in repayment for all the gifts [we've received] from the past. Our "choices" are sacrosanct and beyond any criticism.[38]

If there are no fixed points, no boundaries that divide truth from untruth, or good from evil, if everything is a matter of perspective or interpretation, then the very concept of objective truth is defined out of existence. Is it any surprise that "post-truth" was selected in 2016 by Oxford Dictionaries as the international word of the year—after a 2,000 percent increase in usage from 2015? The dictionary defined "post-truth" as "relating to or denoting circumstances in which objective facts are less influential in shaping public opinion than appeals to emotion and personal belief."[39]

POST-TRUTH CULTURE

As truth gives way to "post-truth," we are discovering to our regret that "some notion of truth is central to the proper functioning of nearly every realm of human endeavor."[40] Society quite literally disintegrates without some shared understanding of objective truth. As self-interest takes over from a shared understanding of reality, we should not be surprised by events such as the recent housing crisis, when banks bundled and sold financially shaky mortgages, homeowners in large numbers took on debt they couldn't afford (and then walked away from their obligations), and government regulators looked the other way while protecting their friends. We are witnessing the fragmentation of Western societies before our very eyes.

In the academy, where honesty is both necessary and expected, truth-telling is becoming increasingly rare. According to a 2012 *New York Times* article, "Large-scale cheating has been uncovered over the last year at some of the nation's most competitive schools, like . . . the Air Force Academy and, most recently, Harvard. . . .

Studies of student behavior and attitudes show that a majority of students violate standards of academic integrity to some degree."[41]

In a post-truth culture, not only do students cheat, but people more readily mislead, violate contracts and agreements, or deceive others in order to get ahead or further a particular agenda. This rising tide of dishonesty erodes trust, which is the glue that holds a society together. Without a commitment to truth, relationships fracture. Mistrust, suspicion, and cynicism become pervasive, divorce rates skyrocket, and institutions falter.

At a societal level, without *public* truth; without shared understandings of what is real, true, good, or evil; if even words and texts no longer have a shared public meaning; then there is no center around which different groups can communicate, much less unify. We have no way to achieve consensus or to pursue the common good. Rather, we retreat into our "identity group" bubbles and find it almost impossible to speak to each other, much less agree. Post-truth culture thus is marked by disunity, distrust, even hatred.

With objective truth out of the way, naked power fills the vacuum. As Pearcey explains, "If there is no objective or universal truth, then any claim to have objective truth will be treated as nothing but an attempt by one . . . community to impose its own limited, subjective perspective on everyone else. An act of oppression. A power grab."[42]

Peterson describes the postmodern world as "a Hobbesian battleground of identity groups. They do not communicate with one another because they can't. All there is, is a struggle for power."[43] In his book *Impossible People*, Os Guinness describes the same dynamic:

> Nietzsche rejected any notion of absolute or objective truth and replaced it with the will to power. His French disciple Michel Foucault made a career of analyzing everything in terms of power. So there is hardly a

discussion [today] in which the power factor will not be raised. What is the real agenda here? What are the power relationships in the equation? Whose interests are being served? Whose ox is being gored?[44]

According to the dominant postmodern, neo-Marxist narrative of Western cultural elites, the very notions of objective truth, reason, logic, evidence, and argument are viewed as weapons employed by white, male oppressors to maintain their hegemony over their victims.

To turn the tables on the oppressors and grab the reins of cultural power and authority, academic critical theorists developed the concept of "Standpoint Epistemology." Simply put, a knowledge of "truth" doesn't come through careful thought, research, reason, logic, or evidence based on wisdom, age or experience, but by listening to so-called victims, who, based on their lived experience of oppression, have greater insight than oppressors. Victims define what is real and true, and no debate is possible.

When reason and logic are discarded, feelings and emotions take center stage. Discussion and debate to discover the truth are replaced with hyperbolic claims of emotional duress. Hurt feelings and claims of deep offense are all that are required to defeat opponents.

In the absence of a shared, objective truth, we are left with competing identity groups jockeying for power. Increasingly, this happens through narrative creation and perpetuation. Postmodern evangelists sell narratives as truth, but they are highly distorted accounts of current or past events created to achieve particular outcomes. They highlight only those facts that make the case for those outcomes and ignore facts that don't. In some cases, they completely fabricate details or events to achieve their ends.

These narratives are conveyed in a manner designed to bypass reason and appeal to emotion—to capture the imagination and sway the masses. They cast people in the roles of hero, villain, and victim. The heroes and victims are always on the side of justice and righteousness—*their* side. The purported villains or oppressors are always on the *other* side, where injustice and oppression reign— even when reality may be closer to the inverse.[45]

Today, we are witnessing a rapid proliferation of narrative creation and perpetuation. To ensure their narratives go unchallenged, powerful elites use an array of methods to silence dissenting voices, including overt censorship, along with charges of "fake news" and "conspiracy theory" as well as attacks against so-called "misinformation," "disinformation," and "malinformation."

All are direct results of postmodernism's denial of objective truth. Any institution or field formerly based on an unbiased quest for facts and truth has been undermined. This includes the university, and the fields of history, journalism, science, law, and justice. All of these in different ways have replaced their older charter—the quest for a knowledge of the truth—with a new one: narrative creation and perpetuation.

In this new regime, politicians, historians, and journalists use their disciplines to achieve preferred outcomes by perpetuating narratives. Universities increasingly perpetuate postmodern ideology and intimidate, silence, or stifle opposing viewpoints. Even science is not immune. Ideally, scientists are compelled by their disciplines to follow the evidence wherever it leads, but more and more scientists feel pressure to manipulate data and findings in ways that lead to preferred outcomes.[46]

In the fields of law and justice, judges increasingly are unmoored from the Constitution. They use their powerful positions to impose their interpretations on legal texts in order to achieve preferred outcomes. The bedrock of the justice system, due process, cannot survive if judges, attorneys, and witnesses no longer feel a sense of fidelity to the truth, and instead lie or otherwise twist facts. In short, we no longer have the rule of law but the rule of the most powerful.

Many of us simply shrug our shoulders, no longer believing we can know the truth about *anything*. Everything that exists is spin, distortion, and false narrative. Everyone's data, evidence, and findings are suspect. No one can be trusted.

The *Harvard Business Journal* reported in 2017 that the general population no longer trusts leaders in government, business, the media, and nonprofits to "do what is right." There is "a staggering lack of confidence in leadership."[47]

So much is lost when we abandon truth. It becomes impossible to affirm what is good and fight what is evil. Rational, civil discussion and debate are undermined. Agendas and outcomes are pursued using all means possible, including lies, deception, censorship, and manipulation. Simply put, without a commitment to objective truth, humane civilization collapses. A society that abandons truth will devolve into a dark and dystopian world of tribalism, chaos, and tyranny. George Orwell foresaw this in his disturbing novel *1984*. The climax comes with the inquisition of the protagonist, Winston Smith, at the hands of his torturer, O'Brien, a representative of "the Party."

"Only the disciplined mind can see reality, Winston. You believe that reality is something objective, external, existing in its own right. You also believe that the nature of reality is self-evident. When you delude yourself into thinking that you see something, you assume that everyone else sees the same thing as you. But I tell you, Winston, that reality is not external. Reality exists in the human mind, and nowhere else. Not in the individual mind, which can make mistakes, and in any case soon perishes: only in the mind of the Party, which is collective and immortal. Whatever the Party holds to be the truth, is truth. It is impossible to see reality except by looking through the eyes of the Party. That is the fact that you have got to relearn, Winston."[48]

Orwell is exactly right. If we choose to abandon ultimate reality—the God of Creation—then reality will be defined on the human plane—by "the Party," representing the group who holds power. Those are the options. The notion that people can be their own little gods or goddesses and determine reality for themselves is unworkable and unlivable. It will inevitably lead to societal chaos, which, in turn, will lead to "the Party" stepping in to restore order and define reality for everyone.

Is there any hope that we might escape this fate? Yes, but it largely depends on how the church responds.

HOW SHOULD WE THEN LIVE?

Before He went to the cross, Jesus comforted His followers with these words: "I will ask the Father, and he will give you another Counselor to be with you forever—the Spirit of truth . . . . When he, the Spirit of truth, comes, he will guide you into all truth" (John 14:16, 17; 16:13, CSB). Filled and empowered by the Spirit of truth, faithful followers of Jesus are called to speak the truth in love (Ephesians 4:15). To be ambassadors of truth, pushing back against the lies and deceptions Satan uses for his destructive ends.

Our approach must be characterized by gentleness and respect. "The Lord's servant must not be quarrelsome but kind to everyone, able to teach, patiently enduring evil, correcting his opponents with gentleness," admonishes the apostle Paul. "God may perhaps grant them repentance leading to a knowledge of the truth, and they may come to their senses and escape from the snare of the devil, after being captured by him to do his will" (2 Timothy 2:24–26).

Ultimate reality exists, and His name is Jesus! There is salvation in no other name (Acts 4:12). But we are to speak the truth about much else besides. We are to speak about what it means to be human. We are to speak about the sanctity of life, about love, and justice, and freedom. We are to love our neighbors by working to build just and humane cultures that lead to human flourishing. We cannot do this if we abandon truth, for such cultures only grow on the solid foundation of objective truth. Speaking the truth in love is the very essence of being "salt and light" (Matthew 5:13–14).

We are called to do all this great task in great humility, knowing that, as social beings, we too are profoundly shaped by our surrounding culture. We've likely imbibed its basic assumptions in ways we don't fully realize. Sadly, all too often the church has accommodated postmodern ideology rather than critique it biblically.

Christians, however, are called to inhabit the culture of God's Kingdom and to think with "the mind of Christ" (1 Corinthians 2:16). We are called to "take every thought captive" (2 Corinthians 10:5) and "be transformed by the renewing of our minds" (see Romans 12:2). In short, we are called to think and act differently— not according to the accepted norms, attitudes, and behaviors of our surrounding culture, but according to reality as presented in God's Word.

Let us pray that God would remove our cultural blinders and reveal the truth, confident that His Holy Spirit can indeed "guide us into all truth." As we see how our thinking has been shaped by false cultural assumptions, we must repent. Repentance literally means to "change your mind."[49] It means to turn from lies to the truth, from illusion to reality. Such repentance will change your life!

As a young man in the 1960s, Darrow Miller traveled to Europe and eventually found his way to L'Abri in Switzerland, and to the home of Francis and Edith Schaeffer. Darrow worked on staff at L'Abri for several years. During that time, he met Udo Middelmann. Darrow and Udo often talked late into the evening about the big questions of life.

Once, on a winter night, with snow gently falling outside and the warm glow of candles softly lighting the room, Udo turned to Darrow and said, "You know, Christianity is true even if you don't believe it." After two sleepless nights, Darrow finally realized that what Udo was saying was that "Christianity is true, even if nobody believes it." This simple idea shook Darrow to the core. He had always assumed (because he had been taught) that Christianity was true *because* he believed it. When he realized that God existed, objectively, wholly apart from anyone's beliefs about Him, Darrow repented. The course of his life was changed forever.

Like Darrow, many Christians don't know how to handle the idea that Christianity is objectively true. It is still common for even committed Christians to speak of their faith in personal, private terms. Christianity is "what I believe" or "is true for me." But as Darrow discovered that night in Switzerland, Christianity isn't a private belief, but a public reality. It isn't "my truth" or "your truth." It is *the* truth. The great British missiologist Lesslie Newbigin said it well: "[We must] affirm the gospel not only as an invitation to a private and personal decision but as public truth which ought to be acknowledged as true for the whole of the life of society."[50]

This will only happen if we have full confidence in the truth. As James said, "the one who doubts is like a wave of the sea, blown and tossed by the wind" (James 1:6). Our confidence grows when we understand the incomparable power and beauty of the biblical worldview. "Christianity has greater explanatory power than any other worldview or religion," Pearcey reminds us. "It fits the data of general revelation better. And it leads to a more humane and liberating view of the human person."[51]

Only the biblical worldview provides a comprehensive view of truth. It links metaphysical truth, physical truth, and moral truth into a unified whole. It allows for the affirmation of human dignity and human rights. It allows us to affirm the good and reject the bad. It provides a basis for understanding truth in the physical world through science and reason. It doesn't reduce truth either to the material realm or to the mind. It affirms both. The biblical worldview fits reality because it *is true*. It, alone, provides the necessary foundation for free, just, and flourishing societies.

That all sounds wonderful, but can we demonstrate it? Yes! We can test the truthfulness of any worldview with three questions: *Is it internally consistent? Does it align with reality? Can it be lived?* Only the biblical worldview passes all three tests. Materialism and postmodernism suffer from fatal contradictions; they "commit suicide."[52]

Postmodernism denies the existence of objective truth, yet the very denial is an objective truth claim. It decries all worldviews as impositions of power, and yet puts forward its own comprehensive worldview as objectively true. Materialism's fatal contradiction lies in its assertion that human beings can know truth through science and reason alone. But if human beings merely are highly evolved animals, at best, or machines, at worst, then we have no basis for believing that we can discover the truth about anything, much less "all truth," as hardcore materialists such as Hawking have claimed.

Most materialists fail to realize that postmodernism arose largely as a result of this fatal flaw. Though they have no foundation for logic, postmodernists draw the logical conclusion from this flaw. They are right to challenge the hubris of materialistic truth claims, but they go too far in claiming that objective truth cannot be known at all.

To strengthen our grasp of the truth, we Christians need to strengthen our confidence in the authority of God's Word, the Bible. We must reject the postmodern idea that the Bible, or any text, has no objective meaning, but only a multitude of interpretations. We must grow in our confidence that the truth of the Bible can be known, through careful study, the guidance of the Holy Spirit, and the help of respected teachers in the church, past and present.

There is no doubt, however, that we will be made to feel ashamed and embarrassed about our stand for objective truth, but we have nothing to be ashamed of. Objective truth is the most loving thing we can give to this mixed up and deluded world. Truth and love are two sides of the same coin. In our post-truth culture, truth and love have been scandalously sundered. We are told in countless ways, for instance, that if we fail to accept and affirm people's chosen identities, we fail to love them. If we insist on objective truth, we are branded intolerant "haters." But dividing truth from love will give us neither.

To be silent or passive in the face of destructive, even deadly, cultural lies is to fail in our Christian duty to love our neighbors. This dereliction of our Christian duty borders on apostasy. According to Chaput, Christians "don't need to publicly renounce their [faith] to be apostates. They simply need to be silent when their [faith] demands that they speak out; to be cowards when Jesus asks them to have courage; to 'stand away' from the truth when they need to work for it and fight for it."[53]

It is a warning that all who claim Christ must heed. Our standard is always to speak the truth in humility and gentleness— but speak it we must. "Biblical truth and wisdom are the highest love for human beings."[54]

Our work as ambassadors of truth must begin at the most basic level—with our personal honesty. Are we careful to speak truthfully, to not lie or shade the truth? Do we keep our word, even when it is costly? Do we keep our agreements, contracts, and vows? While none of us is perfect, we must grow in this area. If we are known as trustworthy, honest, and reliable, we can have tremendous influence.

This, after all, is what God is like. He never lies. He is solid and firm, and we are to imitate Him. Let's remember the simple but profound truth that honesty leads to trust, and trust is the glue that binds relationships—and society. As the world fractures and fragments, we can do our part to push back by strengthening relationships—with our spouses, friends, co-workers, neighbors, and customers—by living lives of honesty.

We also serve as ambassadors of truth by finding creative ways to push back against the core assumptions of our post-truth times. Newbigin rightly said "a serious commitment to evangelism, to the telling of the story which the Church is sent to tell, means a radical questioning of the reigning assumptions about public life."[55] Today, these "reigning assumptions" are materialist and postmodern.

Questioning them is not easy. We won't do it if we want to be admired by cultural gatekeepers and powerbrokers. Standing for unwelcome truth today requires courage and a willingness to be misunderstood, even hated. It may cost us our livelihood, our career, or worse. "Truth demands confrontation," Francis Schaeffer once said. "It must be loving confrontation, but there must be confrontation nonetheless."[56] Such loving confrontation, of course, must always done "with gentleness and respect" (1 Peter 3:15) as we share our hope in Christ.

We must affirm the goodness of reason and logic, and of free, open, and civil discussion and debate. Our post-truth culture has undermined all of these things, while elevating emotion and power tactics, including shaming, silencing, censoring and threatening. Of course, emotions are a God-given good, but reason must pull the train. Of all people, Christians should be the most outspoken champions of free speech, free and open inquiry, and civil discussion. As Catholic economist Michael Novak put it: "Only when truth is cherished as an imperative does civilization becomes possible. Only then can human beings enter into rational conversation with one another. For civilization is constituted by conversation. Barbarians bully; civilized people persuade."[57]

This will not be easy. There will be many disappointments, misunderstandings, and setbacks. We must therefore avoid falling into a pit of cynicism. Yes, we live in a world filled with lies, deceptions, spin, and distorted narratives. While our post-truth culture will tell us that this is all there is, we must never lose our confidence that truth exists, and we are called to search it out. God gave us minds so that we could be truth-seekers and critical thinkers, not herd-followers. Truth-seekers welcome questions, encourage dialogue, and keep an open mind.

We do this with the knowledge that, as finite beings, our grasp of truth will always be partial and limited. But God has given us the capacity to know truth, and we honor Him by seeking it. This is how we love God "with all your mind." (Luke 10:27). We dishonor Him by cynically throwing our hands up and asking, "What's the point?" Uncovering the truth of a matter can be difficult, particularly in our time. In some cases, it takes years of searching, investigating, listening, discussing, and debating. But that is our job.

This confident searching for truth should be the determined purpose of Christian journalists, historians, scientists, and academics of all stripes. It must be the purpose of all Christians to discover the truth of any matter. We must reject the post-truth practice of crafting, selling, or in any way furthering distorted narratives that cherry-pick facts and evidence in support of a desired viewpoint or outcome, while ignoring those that don't. We must pursue truth and facts, wherever the evidence leads. After all, as J.I. Packer reminded us:

> The Evangelical is not afraid of facts, for he knows that all facts are God's facts; nor is he afraid of thinking, for he knows that all truth is God's truth, and right reason cannot endanger sound faith. He is called to love God with all his mind. . . . A confident intellectualism expressive of robust faith in God, whose Word is truth, is part of the historic evangelical tradition. If present-day evangelicals fall short of this, they are false to their own principles and heritage.[58]

Our task is to keep the light of truth burning in our generation, no matter the cost. Unfortunately, that cost is growing higher by the day. Having rejected objective good and evil, post-truth culture has birthed a new totalitarian spirit that has no qualms in using "any means necessary" to crush dissent. It will take real courage to stand for truth, and real conviction—the kind displayed by the great Soviet dissident Aleksandr Solzhenitsyn. Let his credo be ours as well:

> The simple act of an ordinary brave man is not to participate in lies, not to support false actions! His rule: Let that come into the world, let it even reign supreme— only not through me.[59]

We can also learn how to respond from another famous Soviet dissident, Václav Havel, the Czech dramatist former prime minister. He contrasted "living within the lie" and "living within the truth."[60] He told the story of greengrocer who, out of fear, puts up a poster that says, "Workers of the World—Unite!" By so doing, the merchant chooses the path of least resistance. Yet, by tacitly supporting the deception the Party uses to maintain power and exert control, he compromises part of his humanity. He "lives within the lie." Then:

> . . . one day something in our greengrocer snaps and he stops putting up the slogans merely to ingratiate himself. He stops voting in elections he knows are a farce. He begins to say what he really thinks at political meetings. And he even finds the strength in himself to express solidarity with those whom his conscience commands him to support. In this revolt the greengrocer steps out of living within the lie. He rejects the ritual and breaks the rules of the game. He discovers once more his suppressed identity and dignity. He gives his freedom a concrete significance. His revolt is an attempt to live within the truth.

In this simple but courageous act of resistance, Havel says, "the greengrocer has addressed the world. He has enabled everyone to peer behind the curtain. He has shown everyone that it is possible to live within the truth."[61]

What about *you*? Are you prepared to live within the truth? If so, your light will shine brightly in an ever-darkening world, and yours will be the salt that slows its decay. As Christ-followers, we fix our eyes on our Savior, confident that the "truth will come out" because Jesus is on the throne. The lies of the devil may confuse us for a time, but the truth of God will prevail . . . forever.

One word of truth outweighs the entire world.

ALEXANDER SOLZHENITSYN[62]

CHAPTER 2

HUMAN

When I look at your heavens, the work of your fingers,
the moon and the stars, which you have set in place,
what is man that you are mindful of him,
and the son of man that you care for him?
Yet you have made him a little lower than the heavenly beings
and crowned him with glory and honor.
You have given him dominion over the works of your hands;
you have put all things under his feet,
all sheep and oxen, and also the beasts of the field,
the birds of the heavens, and the fish of the sea,
whatever passes along the paths of the seas.

PSALM 8:3-8, ESV

HUMAN

Pertaining to man (male and female), mankind, humans are physical and spiritual beings, created by God in His image, with intrinsic dignity, incalculable worth, and unalienable rights to life and liberty. Humans are created for an intimate relationship with their Creator, as well as relationships with one another. God created humans to wisely steward and govern the created world, and they are accountable to Him for how they carry out this task.

HUMAN REDEFINED

(1) A form of animal life, the product of a purposeless process of material evolution; a biological machine. (2) A radically autonomous, willing creature. An independent, self-determining agent. (3) A socially and historically determined being, a representative of a particular culture or identity group.

Hearing God's call to be a missionary, Luiza Diaz[1] left her hometown of Belém, Brazil, for dusty Nouakchott, Mauritania. One day, she came across a baby girl, lying in the road. The softly crying infant was ill, undernourished, and dying. She was with her grandmother, who was using her as a prop while begging for money.

Unlike the others hurrying past, Luiza, like the good Samaritan, stopped—and in that moment, two worldviews clashed, and Luiza's life was changed. Luiza gave the baby some water and asked for her mother. The grandmother replied, "She is gone, taking care of the other children. The doctor and the witchcraft we tried couldn't heal this child."

When Luiza attempted to put the baby next to her, the woman weakly shook her head, saying quietly in Arabic, "It is Allah's will that this child dies." Luiza indignantly replied, "No, it's God's will for this child to live an abundant life!"

Luiza ordered the grandmother to bring the infant to her home or be sent to the women's prison. The woman complied, and the baby's mother also came, offering to help with the child. Eventually Luiza, a single woman, legally adopted the child, changing her name to *Aleah*, which means "sublime" or "exalted."

Today, Aleah and her sister, Amina (meaning "honest" or "trustworthy")—who was adopted as a baby from the women's prison—are healthy, beautiful, and godly teenagers. Working with their mother from their home in southern France, they rescue teenage girls from Morocco who have been sold into European sex slavery.

HUMAN DEFINED

What does it mean to be human? How we answer this question will profoundly shape how we see ourselves, the kind of lives we lead, and how we treat others. This no less true on a cultural level. How our culture defines "human" will be established in policy, law, and practice—with life-and-death consequences.

Most fundamentally, humans are *created beings*. The Psalmist says: "You [God] knit me together in my mother's womb" and "I am fearfully and wonderfully made" (Psalm 139:13–14). We are *God's* creatures—and as such, we are contingent and dependent. We rely on God "for life, and breath and everything" (Acts 17:25). All of our days are ordained by God, "written in [His] book before one of them came to be" (Psalm 139:16). We exist by His will and for His purposes. We are not our own. Human life is a gift, a stewardship.

> **HUMAN**
> Pertaining to man (male and female), mankind, humans are physical and spiritual beings, created by God in His image, with intrinsic dignity, incalculable worth, and unalienable rights to life and liberty. Humans are created for an intimate relationship with their Creator, as well as relationships with one another. God created humans to wisely steward and govern the created world, and they are accountable to Him for how they carry out this task.

As His special creations, God knows and cherishes us. After completing His work of creation, God evaluated His handiwork and proclaimed it "very good" (Genesis 1:31). God loves His creation, and particularly His crowning achievement, human beings. Jesus said "the very hairs of your head are all numbered" (Luke 12:7). That's how important you—and all human beings—are to God. Because He created us and loves us, human life is imbued with profound dignity and incalculable worth, from the moment of conception to final breath.

Incredibly, God identifies Himself with human beings, and particularly with the weakest and most vulnerable among us. When we show compassionate care for our fellow human beings— for widows, prisoners, the hungry, and the naked—Jesus says, "whatever you did for one of the least of these brothers and sisters of mine, you did for me" (Matthew 25:40).

Humans are, of course, only one of the many creatures God made, and we share many of the same attributes as those in the animal kingdom. We have physical bodies; we reproduce after our own kind; we eat, sleep, breathe, and possess a survival instinct. Yet human beings are profoundly unlike, and distinct from, our fellow creatures, for we are uniquely made like God. God formed human beings from the dust of the earth, yet breathed into man His spirit (Genesis 2:7). We are embodied, spiritual beings who span the divide between heaven and earth. Our life began at the moment of conception, but it extends beyond physical death into eternity.

God is spirit (John 4:24), so bearing His image does not refer to physical resemblance. Rather, we resemble God's *nonphysical* qualities. God is a *person*, and so are we. He can think, feel, and reflect, and we can as well. He is a moral being, and so are we. He uses speech and language, as we do. He is a creative, working God, and we too are made to work and create. He is volitional and so are we. God reigns as King of heaven and earth, and we too have a realm and a dominion.

Because we share these attributes with God, we have the capacity for intimate fellowship with our Creator (as well as with other human beings). Indeed, we were *made* for a relationship with our Creator. As the great church father Augustine said, "You have made us for yourself, O Lord, and our heart is restless until it finds its rest in you."[2] These attributes set us apart from the rest of creation. We are creatures, but human beings are uniquely *God-like* creatures.

Our spiritual nature allows us to transcend the created world. We are not trapped in a cause-and-effect, mechanistic universe. We have the potential, like God, to shape the course of history. According to philosopher and theologian Dallas Willard, "human beings possess the capacity for '*radical* and *underivative* origination of events and things. What comes from us comes from nothing else but us. . . .'

This radical creativity is what makes the [human] person absolutely unique and irreplaceable, and therefore, an 'end in itself.'"[3]

"God created man in his own image, in the image of God he created him; *male and female he created them*" (Genesis 1:27, emphasis added). God is Community—Father, Son, and Holy Spirit. Part of our being made in God's image is that we have been made for community, as male and female. This is because one male cannot reflect all that it means to be the image of God. In fact, *two* males, or two females, cannot do this. It takes female *and* male to produce a community that reflects God's likeness.

Both sexes possess equal, God-given dignity and immeasurable value. All human beings share a unity and an equality—but not a uniformity. We share a common human nature, yet we display tremendous diversity. Our personalities, appearances, giftings, ethnicities, and sexes reflect our diversity. This is particularly true of male-female diversity.

As part of God's marvelous plan and intention, this diversity should be celebrated. Appreciating human diversity sets us free to be the people God created us to be.

These twin truths of human equality and human uniqueness provide a solid foundation for human community. Diversity without unity leads to conflict and bigotry ("Because we are different, I am better than you!"). Unity without diversity leads to the loss of individuality.

Only a biblical balance of equality and uniqueness allows human flourishing. This unity and diversity in human beings reflects the Triune God's image in us. God, in His own nature, possesses both unity and diversity. God is *one* (Deuteronomy 6:4) yet *three*, Father, Son, and Holy Spirit (Matthew 3:16–17). We'll explore this very important subject in further detail in our chapter on sex.

God created human beings for a purpose. Men and women are made to govern—to function as the kings and queens of creation, or more specifically, as vice-regents accountable to Him, under His authority. Genesis 1:27–28 lays out this basic human job description: "God blessed [Adam and Eve] and said to them, 'Be fruitful and increase in number; fill the earth and subdue it. Rule over the fish in the sea and the birds in the sky and over every living creature that moves on the ground.'" This same job description is stated again, in Genesis 2:15, but with a helpfully different emphasis: "The Lord God took the man and put him in the Garden of Eden *to work it and take care of it*" (emphasis added).

"God blessed" not only Adam and Eve, but *every* human being, with gifts and abilities. With creative minds, with words and language, with priceless bodies—hands, eyes, feet—He created us to "work" in His creation (and to rest, too!) Work is fundamental to our human dignity. We are to use our God-given endowments and blessings to care for and expand the Garden. To leave this magnificent world better than we found it. More beautiful, more fruitful, and more prosperous. This idea is powerfully captured by theologian James K. A. Smith:

> When God calls creation into being, He announces that it's "very good," but He doesn't announce that it's finished! Creation doesn't come into existence ready-made with schools, art museums, and farms; those are all begging to be unpacked . . . the riches and potential of God's good creation are entrusted to His image bearers. That is our calling and commission.[4]

In fact, the Bible teaches that God has special work—a unique calling—for each of us (Luke 19:11–26; Ephesians 2:10). He has endowed us with the gifts and talents necessary to do it. This gives incredible significance to all human life.

The collaborative nature of our shared reign over Creation is beautifully illuminated in Genesis 2:19:

> Now the Lord God had formed out of the ground all the
> wild animals and all the birds in the sky. He brought them
> to the man to see what he would name them; and whatever
> the man called each living creature, that was its name.

God, the senior partner, creates the animals with His spoken word. Then He graciously invites His junior partner and vice-regent, Adam, to exercise his own creativity, speak his own words, and name the animals. Amazingly, God humbly agrees to use the names given by Adam.

In defining "human," we must also admit that, because of our sin, we are not as God intended. He created us with the capacity to love Him, and love entails the freedom to choose. It cannot be forced. Our first human ancestors, Adam and Eve, rejected God, and we have suffered ever since. In the words of the apostle Paul: "sin entered the world through one man [Adam], and death through sin, and in this way death came to all men, because all sinned" (Romans 5:12). That first act of rebellion fractured man's relationship with God. And, as a consequence, all human relationships suffered. This explains why the world is scarred by mistrust, abuse, and violence.

Despite this cosmic rebellion against our Creator, we continue to bear His image. But now, the image is distorted. We are still creative, but now we use our creativity to destroy. We continue to love, but now we love idols, worshiping "created things rather than the Creator" (Romans 1:25). In our broken condition, we are born selfish and proud. Through our fallen nature, evil flows from us into God's good world. The source of evil in the world is not "out there" in other groups, or other political parties. No, it is "in here," in our own hearts. As Solzhenitsyn said, "the line dividing good and evil cuts through the heart of every human being."[5]

But God, in His amazing grace, didn't abandon us in our rebellious, fallen condition. Instead, He inaugurated a plan to restore our broken humanity, a plan that culminated when He entered history in the person of Jesus Christ. The incarnation is proof that God loves us, for, incredibly, He became one of us. Living a life of perfect obedience to His heavenly Father—a life that Adam didn't live, and we couldn't live—Jesus died on our behalf, paying the penalty we deserved. Then He rose to life again and lives forever, offering everyone forgiveness and reconciliation with God in His Name. In Christ, God made possible the restoration of our fallen humanity. Through trusting in Him for our salvation, and by the power of His Holy Spirit, we are progressively restored to be the humans He created us to be.

A HUMANE CULTURE

Wherever these truths about human life have shaped a culture, the results have been revolutionary. Cultures built on the truth about human life affirm and protect the dignity of all people, from conception to natural death, regardless of class, ethnicity, sex, or mental or physical condition. They care for and protect all human life, and particularly the weakest and most vulnerable—the unborn, the aged, the gravely ill, the widow, the homeless, the prisoner, and the impoverished. In the words of Muggeridge, "this life in us . . . however low it flickers or fiercely burns, is still a divine flame which no man dare presume to put out, be his motives ever so humane or enlightened."[6]

In such cultures, hospitals and hospices are founded, along with countless efforts to care for the impoverished and marginalized. At the height of the second great epidemic that swept through the Roman Empire, around 260, a writer named Dionysius composed a tribute to the heroic nursing efforts of Christians, many of whom lost their lives while caring for others.

Most of our brother Christians showed unbounded love and loyalty, never sparing themselves and thinking only of one another. Heedless of danger, they took charge of the sick, attending to their every need and ministering to them in Christ . . . drawing upon themselves the sickness of their neighbors and cheerfully accepting their pains. Many, in nursing and caring for others, transferred their death to themselves and died in their stead.[7]

It's not just that the poor and vulnerable are cared for in these cultures—children are positively *welcomed* as special gifts and blessings. Elizabeth Youmans, executive director of the Chrysalis Foundation, has said, "Every child is a promise—with a name, a passion, a story, and a place in God's story. Every child is unique. There are no ordinary children!"[8] Such cultures place a high value on the nurture and education of children and young adults. They value motherhood and fatherhood. It's no coincidence that education is part of the great legacy of the church. Indeed, some of the most important schools in the world, including Harvard, Yale, Oxford, Peking University, and many more were started by Christians.

Such cultures value men *and* women equally. In other cultures, a pernicious lie has destroyed and impoverished more lives than perhaps any other: *Men are superior to women.* In today's world, females have been systematically slaughtered through sex-selective abortions, abandonment, and infanticide, simply because of their sex.[9] By contrast, cultures that value girls and women, that educate them and prepare them to play their God-ordained roles in history, and that appreciate their distinct but complementary role to men are cultures that thrive.

Such cultures respect the uniqueness and individuality of every person, while also affirming the importance of God-established relationships: with God, family, church, and community. They don't subsume the individual to the state, or to any other social group, nor do they view individuals as merely mouthpieces for identity groups.

On the other hand, they do not see humans as radically autonomous individuals. Rather, they respect the unique importance of every human being while affirming their relational nature. Such cultures view people as invaluable assets—as history-makers, whose lives create ripples that carry on forever.

Cultures established on the truth about human life understand that human beings belong to God and are accountable to Him. They recognize that we are not born to be slaves, to be treated as the property of any person or group. We possess God-given rights to life and liberty that no one else, no matter how powerful, may arrogate. Such cultures protect and respect these God-given rights, particularly the freedom each of us has to accept or reject God.

Cultures that respect human life also value work, knowing that God created us to apply our gifts to uniquely bless this world. They don't treat people as pets or as livestock to be fed and sheltered. They avoid fostering debilitating dependencies that rob people of the joy and dignity that come through honest labor. They understand that the wealth of any nation comes from the creativity and innovation of its people. They understand that wealth happens when human beings take grapes and make wine; language and write books, poetry, and music; or sand and fabricate microprocessors and fiber optics.

Human beings have the unique, God-given capacity to leave this world better than they found it—more prosperous, more beautiful. Cultures that understand this advance government, educational, and economic policies to unleash this vast human potential.

Finally, such cultures take into account our fallen nature, our selfish ambition and pride. They form governments that diffuse power to minimize human evil. They recognize the potential for evil that exists in every heart. They don't divide the world into good and evil "tribes," thinking that if we just marginalize or eliminate

Jews, or women, or blacks, or whites, or Muslims, or Christians, everything will be fine. Until Jesus returns, everything will *never* be fine. We will never create a utopia here on earth . . . but that doesn't mean progress isn't possible. It is, and we can work for families, communities, and nations that are more humane.

HUMAN REDEFINED

Today, this older biblical definition of "human" has been largely replaced in the centers of cultural power. By far, the most significant milestone in the redefinition of human life occurred on November 24, 1859, when English naturalist Charles Darwin published his landmark volume, *The Origin of Species*. Darwin theorized that human life was not the purposeful handiwork of God, but rather was the purposeless product of an unguided process known as "natural selection." Darwin believed that natural selection, not the creative and sustaining providence of God, accounted for the origin and development of all plant and animal life, including human life. As Darwin's theory gained credibility in academia and in the broader culture, secularism replace the Judeo-Christian worldview as the dominant worldview shaping the West. Today, Darwin's theory is taught to children all over the world as an unquestioned scientific fact.

In the wake of Darwin, human life has been stripped of nearly all meaning. We are no longer seen as creatures of a benevolent Creator. The infinite-personal God has been replaced by impersonal, physical particles interacting with one another randomly. Thus, we are said to be impersonal, cosmic accidents, clumps of matter. This new belief system asserts that there is no life beyond the grave and that we are merely part of the physical world, cogs in a cause-and-effect material "machine." This worldview says that what we think, feel, and do is the result of impersonal forces and chemistry.

HUMAN REDEFINED
(1) A form of animal life, the product of a purposeless process of material evolution; a biological machine. (2) A radically autonomous, willing creature. An independent, self-determining agent. (3) A socially and historically determined being, a representative of a particular culture or identity group.

It says we are no longer responsible, for we no longer have the freedom to choose. It says we are no longer accountable, for there is nobody to whom we must give account. It says we no longer possess inherent dignity, value, or rights. It says we have no great task, no dominion, no responsibility toward the rest of creation. It says we exist to survive and pass on our genes to future generations.

When we ask, "Who am I?" we no longer look above to God for the answer. We look down to the animal kingdom, because we believe we *are* animals. As Ingrid Newkirk, cofounder of the People for the Ethical Treatment of Animals, put it, "A rat is a pig is a dog is a boy."[10] In the animal kingdom, however, there *are* no ethical considerations. Animals function by instinct, not by freedom of choice or moral reasoning. Only one law obtains: The survival of the fittest. Instead of beings made in the image of a creative God, we are fundamentally believed to be mere players in a life-and-death competition for survival.

This is all very depressing. It's also unlivable—which is why almost nobody lives as if this definition of human life is true. You won't be surprised to learn that very few parents treat their children as if they are biochemical machines, or livestock. The Copenhagen Zoo unintentionally helped prove this point in 1996 when it exhibited a caged pair of *Homo sapiens*. Peter Vestergaard, a representative of the zoo, explained that the exhibit's purpose was to force visitors to confront their origin and accept that "we are all primates."[11] As Vishal Mangalwadi explains: "The visitors saw the other hairy primates staring at the ceiling, swinging from bars, and picking lice from each other's pelts. However, the caged *Homo sapiens* (Henrik Lehmann and Marlene Botoft) worked on a motorcycle, checked their email . . . read books, and adjusted their air conditioner. . . . After a few weeks, both *Homo sapiens* departed the monkey house. The experiment violated their dignity as human beings."[12]

In a similar fashion, the West has tried to walk away from the most dehumanizing elements of Darwinist philosophy. To preserve human rights and human dignity in the culture, most committed Darwinists "borrow" from the biblical definition of humanity. Atheist philosopher Richard Rorty, for example, admits that Christianity gave rise to the concept of universal rights, derived from the principle that all people are made in the image of God. Rorty admits that he himself borrows the concept of human rights from Christianity. He even dubbed himself a "freeloading atheist."[13] He's not the only one, but at least he's honest.

We might believe that the idea that human beings are made in God's image is a given, taken for granted across the centuries, but it is not so. Nearly every society, at one time or another, has practiced some form of slavery. Most, at one time or another, have treated women as sexual objects or merely as the necessary source of children. In many cultures, children have been seen as cheap labor. Unwanted babies could be left in the elements to die. The disabled or infirm were often left to fend for themselves. The aged were considered burdens—extra mouths to feed.

America's founding took a different path: "We hold these truths to be self-evident, that all men are created equal, that they are endowed by their Creator with certain unalienable rights, that among these are life, liberty, and the pursuit of happiness." Without transcendent truth about human identity and basic human rights sourced in God, human rights become constructs of whoever happens to hold power. They can be taken away whenever the powers that be deem them inconvenient.

Human rights are founded not upon naturalism, pluralism, or relativism, but upon the unchanging truth, as laid out in the Bible, that every human being—male or female—is of equal worth and dignity, having been created by God in His image (Genesis 1:26–27). It is this truth claim of the worth of every individual, developed over many centuries, that inspired William Wilberforce to defeat the British slave trade, that fueled the abolition movement in nineteenth century America, that inspired Martin Luther King Jr. to look forward to the day "when all of God's children, black men and white men, Jews and Gentiles, Protestants and Catholics, will be able to join hands and sing in the words of the old Negro spiritual: Free at last! Free at last! Thank God Almighty, we are free at last!"[14]

The Universal Declaration of Human Rights,[15] proclaimed by the United Nations General Assembly in 1948, reflects this biblical emphasis[16] (though it does not mention God). It recognizes "the inherent dignity and . . . the equal and inalienable rights of all members of the human family." It declares that "[a]ll human beings are born free and equal in dignity and rights." It forbids slavery and torture. It commends equality before the law, including the presumption of innocence. It recognizes the right to marry and to own property. It supports freedom of thought, conscience, and religion, and it defends the right to freedom of association and to express one's opinion. All these freedoms flow naturally from their biblical source—the unchanging truth that every single one of us carries the imprint of our Maker.

Nelson Mandela said, "To deny people their human rights is to challenge their very humanity."[17] To give people their human rights is to acknowledge their very humanity, a humanity based on the biblical truth that we are made in the image and likeness of God.

Today, the dominant voices in our culture attempt to hold two contradictory ideas about human nature simultaneously. They affirm Darwin's account of reality, namely that human beings are mere cosmic accidents with no inherent dignity or value. At the same time, they assert that humans exist at the very center of the universe. Cultural critic Rod Dreher describes the second half of this new operational anthropology: "We think we are autonomous, willing creatures, who owe nothing to nature, to God, the past, or the future."[18] Political philosopher Michael Sandel of Harvard, meanwhile, describes the prevailing concept of human life today as the "unencumbered self," a self "unencumbered by moral or civic ties we have not chosen."[19]

If we are animals, we live to satisfy our appetites, urges, and instincts. As "gods," our appetites, desires, and choices are sacrosanct. According to Carl Trueman, a professor of church history at Westminster Theological Seminary, "The late modern self would seem to be understood primarily as a self-determining agent whose desires are curbed only by the principle of consent when brought into relationship with the desires of another self-determining agent."[20]

With the rise of postmodernism, human choice and desire have been elevated above objective reality. As Nancy Pearcey explains, "The sovereign self will not tolerate having its options limited by anything it did not choose—not even its own body."[21] The BBC features a young woman who identifies as non-binary who expresses this perfectly: "It doesn't matter what living, meat skeleton you've been born into; it's what you feel that defines you."[22] This is classic postmodernism applied to human anthropology. You are defined by your feelings. Reality exists solely in the mind. Your authentic self is wholly separate from your biology or anatomy. This is really a new take on ancient Gnostic dualism.

Michael Novak captured this "brave new world" as well as anyone: "For those who view the human being as without spirit . . . with no sense of an abiding good or of eternal beauty, there remains only flickering evanescent desires. Human life is reduced to acts of changeable will. Nothing remains but the individual's pursuit of one distraction after another, trying desperately to escape inner emptiness."[23]

Today, a form of neo-Marxist postmodernism has largely displaced materialism as the dominant worldview of the Western world. Where materialism reduces human beings to their physical *biology*, postmodern Marxism reduces human beings to their *sociology*. We are creatures whose identity is wholly socially determined. All of our ideas are merely social constructions stitched together by cultural forces.

In her book *Finding Truth*, Nancy Pearcey explains this postmodern, neo-Marxist anthropology: "Everyone's ideas are . . . merely social constructions stitched together by cultural forces. Individuals are little more than mouthpieces for communities based on race, class, gender, ethnicity, and sexual identity."[24]

Human individuality, freedom, and volition are the casualties of this radically dehumanizing anthropology. In the words of Jordan Peterson, it "reduces individuals to puppets of social forces . . . powerless to rise above the communities they belong."[25] The things that make you a unique individual—your personal history, life experiences, choices, and deeply held beliefs—don't matter. The only things that matter in defining who you are, are your group affiliations. This false view of human nature can only divide because it has no basis for unity. It can only segregate us into competing tribes, pitted against each other in an endless power struggle.

Christians can agree with this postmodern, neo-Marxist view of the human person on one point: Human beings are shaped profoundly by groups. The Bible affirms that we are not merely individuals but are social beings made for relationships. As the Bible says, "It is not good for the man to be alone" (Genesis 2:18). We are part of groups (families, churches, ethnicities) that deeply shape who we are. We are acculturated into these groups by shared languages, values, habits, and histories. While this is all true, we forcefully deny that human identity can be reduced to group identity. The groups we belong to *shape* us. They do not *define* us.

The biblical definition of human life is rich, multifaceted, and wholistic. The various redefinitions of human life are, by contrast, one-dimensional and reductionist. When we redefine what it means to be human—when we reduce and devalue human life—the results are catastrophic. In the late 1800s, Darwin's theory of natural selection sparked a redefinition of human life that continues to this day.

A CULTURE OF DEATH

For decades, advocates of human abortion have used euphemisms and obfuscations to hide what goes on. It was called a "procedure," a "woman's choice." The unborn baby was called a "fetus," a "product of conception," or even a "blob of tissue." Even the word "abortion" blurs the fact that a tiny human life is killed. The number of babies' lives terminated, globally, through abortion is staggering. This is not progress. It is the devolving of our humanity.

Given all this linguistic legerdemain, it's not surprising that sixty-three million abortions have been performed since the US Supreme Court's *Roe v. Wade* ruling, in which Justice Harry Blackmun stated, "We need not resolve the difficult question of when life begins. When those trained in the respective disciplines of medicine, philosophy, and theology are unable to arrive at any consensus, the judiciary, at this point in the development of man's knowledge, is not in a position to speculate as to the answer."[26]

And the obfuscation never ends. Some who concede today that the unborn *are* human deny to them the status of personhood. "Life is a process, not an event," Alabama abortionist Willie Parker says. "If I thought I was killing a person, I wouldn't do abortions. A fetus is not a person; it's a human entity. In the moral scheme of things, I don't hold fetal life and the life of a woman equally. I value them both, but in the precedence of things, when a woman comes to me, I find myself unable to demote her aspirations because of the aspirations that someone else has for the fetus that she's carrying."[27]

Apparently, it's wrong to kill a "person," but it's not wrong to kill a "human entity."

The abortion industry has grown fat on this kind of "reasoning." But such plausible deniability of what happens in an abortion disappeared in 2015, at least for a little while. That was when David Daleiden's Center for Medical Progress began releasing a series of undercover videos in which executives and employees of Planned Parenthood—the nation's largest abortion mill—callously discussed abortion and the covert sale of fetal body parts.

One Planned Parenthood figure in Texas taught partial-birth abortion in such a way as to "strive for" intact baby brains. Another admitted engaging in creative accounting to hide the sale of human body parts. One clinic changed the way it did abortions in order to harvest intact fetuses so that a local company could sell them.[28]

Being an unborn human made you a potential supply of raw materials to be bought and sold for the financial benefit of others. That's the secular culture's lowest-common-denominator view of what it means to be human today, and we can already see the bitter fruit. How the dominant culture defines "human" increasingly will be established in policy, law, and practice—with life-and-death consequences for all of us.

Salon essayist Mary Elizabeth Williams wrote in a 2013 article titled "So What If Abortion Ends Life?": "I believe life starts at conception. And it's never stopped me from being pro-choice." She continued: "A fetus can be a human life without having the same rights as the woman in whose body it resides. She's the boss. Her life and what is right for her circumstances and her health should automatically trump the rights of the non-autonomous entity inside her. Always." Or, to borrow a line from Orwell's *Animal Farm*, "some lives are more equal than others." Williams ends her article with these chilling words: "The fetus is indeed a [human] life. A life worth sacrificing."[29]

According to Pearcey, we now "have a new category of individual: the human non-person."[30] In the *Roe v. Wade* decision, Justice Harry Blackmun wrote, "The word 'person' as used in the Fourteenth Amendment, does not include the unborn." Because the unborn is not an autonomous, choosing being, it is not a person.[31]

This deception is at the heart of abortion, but it is now being applied to euthanasia, selling fetal tissue, embryonic stem cell research, genetic engineering, and eugenics. And there is absolutely no scientific basis for it!

We've seen all this before. In 1927, the United States Supreme Court, in its notorious *Buck v. Bell* decision, ruled in favor of compulsory sterilization for those deemed to be "feebleminded" and "unfit." In his majority decision, Justice Oliver Wendell Holmes, Jr., wrote that "It is better for all the world, if . . . society can prevent those who are manifestly unfit from continuing their kind." He even went so far as to suggest the possibility of infanticide in order "to reduce the number of undesirables."[32]

Eugenics—basically animal husbandry applied to human beings—was an early and bitter fruit of Darwinian anthropology. Its main British champion was Francis Galton, Darwin's cousin. He believed that most children were born to what he regarded as "inferior races."[33] Galton wanted to create a "highly-gifted race of men" by weeding out the weaklings.[34] In the United States, Margaret Sanger, founder of Planned Parenthood, wrote that "the most urgent problem [we face] is how to limit and discourage the over-fertility of the mentally and physically defective."[35] Compulsory sterilization laws were eventually adopted by thirty US states, leading to the forced sterilization of more than sixty thousand disabled people.

These laws influenced the much larger sterilization program in Germany, which, in turn, laid the foundation for the Holocaust,[36] in which more than six million Jews were exterminated. The Nazis also labeled the disabled *Lebensunwertes Leben* (life unworthy of life).

According to the Jewish Virtual Library, "The forced sterilizations began in January 1934, and altogether an estimated 300,000 to 400,000 people were sterilized under the law. A diagnosis of 'feeblemindedness' provided the grounds in the majority of cases, followed by schizophrenia and epilepsy. The usual method of sterilization was vasectomy and ligation of ovarian tubes of women. Irradiation (x-rays or radium) was used in a small number of cases. Several thousand people died as a result of the operations, women disproportionately because of the greater risks of tubal ligation."[37]

But who decides who is unfit to reproduce? Those in power. When a culture abandons God, it loses the only sure foundation for human rights, dignity, and worth. Either God defines what a human being is, or man does. But whatever man defines, he can redefine— and does. Whatever rights man gives, he can take. Without God, any definition of "human" will be determined and enforced by whichever group has the most power, almost always in cahoots with the state.[38] Rather than defending a right to life, the state will define *which lives are worth living*. This *should* have been the great lesson of the twentieth century.

The great tyrannies of the twentieth century—Nazism, fascism, and communism—were essentially religious movements. God was replaced by the state, which demanded complete obedience. As in Orwell's *1984*, the state defined reality, including the "reality" of human life. For Hitler and the Nazis, the "Aryan race" was superior, destined to prevail in evolution's "survival of the fittest" contest. For Marx and his many disciples, the state was a substitute God. Property owners who didn't willingly surrender their assets to the state were robbed, starved, murdered, or rounded up and sent to the gulags.

All told, more than one hundred million people were killed as communist regimes seized power in the former Soviet Union, Maoist China, Cambodia, Cuba, North Korea, Vietnam, and elsewhere.[39]

As horrific as these twentieth century totalitarian movements were, their death tolls pale in comparison with the even greater horror occurring today. We have already mentioned the Supreme Court's disastrous 1973 *Roe v. Wade* decision, followed by the legalized murder of sixty-three million children through abortion. Then we must add the seventy million unborn baby girls who were aborted in China since its despicable one-child policy was instituted in 1979.[40]

Add to that the millions of abortions performed worldwide, and it becomes clear that we are living through the greatest genocide in human history—right now, on our watch. And while the deadly ideologies undergirding American slavery, Nazism, and fascism have been largely discredited, the champions of the dehumanizing ideology undergirding abortion retain their prestige in academia, entertainment, law, and government. Every year, the largest abortion provider in the United States, Planned Parenthood, receives more than $500 million from taxpayers.[41]

Unborn children are not the only victims of abortion, of course. Abortion puts the burden of a life-and-death decision on mothers in crisis pregnancies. Many are deeply troubled by the idea of aborting their children, but they feel trapped, and abortion provides a seductive solution. For many more, aborting the child is not their choice at all. They are literally forced into it (often kicking and screaming) by boyfriends or husbands. The profound guilt and trauma that these women bear because of their abortions can haunt them for the rest of their lives.

What message has all this carnage sent? Life is cheap and meaningless. *Lebensunwertes Leben.* When young people ask, "Who am I?" today, the answer seems to be: "An accident. A meaningless lump of matter." This is the basic message of Darwinian evolution, taught as fact to generations of students in our public schools and globally. More and more young people are taking their own lives. The annual US suicide rate increased by 24 percent between 1999 and 2014. As of 2023, suicide is the second-leading cause of death for young people aged fifteen to twenty-four.[42]

Today, we see other troubling trends. Eugenics is making a comeback. A 2017 report from CBS News proclaimed that Iceland was "on the verge of eliminating Down syndrome."[43] But the country isn't eliminating Down syndrome; it's eliminating *people* with Down through prenatal testing and abortion. The related "population control" movement is also gaining momentum, driven by a human anthropology that sees people as blights on the environment. The late British political philosopher John N. Gray portrays humanity as a ravenous species engaged in wiping out other forms of life. In his book *Straw Dogs: Thoughts on Humans and Other Animals*, he wrote:

> Homo rapiens [sic] is the only one of very many species, and not obviously worth preserving. Later or sooner, it will become extinct. When it is gone the Earth will recover. Long after the last traces of the human animal have disappeared, many of the species it is bent on destroying will still be around, along with others that have yet to spring up. The earth will forget mankind. The play of life will go on.[44]

This profoundly anti-human view is all too common among leaders of the contemporary environmental movement. It harkens back to Thomas Malthus and his understanding of man as essentially a rapacious, consuming animal. A recent headline proclaims: "Want to save the planet? Don't have children! Study finds bringing new life into the world is the most destructive thing you can do to the environment."[45]

If you view children as destroyers of the planet, or as expensive and time-consuming barriers to personal autonomy, you naturally will have fewer of them. This is exactly what is happening. In the United States, the birth rate has fallen to its lowest level in thirty years,[46] and all over the world, industrialized and secularized countries are shrinking in population.[47]

Then there is *transhumanism*, a movement to evolve the human race beyond its current physical and mental limitations using science and technology. One of the most prominent advocates of transhumanism is geneticist Lee Silver of Princeton University. In *Remaking Eden: Cloning and Beyond in a Brave New World*, Silver spins out a scenario in which humanity will split into two separate races—genetic super-persons who rule over sub-persons. The first group will become the controllers of society. The second group will become the low-paid laborers and service-providers. For Silver, presumably assuming he will be in the first group, this new world will be a kind of utopia.[48]

Other transhumanists, such as Ray Kurzweil, Google's director of engineering, believe that advances in artificial intelligence will enable people to download the brain to a computer, making possible a certain kind of digital immortality. "The whole idea of a 'species' is a biological concept," he says. "What we are doing is transcending biology."[49] Philosopher Mortimer Adler, however, saw a different kind of future. Back in the '60s, he warned, "Groups of superior men [will] be able to justify their enslavement, exploitation, or even genocide of inferior human groups, on factual and moral grounds akin to those that we now rely on to justify our treatment of animals we harness as beasts of burden."[50]

Yet another bitter fruit of this view of human life is the rise of the welfare state. Welfare programs undermine the human capacity to work, innovate, and steward resources. By fostering dependency on recipients, people made in God's image are robbed of the dignity that comes through work, and the profound meaning in life that comes through providing for oneself and others. Similar programs, including foreign aid, international development projects, and even well-intentioned missionary work also can be dehumanizing and destructive.

This is just a sampling of the terrible fruit that has resulted from our culture's tragic redefinition of "human." It is the great task of the church in each generation to push back against lies that demean and destroy human life, and to cherish, champion, and pass along the profound truth of what it really means to be human.

HOW SHOULD WE THEN LIVE?

In his book *Something Beautiful for God*, Malcolm Muggeridge recalled a television interview with Mother Teresa, the famous missionary to the poor of Calcutta. Muggeridge posed questions that reflected the opinion of many sophisticated people in England and around the world: Were there not already too many people in India? Was it really worthwhile to salvage a few abandoned children who might otherwise be expected to die of neglect, malnutrition, or a related illness?[51]

According to Muggeridge, "[It was a question] so remote from her whole way of looking at life that she had difficulty grasping it. The notion that there could in any circumstances be too many children was, to her, as inconceivable as suggesting that there are too many bluebells in the woods or stars in the sky."[52]

Mother Teresa knew that all human life, from the moment of conception to the last breath, has immeasurable value, and she lived that way. God created humans in His image and deeply loves each of us, whether we are male or female, rich or poor, and whatever our race, caste, creed, or disability. In every society where this truth penetrates, slavery is abolished, the treatment and status of women and children are improved, the unborn and the dying are cared for, and the poor, broken, and outcast are served.

Writing about the distinctive characteristics of early Christianity, sociologist Rodney Stark concluded that, above all else, Christianity brought a new conception of humanity to a world saturated with cruelty. "What Christianity gave to its converts," he said, "was nothing less than their humanity."[53]

What drew the early converts to Christianity was a better anthropology. Christ-followers articulated and demonstrated the truth about what it means to be human, and it attracted people—particularly women, the marginalized and dispossessed—like moths to a light. The church, at her best, faithfully proclaims and champions this powerful, transforming truth to each generation.

The ultimate goal must be to change the hearts and minds of our countrymen. We must make crystal clear the vast difference between grubby notions of "human non-persons" and the exalted Christian concept of personhood, which depends not on what I can *do* but on who I *am*—that I am created in the image of God. Human beings need not earn a standing as creatures of great value. Our dignity is *intrinsic*, rooted in the fact that God made us, knows us, and loves us.

We'll have to roll up our sleeves in trusting faith. "Bad philosophy needs to be answered with good philosophy," Ryan Anderson says. "Bad science needs to be responded to with good science. . . . This takes work. We have to work twice as hard as our opponents. We have to understand their arguments better than they understand them themselves—so we can then explain, at the level of reason, where they've gone wrong."[54]

Can we explain how the "pro-choice" position fails to uphold their cherished cultural value of inclusion? Abortion, after all, is exclusive, not inclusive. Abortion says that "some people don't measure up. They don't make the cut. They don't qualify for rights of personhood."[55]

Why not gently turn the tables on those who appeal to personal choice and autonomy? Proponents of a subhuman view of humanity love to say, "If you're against abortion, don't have one," "If you're against assisted suicide, don't do it," and "If you're against gay marriage, don't have one." But are these things only matters of private individuals making personal choices? No. Like the air we breathe, they impact *everyone*. They define the kind of society we all live in.

Let's help our neighbors see this by using the same approach with other issues: "Don't like murder? Then don't kill anyone." "Don't like slavery? Then don't own slaves." They would never go along with this kind of sophistry, understanding that some issues have a profound impact on our shared society, our community. We must help them see that human rights and human dignity apply to everyone.[56]

We not only have to win minds, but also hearts. Let's do this by obeying Jesus, who said, "love your enemies, and pray for those who persecute you" (Matthew 5:44). We must view our opponents as human beings, loved by God, and therefore worthy of our respect. "The Lord's servant must not be quarrelsome but must be kind to everyone. . . . Opponents must be gently instructed, in the hope that God will grant them repentance leading them to a knowledge of the truth" (2 Timothy 2:24–25).

We also do this by tenderly caring for the many victims of abortion, and particularly for the countless women whose lives have been shattered. They need to know that forgiveness and loving care are available from Jesus and His church. Isn't it wonderful that crisis pregnancy centers outnumber abortion facilities four thousand to seven hundred in America?[57]

Let's also expose the "fruitless deeds of darkness" (Ephesians 5:11). Since evil thrives in darkness, where it is out of sight, one of the most effective things we can do is to expose it. Besides the Center for Medical Progress, other heroic Christians have shined a light on the evils of abortion, including Lila Rose and the LiveAction Network, Voices for the Voiceless in Phoenix, and Ryan Bomberger's Radiance Foundation.

Because of all this, the momentum on abortion is shifting. Anderson, a Millennial and a scholar with the Heritage Foundation, captured this shift powerfully:

> Think of pro-lifers in February 1973, just weeks after *Roe v. Wade*. Public opinion was against them, by a margin of 2:1. With each passing day another pro-life public figure—Ted Kennedy, Jesse Jackson, Al Gore, Bill Clinton—evolved to embrace abortion on demand. The media kept insisting that all the young people were for abortion rights. Elites ridiculed pro-lifers as being on the wrong side of history. The pro-lifers were aging; their children, increasingly against them.
>
> But courageous pro-lifers put their hand to the plow, and today we reap the fruits.
>
> My generation is more pro-life than my parents' generation. A majority of Americans identify as pro-life, more today than at any other point. More state laws have been passed protecting unborn babies in the past decade than in the previous 30 years combined.
>
> What happened?
>
> Academics wrote the books and articles making the scientific and philosophical case for life. Statesmen like Henry Hyde, Ed Meese, and Ronald Reagan crafted the policy and used the bully pulpit to advance the culture of life. Activists and lawyers got together; coalitions were formed and strategies were devised. Witness to the truth was borne.
>
> And the Christian community woke up—the Southern Baptists at the time, we sometimes forget, were in favor of abortion rights and supported *Roe*. Today they are at the forefront of the cause for life.[58]

Anderson rightly says that in the pro-life movement, "there's work for everyone, for artists and musicians, for pastors and theologians, for statesmen and lawyers, for scholars and activists." What role will *you* play?

Our goal is not to win a culture war, or to impose our views. It's to love our neighbors, which means working for their good. When a deadly lie emerges, a lie that dehumanizes, we *must* act—out of love. We cannot sit back passively, or "go along to get along." We must confront the lie and articulate the countervailing and life-affirming truth, helping our neighbors see how the materialistic and postmodern redefinitions of human life that they have believed are reductionist, dehumanizing, and ultimately unlivable. They don't fit who we are; they don't match the real world.

It is up to the church to have the courage of her convictions and keep the flame burning in each generation. "The only way to find the courage, and the strength to do this, and to have the hope to fulfill our vocation in life," says Anderson, "is to rely on the grace of the One who called us to that vocation."

> History isn't a blind force. We aren't passive observers. History will be shaped by the actions of people like you and me, by our response to God's call. And so it is not history that will judge us. We know that we will be judged instead by the Lord of history. The same Lord who reversed history's greatest evil when He rose from the grave the following Sunday.[59]

Mother Teresa was right. In the end, we will be judged by how we cared for the most vulnerable, by how we emulate our heavenly Father: "A father to the fatherless, a defender of the widows, is God in his holy dwelling" (Psalm 68:5); "He will deliver the needy who cry out, the afflicted who have no one to help. He will take pity on the weak and the needy and save the needy from death. He will rescue them from oppression and violence, for precious is their blood in his sight" (Psalm 72:12–14). Our greatest apologetic as we share God's love will be how we care for weak and vulnerable people made in God's image.

Who are those out of sight and out of mind in your life or circle of influence? The unborn and infant, elderly and dying, the sick, lonely, and isolated, the refugee or alien? They might be in our own home, or next door, or down the street. Start there. And as you do, remember that "no matter who we are addressing, or what moral issue the person is struggling with, their first need is to hear the gospel and experience the love of God. The most important question of their life is whether they will have a relationship with the living God that lasts into eternity."[60]

CHAPTER 3

SEX

So God created mankind in his own image,
in the image of God he created them;
male and female he created them.

GENESIS 1:27

At the beginning the Creator
made them male and female, and said,
"For this reason a man will leave his father and mother
and be united to his wife, and the two will become one flesh."
So they are no longer two, but one flesh.

MATTHEW 19:4-6

SEX

(1) The God-created male-female division. (2) Sexual intercourse between a man and a woman; a comprehensive one-flesh union of heart, mind, spirit, and body, often issuing in the gift of children. Sexual intercourse is a gift from God exclusively for the uniting of husband and wife in marriage.

SEX REDEFINED

(1) Synonymous with gender, a social construct; a person's subjective sense of their sexual identity, without regard to biology or anatomy. (2) The ultimate source of personal identity and meaning. (3) Any form of recreational sexual activity done to give pleasure.

Michael Hobbes describes in heartbreaking detail how profoundly the Sexual Revolution impacted his friend Jeremy:

"I would stay up all weekend and go to these sex parties and then feel like [expletive] until Wednesday. About two years ago I switched to cocaine because I could work the next day. . . . The drugs were a combination of boredom and loneliness," he says. "I used to come home from work exhausted on a Friday night and it's like, 'Now what?' So I would dial out to get some meth delivered and check the Internet to see if there were any parties happening. It was either that or watch a movie by myself."

Jeremy (not his real name) is not my only gay friend who's struggling. There's Malcolm, who barely leaves the house except for work because his anxiety is so bad. There's Jared, whose depression and body dysmorphia have steadily shrunk his social life down to me, the gym and Internet hookups. And there was Christian, the second guy I ever kissed, who killed himself at 32, two weeks after his boyfriend broke up with him. Christian went to a party store, rented a helium tank, started inhaling it, then texted his ex and told him to come over, to make sure he'd find the body.

For years I've noticed the divergence between my straight friends and my gay friends. While one half of my social circle has disappeared into relationships, kids and suburbs, the other has struggled through isolation and anxiety, hard drugs and risky sex."[1]

Michael, Jeremy, Jared, Malcolm, Christian. All are God's precious creations, made in His image, with dignity, purpose, and incalculable worth. They, and countless others, are victims of the Sexual Revolution and its celebration of neopagan sexuality.

Over the last sixty years, this revolution has overthrown a millennia-old order and replaced it with a new one. The new order

is defined by a new god, a new anthropology, and a new morality—
what was formerly called evil is now called good, and vice versa.
It has redefined critical, load-bearing words in the culture—sex,
marriage, family, and even male and female. Though a seeming
novelty only a few years ago, it has quickly become institutionalized
in government, law, education, and business. It is relentlessly
championed in music, film, television, and literature.

While it arose in the West, this revolution now has set its
sights on the rest of the world. Every American has been profoundly
impacted by the revolution in ways obvious and subtle. Christians,
too, have been caught up in these momentous changes. Bible-
believing churches have been cast as the enemy. The most ardent
revolutionaries pushing for the church to surrender . . . or perish.
To grasp how far we have fallen as a culture, let's look first at the
biblical definition.

SEX DEFINED

To understand sex, we begin with truth about the body. Our bodies
aren't meaningless matter. They are the handiwork of a loving God.
They exhibit order, design, and purpose. Scripture treats body and
soul with equal importance, as parts of a deeply interconnected
whole.[2] Masculine and feminine are the architectual drawings for
the physical product of male and female.

This high view of the human body was a relative newcomer
in the history of the world. Ancient pagan cultures, Nancy Pearcey
says, were "permeated by world-denying philosophies such as
Manichaeism, Platonism, and Gnosticism, all of which disparaged
the material world as the realm of death, decay and destruction—
the source of evil."[3] Christianity revolutionized the pagan world by
teaching that matter—including the human body—was not evil, but
good—so good, in fact, that God entered creation in human form,
as a sexed human being, a male, Jesus, born of a female, Mary.

SEX AND GENDER

Today, the word *sex* primarily connotes sexual activity, although historically it has mainly referred to being biologically male or female. Today, however, that latter definition is used almost interchangeably with the word *gender*. Let us keep in mind that the words *sex* and *gender*, though related, actually are quite different.

Historically, *gender* has referred to how people live out their sex, how they act or behave in light of being biologically male or female. This varies somewhat from one culture to the next. For example, in the West, it is common for baby boys to be associated with the color blue, and baby girls with pink.

Today in postmodern culture, for the purpose of eliminating the importance of biological distinctions, sex (a God-given, objective reality) is equated with gender (a subjective, culturally influenced concept). Sexual revolutionaries say that since gender is a subjective concept, sex is too. This is completely false. Our sex is not a personal choice shaped by our culture. It is a God-given biological reality. You either have a Y chromosome or you don't.

Let's look at what the Bible says. It informs us that the Triune God formed man male and female for life together. We see this in the first chapter of the first book of the Bible: "Then God said, 'Let us make man in our image, after our likeness.' . . . So God created man in his own image, in the image of God he created him; *male and female he created them*" (Genesis 1:26–27, italics added).

SEX

(1) The God-created male-female division. (2) Sexual intercourse between a man and a woman; a comprehensive one-flesh union of heart, mind, spirit, and body, often issuing in the gift of children. Sexual intercourse is a gift from God exclusively for the uniting of husband and wife in marriage.

Incredibly, God's divine image is reflected in embodied, sexual human beings. Notice that it says let "us" make man in "our" image. It does not say let "me" make man in "my" image. Before the creation of the world, there was community, communication, and communion within the Godhead—Father, Son, and Holy Spirit. The Trinity is marked by unity without uniformity and diversity without superiority. So when God created man in His image, He didn't create a single, solitary individual, "a genderless monad."[4] He created a complementary pair—male and female—marked by unity without uniformity and diversity without superiority.

As Glenn Stanton says, "When God said, 'Let us make man in our image, in our likeness,' and then created Adam and Eve and bid them to be sexually fruitful, it tells us something important about who God is. Male and female, in their body, soul and mind and in their sexuality, must be some kind of earthly icon of the heavenly God. We don't know *how* this is, but we must know *that* it is."[5]

One single male, or one single female, cannot reflect all that it means to be made in the image of God, nor can two males or two females. It takes *female and male* to reveal God's comprehensive nature.

As Simon Chan, the Earnest Lau Professor of Systematic Theology at Trinity Theological College in Singapore, acknowledges, "Feminine images are used throughout Scripture to describe God's compassionate and loving nature. Examples include the frequent images of God protecting and comforting his children (Isa. 66:12–13; Hos. 11:1–4). But it's important to note that God is never addressed as *Mother*."[6]

Together, female and male are integrated as the comprehensive, complementary, transcendent nature of the image of God. No wonder the devil so often seeks to distort human sexuality, which Stanton says reflects "one of the deepest and most mystical parts of the very image and likeness of God in the world."[7]

"This centrality of human sexuality to the divine image can also be seen in what God's terrible enemy attacks at the beginning of Creation," Stanton says. "A smart adversary attacks the most strategic and valuable outposts of his enemy. What is it that Satan attacks in creation? It is not just Adam and Eve, but Adam and Eve as God created them to be as images of His likeness. As lovers, intimate and self-giving, life-creators."[8]

Satan attacked their fundamental purpose to create families, the building blocks of society, and together to fulfill their divine purpose of the cultural mandate.

So sex is an essential part of our identity. It is not some evolutionary accident. It is a gift we receive, not a choice we make. God expects us to gratefully receive, and live in conformity with, the body He gave us.[9] "At the heart of the church's historic teaching on human sexuality," says Todd Wilson in his excellent book *Mere Sexuality*, "is the belief that sexual difference, being male or female, is both theologically and morally significant. It matters to God, and it ought to matter to us."[10]

> When God created you in his image as male or female, he called you to a certain way of life—as either a male or female . . . you have a call on your life; you have a vocation. It is your most basic vocation, your most fundamental job in life: to joyfully embrace and faithfully embody your sexuality—whether male or female—for the good of others.[11]

As Elisabeth Elliot said, men and women are "two creatures amazingly alike and wondrously different."[12] How different? In a popular TED talk, cardiologist Paula Johnson tells us, "Every cell has a sex—and what that means is that men and women are different down to the cellular and molecular level. It means that we're different across all our organs, from our brains to our hearts, our lungs and joints."[13]

Bruce Goldman of Stanford University, explaining differences in the brains of women and men, says that on average, women's reading comprehension and writing ability consistently exceed those of men. Likewise, women outperform men in fine-motor coordination and perceptual speed—and they're more adept at retrieving information from long-term memory. Men, on average, can more easily juggle items in working memory. They're better at visualizing what happens when a complicated two- or three-dimensional shape is rotated in space, at tracking moving objects and at aiming projectiles.[14]

The brains of men and women both have grey and white matter. Grey matter deals with facts and is used for the rational processing required for science and math. White matter deals with meaning and is used to assimilate and sort information. Females have ten times more white matter than males. And males have six-and-a-half times more grey matter than females. Both are needed for fully functional societies. All of this should cause us to grow in our appreciation for the complementary strengths male and female bring to every task.[15]

"The opposite sex isn't just some strange creature from another planet," Wilson says, "but it is God's gift to you, as your complement, whether you are male or female."[16] As 1 Corinthians 11:11–12 says: "In the Lord woman is not independent of man, nor is man independent of woman. For as woman came from man, so also man is born of woman." Biologically, physiologically, chromosomally, and anatomically, males and females are counterparts to one another. "To have a male body is to have a body structurally ordered to loving union with a female body, and vice versa," says Anglican theologian Oliver O'Donovan.[17]

The sexed body has a built-in purpose, seen in Genesis 1:28, ESV: "God blessed them. And God said to them, 'Be fruitful and multiply and fill the earth and subdue it, and have dominion over the fish of the sea and over the birds of the heavens and over every living thing that moves on the earth.'" Notice that this purpose (sometimes referred to as the Cultural Commission) is for "them." It is a joint task for both male and female, with two distinct aspects.

The first is "be fruitful and multiply." Bear and raise offspring, form families, cultures, and nations. The second aspect is having dominion—stewarding creation as God's vice regents. Just as it takes male and female to fully reflect the image of God, so it takes female and male to fulfill the Cultural Commission.

Despite the headlines in recent years proclaiming, "man has a baby," it is biologically *impossible* for two men or two women to procreate. This requires two distinct sets of sexual organs, one male and one female, to create a unique, priceless human being who will live in time and eternity. Because God designed sexual intimacy between male and female to bear the fruit of new human life, it is incredibly powerful and must be channeled with great care. Today, inexpensive and readily available birth control has given rise to the myth of "safe sex." But as Wilson reminds us, "there is no such thing as safe sex. Sex is too powerful to ever be safe. It isn't safe, but it is good."[18]

Only one place exists where the power of procreation is both safe and good—within the context of the lifelong covenant of marriage. It is the God-ordained community intended to firmly cement husband to wife, and both to the offspring their union produces.

Ryan Anderson puts it succinctly: "Marriage exists to bring a man and a woman together as husband and wife to be father and mother to any children their union produces. Marriage is based on the anthropological truth that men and women are different and complementary, the biological fact that reproduction depends on a man and a woman, and the social reality that children need both a mother and a father."[19]

Some liken sex to a river. When it flows in its God-ordained channel (marriage), it is powerful, beautiful, and life-giving. But when it overflows, it is destructive. Sexual immorality is defined in Scripture as any sexual activity outside the bounds of marriage. "It cannot be overstated," says Kevin DeYoung, "how seriously the Bible treats the sin of sexual immorality."[20] Sex isn't restricted to marriage because God is some kind of cosmic killjoy. After all, He designed sex! He knows its life-giving potential. He knows best how to maximize it for human flourishing. Out of His pure love, He graciously warns us of the brokenness that is unleashed when sex is abused.

Wilson notes:

> Sex isn't a toy or plaything: it's a sacred and sovereign power—strong enough, in fact, to bring new life into being. . . . Our sexual capacities are powerful, far too powerful to be used anywhere outside of marriage. They need the safe and stable environment that comes with a "till death do us part" commitment.[21]

In God's plan, the purpose of sex goes beyond procreation. It includes the bonding of husband and wife; what theologians call its unitive function. The Hebrew word *echad* means "united," "compound," or "bound together." This word is used of the nature of the Trinitarian God (combined one Lord) and the nature of the union of a man and woman in marriage. We do not have a similar word in English. But this reinforces that we are made in the image of God, as complementary community. Sexual intercourse expresses bodily the one-flesh covenant of marriage. Timothy Keller writes, "Sex is God's appointed way for two people to say reciprocally to one another, 'I belong completely, permanently, and exclusively to you.'"[22]

Scientists first learned about a hormone called oxytocin because of its role in childbirth and breastfeeding. It is released when a mother nurses her baby, and it stimulates an instinct for caring and nurture. For this reason, it is referred to as "the attachment hormone." As Pearcey explains, "More recently, scientists have discovered that oxytocin is released during sexual intercourse, especially (but not exclusively) in women."[23] God designed the one-flesh union of sexual intercourse to bond a husband and wife physically, emotionally, spiritually—and even biochemically.

Yet for all this, sexual intercourse is not to become an idol, a source of ultimate purpose or meaning. As strange as it may sound in the hypersexualized West, intercourse *isn't* essential for human flourishing. Jesus is our model of a life perfectly lived. He was a sexed human being with all the longings and desires of any man, yet he was content to be celibate. Wilson reminds us that "he didn't need sex—not because sex is sinful or somehow beneath his dignity, but because [sexual intercourse] isn't essential to being human."[24]

SEX, CULTURE, AND CIVILIZATION

God never intended that sex merely be a private act between consenting adults. It has massive public consequences. In fact, sex is at the very foundation of civilization. Whether that civilization thrives or decays will depend largely on how it treats sex.

Why does sex have such profound societal consequences? One word: children. Chesterton once wrote, "Sex is an instinct that produces an institution . . . the family; a small state or commonwealth."[25] What happens in that "small state" will have a massive impact on the larger society, from economic to educational, from religious to charitable.

As sex goes, so goes the family. As the family goes, so goes the nation. What goes on in the foundational relationships between sexual partners and their offspring will literally make or break a society.

Flourishing nations require healthy children. A mountain of research confirms that children need, more than anything, the female mother and male father who together made them. Their very identity hinges upon this. They need their parents' love—and they need their parents to love each other—with adoption available for children whose natural parents are unable or unwilling to care for them. "Children," writes Katie Faust, "have a natural, fundamental right to the dual-gender influence of their biological parents."[26]

A culture that upholds these truths will thrive. Societies that discard them will collapse. Ancient pagan cultures, according to Pearcey, "placed no moral limits on sexual behavior."

> It was morally acceptable for a man to have sex with men and youths as freely as with women and girls. For the dominant male in ancient Rome, virtually anyone was fair game, without regard to sex or age. Ancient culture gives us a concrete historical example of the kind of social chaos that results when sex is untethered from marriage and family.[27]

Judeo-Christian faith was revolutionary because it channeled sexual desire into marriage as the only acceptable outlet. Dennis Prager, a Jewish writer, commentator, and cultural critic, notes, "When Judaism demanded sexual activity be channeled into marriage, it changed the world. The Torah's prohibition of non-marital sex quite simply made the creation of the Western civilization possible."[28]

The societal consequences were massive, as the Judeo-Christian understanding of sexuality significantly elevated the cultural standing of women. No longer did a wife have to compete with others for her husband's love. "No wonder women were especially attracted to Christianity," Pearcey notes.[29] The revolution also ensured that most children were raised by their biological parents, which produced a host of positive societal outcomes.

"Christianity," Rod Dreher writes, ". . . worked a cultural revolution, restraining and channeling . . . *eros*, elevating the status of both women and of the human body, and infusing marriage—and marital sexuality—with love."[30]

Since the 1960s, tragically, we've experienced an inverse Sexual Revolution, one that has returned sex to the understanding common in pre-Christian animistic cultures. Neopagan sexuality is again mainstream.

SEX REDEFINED

In our secular, postmodern age, human sexuality either loses all meaning and purpose, or it becomes a source of ultimate meaning—a substitute god. The loss of meaning is reflected in this quote from a drummer in Austin, Texas, who told *Rolling Stone* that sex is just "a piece of body touching another piece of body."[31] In other words, sex is no more meaningful than any other amusement, such as attending a concert or football game. A video from Children's Television Workshop, widely used in sex education classes in America, reduces sex to "something done by two adults to give each other pleasure."[32]

On the other hand, for many, sex has become an idol, the source of their identity, and even salvation. According to Wilson, for many "sexual activity is viewed as the most direct path to personal fulfillment and self-realization—to being truly human and fully alive . . . to deny yourself sexual experience is to undermine your own humanity."[33]

> ### SEX REDEFINED
> (1) Synonymous with gender, a social construct; a person's subjective sense of their sexual identity, without regard to biology or anatomy. (2) The ultimate source of personal identity and meaning. (3) Any form of recreational sexual activity done to give pleasure.

Human sexuality used to be part of a comprehensive whole that united male and female as husband and wife in a loving, lifetime commitment, and bound them to their offspring, and to future generations. Today, this beautiful sexual mosaic has been shattered. Sex is now separated from marriage, from children, and even from male-female biology. How did this happen?

A series of worldview shifts that began in the 1800s underpin our present-day Sexual Revolution.

Charles Darwin (1809–1882) taught that humans are not created by God in His image but are highly evolved animals formed through an unguided, purposeless process of natural selection. Animals mate and reproduce out of instinct, and the same holds true for people. Today in America's public schools, young people are viewed as little more than animals in heat, with no moral consideration or ability to control their sexual appetites.

Friedrich Nietzsche (1844–1900) taught that we need to move beyond notions of the Christian God, and particularly Christian sexual morality—and determine what is right and wrong for ourselves.

Sigmund Freud (1856–1939) taught that sexual repression rooted in Judeo-Christian morality accounts for nearly every psychological disorder.

Margaret Sanger (1879–1966) viewed sex as a source of earthly salvation. Her lifetime mission was to separate sex from procreation and child rearing. She pioneered artificial birth control, believing it would open the gates of utopia. She founded Planned Parenthood, which is behind the abortion deaths of millions of children worldwide.

Alfred Kinsey (1894–1956), unencumbered by antiquated Christian ideas about sexual morality, thought that any sexual behavior that people practice should be viewed as normal and healthy. This idea contributed to movements seeking to mainstream adultery, masturbation,[34] incest, homosexuality—even pedophilia.

Mary Calderone (1904–1998) cofounded the Sexuality Information and Education Council of the United States (SIECUS) with funding help from *Playboy* founder Hugh Hefner. Today SIECUS is the most influential organization shaping sex education curricula in America's public schools.

This revolution is reflected and reinforced in music, films, novels, corporate policies, and government laws and regulations. And, for all its destructive power, it shows little sign of fading. Darwin's theory of purposeless evolution continues to be uniformly represented as an indisputable scientific fact. Our culture's gatekeepers agree with Nietzsche and Freud that the Christian sexual ethic is an immoral, harmful, and repressive myth—a means of empowering the despised "patriarchy" to subjugate women.

Margaret Sanger was recently lionized with a statue in the Smithsonian. The Kinsey Institute still proudly operates at Indiana University. SIECUS still determines what our children learn about sex in public schools.

FRUITS OF THE SEXUAL REVOLUTION

The fruits of the Sexual Revolution have been devastating. We saw the wreckage it causes in the lives of people such as Michael, Jeremy, Jared, Malcolm, and Christian at the beginning of this chapter. We see it on a macro scale in our society's alarmingly high rates of premarital sex, cohabitation, adultery, divorce, out-of-wedlock births, abortion, dysfunctional sexual relations between spouses, the hook-up culture, sexual abuse, sex trafficking, sex slavery, the proliferation of pornography and porn addiction . . . and the list goes on.[35]

With the advent of inexpensive and widely available birth control, according to Pearcey, "sexual intercourse, the most intimate of bodily relations . . . [became] cast as a purely recreational activity that can be enjoyed apart from any hint of love or commitment."[36]

> According to the rules of the game, you are not to become emotionally attached. No relationship, no commitment, no exclusivity. You are supposed to be able to walk away from the sexual encounter as if it did not happen. . . . The hookup culture "creates a drastic divide between physical intimacy and emotional intimacy" according to researcher Donna Freitas. . . . If you admit you want more than sex, students told Freitas, you will be labeled needy, clingy, and dependent.[37]

A college student named Alicia says, "Hookups are very scripted. . . . You learn to turn everything off except your body and make yourself emotionally invulnerable."[38] Of course, it is simply not possible to separate your body from your emotional and spiritual self. The hook-up culture empties sex of its meaning and leaves people lonely, isolated, and starving for genuine relationship. No wonder that the top two prescribed drugs on our college campus health centers are anti-depressants and the birth-control pill.[39]

"Where did we ever get the idea," Stanton asks, "that we can separate our bodies from our minds and spirits and that our bodies could do whatever they like without consequence for the rest of our being? The human cannot be gnostic. To do so is reductionistic and untrue to a full Christian anthropology."[40]

The most extreme form of depersonalized and reductionist sexuality is pornography. Porn turns women and men into mere bodies—sex objects—not human beings made in God's image. The internet has made pornography pervasive, of course. Porn sites receive more traffic than Netflix, Amazon, and Twitter (now "X") combined.[41] It has grown into an estimated $97 billion per year global industry, with $10–12 billion of that coming from the US.[42]

The explosion of pornography has spawned a public health crisis as more and more men and women become porn-addicted. Early exposure to porn produces a host of detrimental consequences, including early sex, high-risk sex, a variety of sex addictions, and sexual violence.[43] *TIME* magazine reports on an unexpected and tragic consequence of this porn addiction: "Many [men] are simply unable to experience a sexual response with a real live woman. They are only able to respond to pornography. In fact, they prefer pornography."[44]

Another tragic consequence of sundering sex and procreation is how pregnancy has been devalued and the unborn have been dehumanized. For many, pregnancy is viewed as a disease and unborn children as a problem to be overcome, or even worse, an enemy to be defeated.[45]

The prevention and termination of pregnancy are now described as "essential healthcare" by "prochoice" feminists and most of the modern Democratic Party. As we discussed in the previous chapter, the abortion genocide is the fruit of this deadly dehumanization of unborn children.

Sex has been not only separated from marriage and procreation, but from male-female biology. The result is an all-out assault on the male-female binary at the foundation of human sexuality. That's because postmodernism grants the mind a godlike creative power. It says one's feelings and choices define reality. You can be whoever (or whatever) you want. Human choice and desire are elevated *above* objective reality.

For postmodernists, the male-female binary is not an objective biological reality, but a cultural construction, an oppressive relic of Judeo-Christian morality.

The "T" in the LGBTQ movement stands for "transgender," representing people who believe their biological sex (which they claim was "assigned at birth") can be changed to fit with their feelings through hormones, drugs, or surgery. Postmodernism rests on the materialist belief that the body is a meaningless biological organism. But postmodernism goes further, by disconnecting the body from the mind—what it calls the "the authentic, choosing self."

According to Pearcey, "The facts of physiology, anatomy, chromosomes, and DNA are less real or knowable than the subjective feeling someone has." She concludes that "this is a devastatingly reductive view of the body."[46]

The discarding of the male-female sexual binary has given rise to a chaotic proliferation of sexual categories that grows longer with each passing day. In 2014, Facebook added a feature that allowed users to "customize" their sexual identity by choosing from more than *fifty* alternatives. In 2016, the New York City Human Rights Commission released a list of thirty-one terms of gender expression— androgynous, genderqueer, non-binary, pangender, bi-gendered, gender fluid, third sex, two spirit, and so on. According to a 2023 Gallup survey, 7 percent of adult Americans identify as one (or more) of these categories. More than double the number a decade ago.[47]

Activists are now signaling their desire to move beyond the growing list of acronyms. A psychotherapist writing in a magazine billed for "queer people" explains that people "don't want to fit into any boxes. . . . They want to be free to change their minds. . . . We're seeing a challenge to the old, modernist way of thinking 'This is who I am, period' and a movement towards a postmodern version, 'This is who I am right now.'"[48]

Pressure is growing on parents and doctors to forego announcing the sex of infants at birth, in favor of allowing children to determine their sexual identity based on an "internal sense" of who they are. Tragically, pressure is growing on children to pronounce on their so-called "gender identity" at increasingly young ages. This radical sexual movement has made children their primary target, with a plethora of sexually explicit books and comics, often available in elementary school libraries and classrooms, that encourage them to ignore their biology and determine their sexuality based on feelings and desires.[49] *The Adventures of Toni the Tampon* informs young children that men as well as women are capable of menstruating.[50] This is now being taught in public schools across the country. For example, one Chicago-area public school

> Has adopted a radical gender curriculum that teaches pre-kindergarten through third-grade students to celebrate the transgender flag, break the "gender binary" established by white "colonizers," and experiment with neo-pronouns such as "ze," "zir," and "tree" . . . "It is a myth that gender is binary," one lesson explains. "Even though we are all given a sex assigned at birth, you are NOT given your gender. Only you can know your gender and how you feel inside."[51]

Children and youth are then encouraged to "come out" and publicly express their "authentic" gender identity by changing their names, "preferred pronouns," clothes, haircut, voice, and behaviors. An entire industry has developed to facilitate these changes through easy access (often without parental consent), to powerful hormonal drugs and even barbaric sex-reassignment surgeries that often render those that undergo them infertile, as well as physically, emotionally, and spiritually traumatized.

Everyone else, including the parents of the children, are encouraged and coerced into affirming and "celebrating" these life-altering choices. "Misgendering," or failure to use someone's preferred pronoun may lead to your being fired, or fined, in some cases up to $250,000.[52] It may even lead to state officials removing your children from your custody. In California, "parents, who fail to acknowledge and support their child's gender transition, could face potential consequences, including the loss of custody rights to another parent or even the state itself."[53] In an egregious form of emotional blackmail, you will be told that failure to affirm someone's gender identity will likely make you an accomplice to their death by suicide. Those who refuse to support this radical gender revolution will not be tolerated.

We are only now coming to grips with the profound societal and cultural implications of discarding the male-female binary. Everywhere male-female distinctions existed in society are now being erased, including sports, bathrooms, locker rooms, prisons, and clothing departments in major chain retail stores. But the consequences go far beyond these issues. When the male-female binary is abolished, so too is the natural family. If the law no longer recognizes biological sex, then it can no longer recognize biological parents, and children's right to them.[54]

The loss of the natural family is leading to a profound sense of alienation and loss of identity.[55] This helps to explain why, for many, sex has become the core of their identity. The fragmentation of sex, marriage, procreation, and the male-female binary has left the natural family on life support. Because the family is so central to determining a person's identity, young adults are increasingly adrift, hungering for something to fill the void. Sexual identity, and the communities associated with those identities, fill that void for many. Young people are told that their sexual desires *define them as human beings.*

The Sexual Revolution is not merely a social or political movement, but a religious one. The god is sexual desire—and it is a jealous god, labeling anyone who would challenge it as hateful and bigoted. Adherents of this new religion increasingly turn to the state, passing laws and regulations that target dissenters. The new religion entails a new morality, one that inverts Judeo-Christian sexual morality. Salvation is found in unbounded sexual expression.

In a June 2017 interview in *Rolling Stone*, tech multimillionaire Tim Gill, a major funder of the LGBTQ movement, openly revealed his strategy: promote the passage of SOGI (sexual orientation and gender identity) laws in order to "punish the wicked."[56] Such promoters of the Sexual Revolution define those who adhere to a Judeo-Christian sexual ethic not as ignorant or well-meaning but as evil. Their inverse morality is seen in the symbol of their movement, the rainbow. They take God's symbol for mercy, and patient forbearance, and invert it in open defiance of God and His design and purpose in human sexuality.

This religious zeal also helps explain why the revolution has advanced so rapidly. For its champions, it isn't merely a push for sexual freedom, but for basic human rights. Its most powerful advocates are academics in the social sciences, and particularly in fields such as women's studies, gender studies, and other fields. They are supported by a network of powerful nonprofit advocacy organizations, such as the Human Rights Campaign and Planned Parenthood, with backing from extraordinarily wealthy donors such as Tim Gill. These in turn are supported by artists and leaders in film, television, media, and business—think of Target and AirBnB as examples.

Central to their strategy is the crafting of a powerful narrative aimed at changing perceptions of everyday Americans toward "sexual minorities." Why, and how, this new narrative was crafted is chronicled in the landmark 1989 book, *After the Ball: How America*

Will Conquer Its Fear and Hatred of Gays in the 90's, by Marshall Kirk and Hunter Madsen.

The narrative portrays members of the LGBTQ community as victims—as normal, everyday Americans trying to go about their lives peacefully, desiring the same rights as everyone else. A powerful and oppressive group of Christian traditionalists (the villains), however, is bent on marginalizing and dehumanizing them. According to the narrative, the LGBTQ community is routinely bullied, threatened, harassed, and attacked. Its members are refused service from businesses, unable to secure hotel rooms and restaurant tables.

As with all powerful narratives, there is a grain of truth here, but the narrative is built upon distortion. The goal is to create sympathy for the victims and animosity for the oppressors.

This carefully cultivated narrative powerfully links the Sexual Revolution to the earlier fight for racial equality. Accordingly, there is a concerted push for "sexual minorities" to be included as a protected class in existing civil rights legislation through the passage of SOGI laws—laws that make it illegal to discriminate against homosexuals and the transgendered in hiring. This link to civil rights allows the sexual revolutionaries to paint opponents—including Christian organizations—as hateful bigots in the mold of the Ku Klux Klan.

This narrative has now taken hold. It shapes how most Americans view this issue, including many younger evangelicals and those on the evangelical left. This has allowed the sexual revolutionaries to describe their cause as inevitable—the change is coming and it is futile to resist. If you do, you are "on the wrong side of history."

Next, the revolution works to infiltrate, influence, and build alliances across American institutions. Particularly striking has been its success in recruiting large, influential corporations, including Apple, Amazon, and Starbucks. The big-time sports leagues have jumped on the bandwagon, including the NFL and the NCAA. These corporations wield enormous political and economic power. If state or local governments fail to support LGBTQ rights to the revolution's satisfaction, boycotts are mobilized and threats are made to withhold business expansion or to withdraw from major sporting events, such as the Super Bowl or the NCAA basketball tournament. This puts immense economic pressure on state and local governments to support the revolution, and, in almost all cases, they succumb.

Other tactics:

- The revolution identifies sympathetic law firms, judges, and courts in order to establish new legal theories and precedents.
- Television programs and films such as *Will and Grace*, *Glee*, *Brokeback Mountain*, *Modern Family*, and many more have advanced the narrative significantly.
- The revolution targets prominent dissenters and critics and attempts to ruin them through social and legacy media. A case in point is Brendan Eich, who was fired as CEO of Mozilla after being "outed" on social media for contributing $1,000 to the California campaign in support of traditional marriage.[57]
- The revolution exploits existing divides between mainline Protestant and evangelical churches, and between older and younger Christians. It supports champions of the revolution within the church and paints critics as rigid, dogmatic, and unloving culture warriors.

- It works to change the popular understanding of religious freedom from a lynchpin of the republic to something negative and nefarious—as a pretext for homophobic, transphobic bigots to practice discrimination. This is exactly what Tim Cook, Apple CEO, did in his 2015 *Washington Post* op-ed, when he referred to religious liberty claims as "very dangerous."[58]
- The revolution ensures that children at every level in the public schools understand LGBTQ rights as basic human rights, and sexual identity as central to human dignity.

At every one of these tactical levels, the revolution has been amazingly successful. But neopagan sexuality is still a false religion. It offers false hope. It reduces human beings to their sexual desires. It treats the incredible gift of the sexed human body as a meaningless "meat skeleton" to be used and manipulated according to personal whim. It inevitably leads to heartache, isolation, and emptiness, and to social chaos, with children paying the highest price.

HOW SHOULD WE THEN LIVE?

Only God knows how the Sexual Revolution will ultimately play out in the West and around the world. But the mandate for the church hasn't changed. "Honor God with your bodies" (1 Corinthians 6:20). Preach the gospel. Love your neighbor. Work for the good of the city and the nation. Be preserving salt. Hold out the light of truth in the midst of darkness.

To hold out that truth, we have to recover it ourselves. We can't merely stand in opposition to sexual immorality. We have to recover, treasure, and champion the positive, life-affirming, and culture-creating truth about human sexuality. Wilson puts it well:

It is time for evangelicals to rediscover the historic Christian vision of human sexuality. Now, more than at any other time since the first centuries of the church, we need a countercultural Christian sexual ethic and, at an even deeper level, a distinctively Christian view of human sexuality. We need a fresh encounter with what has been called the "jarring gospel of Christian sexuality" that transformed the pagan world.[59]

What we do with our sexuality is one of our most important testimonies. For many of us, this kind of countercultural sexuality seems impossible. One study indicates that 57 percent of *evangelical pastors* have struggled with pornography, and many have become addicted. Almost certainly, the numbers are higher among Christians generally.[60] Some have mistresses, engage in premarital sex, or even indulge in the hook-up culture. Some succumb to their feelings of homosexual attraction. Almost always, with a sense of guilt, shame, or apathy, our failures keep us silent and on the sidelines as the battle rages.

If this describes you, please seek help. Our standard as followers of Jesus Christ must be nothing short of sexual purity. (See 1 Corinthians 6:18 and Colossians 3:5.) But overcoming sexual immorality or sexual addictions can't be done alone. We need the church, brothers and sisters in Christ who will hold us accountable. We must lean on the Holy Spirit and prayer.

One of the wisest things any of us can do when tempted is simply to run away. The Bible says we are to "flee from sexual immorality" (1 Corinthians 6:18). For evangelicals who've had abortions, or are porn users or even porn-addicted, grace and forgiveness are available at the cross of Christ. But first, we must recognize and name our sin and repent. Then we must join the battle.

Younger evangelicals often perceive our resistance to the Sexual Revolution as distasteful culture-warring at odds with Christ's command to love our LGBTQ neighbors. Many wonder why older Christians seem so obsessed with sexual sin.

For my younger evangelical brothers and sisters, I would remind you: We didn't start this fight, and we won't pretend it doesn't matter. Today's gross abuse of sexuality destroys the lives of millions of people and puts them at grave risk of eternal separation from a holy and righteous God. 1 Corinthians 6:9, ESV is a sobering reminder: "Do not be deceived: neither the sexually immoral, nor idolaters, nor adulterers, nor men who practice homosexuality . . . will inherit the kingdom of God."

Ignoring these realities isn't loving. Blithely disregarding the core deception of the Sexual Revolution, that a person's identity comes from his sexual desires rather than from his being created in God's image, is not loving. Former lesbian activist and feminist studies professor—and now passionate follower of Jesus Christ— Rosaria Butterfield explains why this matters:

> A few years ago, I was speaking at a large church. An older woman waited until the end of the evening and approached me. She told me that she was 75 years old, that she had been married to a woman for 50 years, and that she and her partner had children and grandchildren. Then she said something chilling. In a hushed voice, she whispered, "I have heard the gospel, and I understand that I may lose everything. Why didn't anyone tell me this before? Why did people I love not tell me that I would one day have to choose like this?" That's a good question. Why did not one person tell this dear image bearer that she could not have illicit love and gospel peace at the same time? Why didn't anyone—throughout all of these decades—tell this woman that sin and Christ cannot abide together, for the

cross never makes itself an ally with the sin it must crush, because Christ took our sin upon himself and paid the ransom for its dreadful cost?

She concludes, "When we . . . bless the relationships that God calls sin, we are acting as though we think ourselves more merciful than God is. May God have mercy on us all."[61]

We must not lose our prophetic voice out of a misplaced desire to be accepted by the elite trend-setters in the culture. However, I fear Owen Strachan's indictment on this point is sadly correct:

> In recent decades, evangelicals have thirsted after cultural approval. Like the world's saddest pageant contestants, we want desperately to be accepted by secular culture. We have exchanged our holy birthright for a Facebook fan page. Our hermeneutic is not motivated by righteous awe, by fear and trembling, by the honor and magnificence of our God. It is driven by a craven desire to be liked, to be culturally acceptable, to be *au courant*. The church should not be a preening wannabe. It should recognize . . . that it is a counterculture.[62]

For the revolution's many victims, as well as for the well-being of the church, communities, and nations, our task is to confront lovingly but firmly the deadly dogmas of the Sexual Revolution, not to accommodate them.

For others who are tempted to lash out in anger and frustration at our cultural opponents, I would remind you that we are called to love our enemies, dealing gently with opponents. We don't fight as the world fights, with the weapons of the world, with angry and cutting words, with threats, with hatred. Rather, we fight with spiritual weapons, with prayer, with the "sword of the Spirit, the Word of God," and in the power of the Holy Spirit.

Let's remember that defeatism is a mistake, knowing that "he who is in you is greater than he who is in the world" (1 John 4:4). We must stand up, speak out, and resist. And victory is not impossible.

Consider the case of Jack Phillips, the owner of Masterpiece Cakeshop in Lakewood, Colorado. Phillips was approached by two customers he knew and liked. The men asked him to create a custom-designed wedding cake for their same-sex marriage. Phillips politely refused, citing his Christian beliefs about marriage. The couple hauled him before the state's civil rights commission, which mocked his claim to religious freedom (comparing it to earlier defenses of slavery and the Holocaust) and ordered him to change his store's policy. Philips refused, and the case eventually wound up at the Supreme Court, which ruled that the commission had failed to exercise religious neutrality. The commission's decision was overturned.[63]

Phillips won, but the fight is far from over. As Princeton professor Robert George, a great warrior for truth about marriage and sexuality, said, "We must be ready and willing to pay 'the cost of discipleship.' Are we serious Christians or are we not? Jesus didn't promise us an easy life. . . . He promised us a cross. We know that Easter is coming, but now is Good Friday. It is going to be hard. We need to pray. Our culture is in big trouble, but prayer is powerful."[64]

Indeed, so let us pray for wisdom. Many of us work in institutions (governments, schools, businesses, etc.) that openly support the Sexual Revolution. When do we speak out and when are we to be silent? How might we bring about reform? Is it time to walk away and find a new job? Should we start a new institution?

Let us also pray for discernment. We need to be far more open-eyed in how we use the internet, social media, and popular culture generally, whether television, film, or literature. As well, we ought to be far more proactive and intentional when it comes to teaching our children about sexuality. Leaving that job to the public schools, their friends, or the media will leave our kids vulnerable to being indoctrinated into the ideology and practices of the Sexual Revolution. Let's exercise far more creativity when it comes to our children's education, doing all we can to teach them to love what is good, true, and beautiful, and protecting them from deadly cultural lies.

Despite all the challenges it brings, the Sexual Revolution presents the church with a massive opportunity. Countless victims left in its noxious wake need help, love, community, healing, and support. That task is tailor-made for the church. William Wilberforce, the great British parliamentarian, mobilized Christians and the political class to overturn the empire's deeply entrenched slave trade and spark a moral revolution in society.

That's just one example. In the early days of the church, believers sparked another moral revolution. As Pearcey reminds us:

> In the ancient world, Christians were distinctive for their humanitarian efforts—taking care of babies and slaves, of widows and orphans, slaves, of the sick and elderly, of the unwanted and abandoned. Today, as the West sinks back into pre-Christian pagan practices, we must be once again be ready to stand with courage and conviction.[65]

Ultimately, we find hope in knowing that God loves broken sinners far more than we do. He's not sitting on the sidelines waiting for us to do something. He is actively working in the lives of lost, sinful people, gently leading them to a knowledge of the truth. Our job is simply to join Him.

CHAPTER 4

MARRIAGE

From the beginning of creation, 'God made them male and female.' 'Therefore a man shall leave his father and mother and hold fast to his wife, and the two shall become one flesh.' So they are no longer two but one flesh. What therefore God has joined together, let not man separate.

MATTHEW 19:6–9, ESV

MARRIAGE

A God-ordained, comprehensive, exclusive, and permanent union that brings a man and a woman together as husband and wife, to be father and mother to any children their union brings into being. It is based on the anthropological truth that men and women are different and complementary, the biological fact that reproduction depends on a man and a woman, and the social reality that children need both a mother and a father.[1]

MARRIAGE REDEFINED

A legally recognized, romantic caregiving relationship between consenting adults who intend to live together as sexual and domestic partners.

In the face of many challenges to the institution of marriage, one young married couple from Scandinavia is on a mission to proclaim its true meaning to a world that seemingly has forgotten it. As part of a documentary, the husband and wife chose to interview Catholic author and essayist Mary Eberstadt. They flew to Washington, D.C., for the interview. Eberstadt recalls the encounter:

> They had gotten in touch with me to discuss a documentary they were creating. . . . Their studio in D.C. turned out to be their hotel room. The entourage

for the shoot included their three very young children, with whom they took turns [watching] throughout the interview. They had made many sacrifices and traveled hundreds of miles because, they said, they were on a mission to tell the truth.

The young woman had grown up without knowing who her father was. Her mother, a radical feminist, raised her to fear and hate men. The young man [grew] up as secular as Scandinavians can be. Both, if encountered earlier in their lives, would have been categorized as [religiously unaffiliated] "nones."

In their own estimations, they had escaped from behind the enemy lines of the Sexual Revolution. Somehow, they found each other. Somehow, falling in love led them to question what had happened in their pasts. Somehow, they encountered a priest. Somehow, they read some books by faithful authors. And what with one improbable development and another, both ended up converting to Catholicism. Now they want to share with others the truths they discovered the hard way.[2]

These formerly secular Scandinavians had been captivated by the sublime truths about marriage, sex, and family. As they began to discover this forgotten wisdom, they experienced a life-changing encounter with the great founder of marriage, God Himself.

This wisdom came not through the example of their parents, or through the ideas and values of secular Scandinavian culture. It came supernaturally, through God-ordained appointments. It changed their lives, and they are not alone. God is raising up a remnant who, captivated by the beauty of marriage, are determined to share its good news with their neighbors, communities, and world.

Marriage, one of God's greatest gifts to humanity, is a uniquely life-giving, multigenerational, culture-forming, and civilization-building institution. Flourishing societies are built on the foundation of healthy families, which are built on the foundation of strong marriages. Marriage is quite literally the cell of the societal body. What is happening in that cell will determine whether the body thrives . . . or dies.

Singleness is also part of God's plan, of course. Some people never marry, and God uses singleness in significant ways, as He did in the life of the apostle Paul, and in our Savior, Jesus Christ. Augustine of Hippo, the great bishop, author, and theologian, was another. Yet for most of us, marriage will shape our lives more profoundly than almost anything else.

Tragically, an unprecedented moral revolution aimed at fundamentally redefining this ancient institution has been underway for more than one hundred years. At least two generations in the West have come of age without even knowing what marriage really is, or why it matters. This loss of wisdom about marriage has devastated not only individual lives, but whole nations.

MARRIAGE DEFINED

Marriage isn't a human invention. It isn't the outcome of a random evolutionary process. It is God's idea. It is His doing, and He defines it. In fact, marriage is the first and most basic social institution He created! Not incidentally, He created it *before* the fall. Marriage is not merely a legally recognized relationship between two people. It is a mysterious and sacred lifelong uniting, by God, of a man and a woman as husband and wife. A pastor or priest may perform a wedding ceremony, but it is God who joins husband and wife together. Jesus said: "What . . . God has joined together, let not man separate" (Mark 10:9, ESV).

Marriage is basic to God's design in creation and His purposes in the world. In fact, marriage is a central theme in the Scriptures. The Bible begins with the marriage of the first couple, Adam and Eve, in Genesis 1 and 2, and ends with a marriage of Christ and the church in Revelation 19. Between these two bookends, Scripture is replete with marriage imagery and the language of husband and wife. Karl Stern goes so far as to say "all being is nuptial."[3]

The marriage of Adam and Eve in the Garden of Eden (Genesis 2:18–24), because it happened before the Fall, serves as a template for all marriages in all cultures, and for all times. Here we see marriage as the exclusive uniting of a man and a woman. Not a man and a man, a woman and a woman, a man and an animal, a man and multiple women, or any other combination. Because God created Adam and Eve male and female, homosexual "marriage" is excluded. Likewise, because Adam "could find no helper suitable" (Genesis 2:20) for himself among the animals, bestiality is excluded. Because God created just one woman for Adam, polygamy is excluded and the pattern of monogamy is established.

MARRIAGE

A God-ordained, comprehensive, exclusive, and permanent union that brings a man and a woman together as husband and wife, to be father and mother to any children their union brings into being. It is based on the anthropological truth that men and women are different and complementary, the biological fact that reproduction depends on a man and a woman, and the social reality that children need both a mother and a father.

Marriage is rooted in the nature of God. Before creation, there was community, communion, and communication within the Godhead between Father, Son, and Holy Spirit. To reflect this divine community of relationship, when God made people in His image. He made them male and female *in relationship*. God declared His magnificent creation "very good" in Genesis 1:31, with one significant exception. "It is *not good* for man to be alone" (Genesis 2:18, emphasis added).

The one word that best describes the relationship that exists within the Godhead is *love*.

As God's image-bearers, we too are made to love, and to be loved. This applies especially in marriage, which is inherently other-centered.

This stands in stark contrast with the radical autonomy that defines marriage in Western culture. Today, marriage is about "me," not "us." It is about serving self rather than serving others. It is about personal freedom without personal responsibility.

But marriage as God intended is just the opposite. It reflects the other-serving love that exists between Father, Son, and Holy Spirit. In marriage, a husband and wife have the unspeakable privilege of manifesting, in some small way, this joyous, transcendent love before a watching world.

Let's take a closer look at this love. Unity without uniformity and diversity without superiority exist in the Godhead. The Father, Son, and Holy Spirit are mysteriously "one" (Deuteronomy 6:4) yet distinct and complementary. Since people are image-bearers of God, this same unity and diversity applies to us. In marriage, the husband and wife are profoundly united as "one flesh" (Genesis 2:24), yet they remain distinct. In the relationship between husband and wife, there is unity without uniformity and diversity without superiority.

Before we go any further, let's note that marriage is about *correspondence* and not *uniformity*. Correspondence is synonymous with compatibility and complementarity. Examples include the two parts of a latch, or button holes and buttons, or the two ends of a seat belt. Differences exist, but they correspond to and complement each other for a greater purpose. This is true of male and female, and particularly true of husband and wife. By contrast, uniformity is all about conformity or interchangeability. It implies a mirror image, something identical. Examples include two earrings, two gloves, two shoes, two men, or two women.

God created man male and female to correspond to and complement each other. There is a *unity*. Both male and female are human beings. Both are equally valued and loved by God. Both have equally important roles to play in carrying out God's purposes in history. But their parts are *different*. We explored some of the profound differences between male and female in the previous chapter. In marriage, there is a corresponding difference in the roles of husband and wife.

The Old Testament word for husband is *ishi*. This implies a self-sacrificing, other-serving authority who offers initiative, protection, and provision. God, rather than culture, defines what it means to be a husband. The Bible describes *God* as a husband to His people, Israel (see Isaiah 54:5, or the Book of Hosea), and Christ as husband to His bride, the Church (Ephesians 5:25–33). God is the archetypal husband—His very nature is *to husband*. We see this in one of the most beautiful passages of Scripture, Psalm 23, ESV. God *leads*: "The Lord is my shepherd. . . . He leads me beside still waters. . . ." He *provides*: "I shall not want. He makes me lie down in green pastures. [He] prepare[s] a table before me. . . . [He] anoint[s] my head with oil; my cup overflows." He *protects*: "Even though I walk through the valley of the shadow of death, I will fear no evil, for you are with me; your rod and your staff, they comfort me."

The authority of the husband in the Bible in no way implies his superiority to the wife or their children. Rather, this authority, or headship, involves a willingness to shoulder responsibility, and to lovingly serve those under authority. As such, a husband is ultimately responsible for what happens in his household. He must sacrificially serve his wife and children, laying down his prerogatives to attend to their needs, even at the cost of his own life. In the words of the apostle Paul, "Husbands, love your wives, as Christ loved the church and gave himself up for her" (Ephesians 5:25).

In Genesis 2, God designates Adams' wife by the word *ezer*, meaning "helper." In Genesis 2:18, God said of Adam "I will make *a helper* suitable for him" (italics added). If God is the archetypal husband, He is also the archetypical *ezer*—helper. "I lift up my eyes to the hills. From where does my help come? My help comes from the Lord, who made heaven and earth" (Psalm 121:1–2). This kind of help doesn't imply weakness or inferiority—far from it! In marriage, the husband needs help, and the wife provides it—a picture of true complementarity.

This begs the question: Help with *what*? The answer is found in Genesis 1:28, ESV, God's original job description for mankind: "And God blessed them. And God said to them, 'Be fruitful and multiply and fill the earth and subdue it, and have dominion over the fish of the sea and over the birds of the heavens and over every living thing that moves on the earth.'"

Notice that this task is for "*them*," both male and female. It has two subordinating mandates, (1) be fruitful, multiply and fill the earth, and (2) to have dominion and exercise stewardship over creation. Both tasks begin with families.

Marriage is a relationship like no other, because it uniquely involves procreation, the raising of children, and the establishing of families, communities, cultures, and nations. There is nothing more miraculous, mysterious, and beautiful than God's partnership with husband and wife in the creation of a new human being—a unique person of incredible complexity and intricate design, complete with immortal spirit, mind, and will, with vast potential and incalculable worth. Filling the earth with such people is among God's chief purposes in marriage.

Marriage, rightly understood, is the *only* proper environment for sexual intimacy, because God designed it to bear the fruit of new human life. Only one place exists where this amazing and sacred procreative power can be properly channeled—the lifelong covenant of marriage. Marriage links sex, procreation, and child-rearing in a powerful, life-giving, and culture-creating mosaic. It bonds husband to wife, and both to the offspring their union produces, and thus to the future of humanity.

All this is true even if a marriage doesn't result in biological children. According to Nathanael Blake, "the fullness of marriage is only realizable between a man and a woman in a union that is naturally open to children. That some . . . couples, whether from age or from misfortune, are unable to have children does not alter this. Infertility is a deprivation that should be mourned as a diminishment of a marriage's full potential."[4]

Yet merely having children is not enough; the Lord wants "godly offspring." Malachi 2:15, ESV makes God's intentions plain: "Did [God] not make [husband and wife] one, with a portion of the Spirit in their union? And what was the one God seeking? Godly offspring."

To achieve this, God designed marriage and the family to "be a community of teaching and learning about God and godliness."[5] Both mothers and fathers play vital roles. Proverbs 6:20–21, ESV says: "My son, keep your father's commandment, and forsake not your mother's teaching."

Every mother and father ought to desire a quiver-full of well-nurtured "children arrows" (see Psalm 127:4, 5) to advance God's purposes on earth. As parents mold their children's characters, they, in turn, will influence their children and grandchildren through many generations. "His offspring will be mighty in the land; the generation of the upright will be blessed" (Psalm 112:2, ESV).

God designed marriage to be an exclusive, lifelong relationship rooted in a solemn commitment of fidelity (Luke 16:18; Romans

7:1–6). This too reflects God's relational nature as a covenant-making, covenant-keeping God. The exclusive nature of this relationship is underscored in the Ten Commandments' prohibition against adultery (Exodus 20:14). The marriage covenant is rooted in the covenant between God and His chosen people. In the Old Testament, God made an exclusive, permanent covenant with His chosen people, Israel: "I will take you to be my people, and I will be your God" (Exodus 6:7, ESV, see also Exodus 29:45 and Leviticus 26:12). In the New Testament, this covenant is extended to believing gentiles—the worldwide church (Ephesians 2:11–22). This is the "new covenant in my blood" that Christ proclaimed in Luke 22:20.

Today, most of us think in terms of contracts, not covenants, but there is a huge difference. As Chris and Lisa Cree explain, "With a contract, if one agreeing party does something in violation of the contract then it is considered broken. The whole contract becomes null and void. . . . With a covenant, both parties agree to hold up their ends regardless of whether the other party keeps their part of the agreement. A violation of a covenant by one party doesn't matter as far as the other party's responsibility to continue to do what they agreed to do."[6]

So when God makes a covenant with His people, it can never be revoked, even if we fail to uphold our end. As it says in 2 Timothy 2:13, ESV, "If we are faithless, he remains faithful, for he cannot deny himself."

In many cultures, a marriage vow is followed by the exchange of rings as a visible symbol of this exclusive, lifelong covenant. At that sublime moment, the husband becomes a living picture of Jesus Christ, who solemnly promises his bride that "neither death nor life, neither angels nor demons, neither the present nor the future, nor any powers, neither height nor depth, nor anything else in all creation, will be able to separate us from the love of God that is in Christ Jesus our Lord" (Romans 8:38-39).

The apostle Paul, in Ephesians 5:31–32, makes the astounding claim that marriage was created by God to be a reflection of this covenant between Christ and his bride, the church: "For this reason a man will leave his father and mother and be united to his wife, and the two will become one flesh. This is a profound mystery—but I am talking about Christ and the church." According to Pastor John Piper, "The . . . ultimate purpose of marriage is to put the covenant relationship of Christ and his church on display . . . a covenant-keeping love that reached its climax in the death of Christ for his church."[7]

Because God created marriage to reflect His character and nature, as well as Christ's covenant love lavished on the church, divorce is an abomination. It not only is a rupture of a covenant, but, more importantly, it makes us lie about the faithfulness of Christ, who will never leave His bride (Romans 8:38–39; Hebrews 13:5). Today, many couples justify divorce by saying, "I just don't love him (or her) anymore." But according to Piper, "Marriage is not mainly about staying in love. It is about telling the truth with our lives. It is about portraying something true about Jesus Christ and the way he relates to his people."[8] Love is not merely a feeling. It is an act of the will. It is the keeping of the covenant.

Although God hates divorce, He allows for it in limited circumstances (Matthew 5:32) in our fallen world. The terrible devastation wrought by divorce is testament to the fact that marriage, unlike any other relationship, is uniquely multigenerational and "brought together" by God.

Hebrews 13:4, ESV says, "Let marriage be held in honor among all, and let the marriage bed be undefiled." Marriage is a beautiful—even sacred—institution created by God to bless the world. While many dishonor marriage in our culture, our calling as Christians is to do the opposite—to speak highly of it, to celebrate it, and to preserve it—even as we strive to faithfully apply God's teaching in our own marriages, and encourage our children and young people to aspire to this holy calling.

THE INCREDIBLE SOCIETAL BENEFITS OF A VIBRANT MARRIAGE CULTURE

Marriage isn't a private relationship between husband and wife. It has enormous social and cultural repercussions. Marriage is the foundation upon which families are built—upon which children are brought into the world and within which their character is formed, and it is that which gives mankind a future and a hope. Families are key to the developmental mandate given by God. As the family goes, so goes the nation . . . and the world.

Family, as God intended, is the elemental community to which we all belong and in which we are loved and supported. "Connecting sex, babies, and moms and dads," says Ryan Anderson, "is the irreplaceable social function of marriage."[9] David Blankenhorn, a self-described liberal Democrat, agrees: "Marriage says to a child: The man and the woman whose sexual union made you will also be there to love and raise you. Marriage says to society as a whole: For every child born, there is a recognized mother and a father, accountable to the child and to each other."[10] Let's look a bit more closely at some of the many cultural benefits of marriage.

Women benefit. In a culture in which sex and marriage are interconnected, women are protected from being exploited by men, who might otherwise enjoy sexual favors for a time and then abandon the women and any children when those relationships are no longer convenient.[11]

Men benefit. Married men gain moral and personal discipline, a stable domestic life, and the opportunity to participate in the upbringing of their children.[12] According to Brad Wilcox, a senior fellow of the Institute for Family Studies at the University of Virginia, and Nicholas H. Wolfinger, professor of family and consumer studies and adjunct professor of sociology at the University of Utah, "Social science confirms that marriage confers enormous benefits for men's wallets, their sex lives, and their physical and mental health."[13]

Children benefit. For healthy development, a child needs the mother and father who together made him, who love him and each other, with humane foster care and adoption available when necessary. According to marriage researchers Sara McLanahan and Isabel Sawhill, "most scholars now agree that children raised by two biological parents in a stable marriage do better than children in other family forms across a wide variety of outcomes."[14]

Men and women are complementary not merely in their reproductive biology, but in their psychology and physiology as well. This is why healthy children require the dual influence of mother *and* father. As Anderson says, "It does not detract from the many mothers and fathers who have of necessity raised children alone, and done so successfully, to insist that mothers and fathers bring distinct strengths to the task."[15]

Today, LGBTQ activists reject this. They argue that the dual-sex influence of a mother and father isn't necessary for children to thrive. But this assertion flies in the face of our experience of male-female diversity in other areas of life. What if a company, organization, or board of directors were comprised solely of males? Or females? Don't you think this would have considerable influence on the entity's work, products, and accomplishments? Today "diversity" is hailed as indispensable in the workplace and on the campus—everywhere except in the critical area of family life, where "two mommies" or "two daddies" are said to be just as good.

Not only men, women, and children benefit from marriage. Society itself *greatly* benefits. For one thing, healthy marriages provide society with healthy, well-adjusted citizens. As Anderson says:

> For highly dependent infants, there is no path to physical, moral and cultural maturity—no path to personal responsibility—without a long and delicate process of ongoing care and supervision to which mothers and

fathers bring unique gifts. Unless children mature, they never will become healthy, upright, productive members of society [and] marriage is society's least restrictive means of ensuring the well-being of children.[16]

Marriage is the greatest poverty alleviation "program" to ever exist. According to Robert Rector at The Heritage Foundation, being raised in a married family reduces a child's probability of living in poverty by an astonishing 82 percent.[17]

Marriage is the greatest crime prevention "program" to ever exist. Children raised by their biological parents are far less likely to engage in criminal activity. This is particularly true for boys, for whom a strong link between crime and fatherlessness exists. McLanahan found that boys raised outside of an intact nuclear family were more than twice as likely as other boys to end up in prison. Another study revealed that 70 percent of juveniles in state reform schools, 72 percent of adolescent murderers, and 60 percent or rapists grew up in fatherless homes.[18]

This is only the tip of the iceberg as far as the personal and social benefits of marriage are concerned. Marriage brings innumerable blessings to anyone touched by it. As the Manhattan Declaration concludes, "Vast human experience confirms that . . . where marriage is honored, and where there is a flourishing marriage culture, everyone benefits—the spouses themselves, their children, the communities and societies in which they live."[19]

MARRIAGE REDEFINED

Despite offering all these benefits for society, the ancient institution of marriage is under attack. The West is undergoing an existential crisis centered on marriage, sex, family, and fertility. LGBTQ activists are not the cause of this crisis. If anything, ordinary heterosexual men and women—Christians very much included—bear most of the blame for the breakdown of marriage. Long before anyone had heard the phrase "same-sex marriage," straight married couples had "disassociated procreation from marriage, embraced easy divorce, and emphasized romantic self-fulfillment above all else" according to Blake. "The effects have harmed, and even devastated, millions. And this has been done by heterosexual men and women, many of who nonetheless self-righteously opposed same-sex marriage."[20]

To see just how significant this revolution has been, consider these two vastly different definitions of marriage. First, look again at Noah Webster's 1828 *American Dictionary of the English Language*:

> [Marriage is] the act of uniting a man and woman for life; wedlock; the legal union of a man and woman for life. Marriage is a contract both civil and religious, by which the parties engage to live together in mutual affection and fidelity, till death shall separate them. Marriage was instituted by God himself for the purpose of preventing the promiscuous intercourse of the sexes, for promoting domestic felicity [happiness], and for securing the maintenance and education of children."

Now, look at this contemporary definition from Microsoft Word's embedded English Dictionary, possibly the most referenced English dictionary in the world today:

> Marriage: A legally recognized relationship, established by a civil or religious ceremony, between two people who intend to live together as sexual and domestic partners.

Take a moment to reflect on how radically marriage has been redefined in the 170 years that separate these two dictionaries. This redefinition happened through a progressive, step-by-step process as the support-bearing pillars of marriage began to fall, one by one.

MARRIAGE REDEFINED

A legally recognized, romantic caregiving relationship between consenting adults who intend to live together as sexual and domestic partners.

First, notice how God, the creator, definer, and main supporting pillar of marriage, isn't even mentioned. The secularization of Western culture throughout the nineteenth and twentieth centuries explains this. God didn't abandon marriage. Following the lead of powerful intellectuals like Darwin, Freud, and Nietzsche, the West abandoned God. Even so, He remains the center of marriage, and when His position at the center is acknowledged, individual marriages (and the institution of marriage as a whole) hold together. But when God is removed from the center, marriage disintegrates. We see the consequences of this tragic rebellion everywhere today.

The next supportive pillar fell in 1960, when the United States Food and Drug Administration approved the birth control pill for general use. This was followed in 1973 by the Supreme Court's *Roe v. Wade* ruling that made abortion a legal form of "birth control" all the way up to the moment of birth.

Widely available birth control and legal abortion effectively led to the stripping of sex from procreation, and both from marriage. Those who championed this separation, such as Margaret Sanger, promised liberation, fulfillment—even salvation—through unconstrained sex. What we got instead was a conscience-searing sixty-three million unborn children murdered in the United States through abortion since 1973, with approximately fourteen million recorded abortions each year globally, including 6.9 million in China.[21]

Prior to 1960 and the mainstreaming of the Sexual Revolution, there remained a social stigma associated with sex outside of marriage. Today, by some estimates, a staggering 95 percent of the

US population engages in sex outside of marriage,[22] and the notion that sex should be reserved for male-female marriage is viewed as unreasonable, bizarre, and even bigoted.

With God removed and sex no longer reserved for marriage, the next pillar to fall was the permanent, exclusive, covenant nature of marriage. The Microsoft Word definition talks about marriage as a "legally recognized relationship" but has nothing to say about an exclusive, lifelong commitment. Before 1960, cohabitation (two unmarried people living together in a sexual relationship) was exceedingly rare and culturally frowned on. Now cohabitation has lost nearly all of its stigma, becoming the unquestioned norm.

Between 1960 and 2011, cohabitation rates in the United States increased by over 1,000 percent, and the rates are similar in almost all Western nations. Today, about a quarter of unmarried women between age twenty-five and thirty-nine are in cohabiting relationships.

Cohabitation is increasingly seen as preferable to marriage, despite the fact that rates of assault, depression, and abortion are all significantly higher among cohabiting couples than married couples, and 40 percent bring children into their shaky, noncommittal relationships.[23]

Before 1970 and the advent of no-fault divorce laws, divorce was relatively uncommon and difficult to get. Today, however, about half of all marriages in the United States will end in divorce.[24] Monogamy itself is increasingly viewed as an oppressive holdover from our regressive, patriarchal Judeo-Christian legacy. Interest in so-called "open marriage" (in other words, flagrant adultery) is surging. A 2011 *New York Times Magazine* profile of Dan Savage, headlined "Married, with Infidelities," introduced Americans to the term "monogamish," referring to relationships in which the partners allow sexual infidelity provided they are honest about it.[25]

With God, sex, procreation, permanence, exclusivity, and covenant all stripped from marriage, the conditions were ripe for the next pillar to fall—the male-female binary. Notice that the Microsoft Word definition says that marriage is between "two people." LGBTQ activist Ricki Wilchins captured the spirit of this revolutionary move powerfully: "Gay and transgender rights advocates have been quietly dodging the issue of binary heteronormativity, but that sound you hear is the other shoe finally dropping . . . hard," concluding, "Ending our culture's obsession with what's 'male' and what's 'female' will be our salvation."[26]

Before 2001, no country, at any time in history, had ever defined marriage as a same-sex institution. In virtually every culture, male and female, sex and procreation had been the beating heart of marriage. But starting with Holland in 2000, nineteen countries officially have declared that male and female are no longer essential to marriage. This happened in the United States in 2015 with the *Obergefell v. Hodges*, in which the Supreme Court redefined marriage for all fifty states.

Anyone who refuses to affirm this new definition of marriage publicly can expect to be shamed, excluded, fired, or fined. LGBTQ activists aren't content to live and let live. They demand that everyone affirm their non-binary standards. In a sharp dissent to the *Obergefell* majority opinion, Justice Samuel Alito correctly foresaw that activists would use the decision's rhetoric to attack people who hold to the historic meaning of marriage:

> It will be used to vilify Americans who are unwilling to assent to the new orthodoxy. In the course of its opinion, the majority compares traditional marriage laws to laws that denied equal treatment for African-Americans and women. The implications of this analogy will be exploited by those who are determined to stamp out every vestige of dissent.[27]

If marriage is genderless, then procreation can be jettisoned. The Microsoft Word definition doesn't mention children, much less their nurture and education. That's because marriage is now an institution exclusively serving the interests of adults—stripped of its intrinsic connection to children, family, or future generations.

E. J. Graff acknowledges that redefining marriage fundamentally changes the "institution's message," which will "ever after stand for sexual choice, for cutting the link between sex and diapers."[28] To be sure, some same-sex couples adopt children, or use assisted reproductive technologies (in-vitro fertilization and surrogacy). But even these cases send the profoundly destructive message that men and women—mothers and fathers—are interchangeable, and that children won't suffer harm from being separated from their biological parents.

Tragically, we've not yet hit bottom. In their statement "Beyond Same-Sex Marriage," more than three hundred "LGBT and allied" scholars and advocates call for legally recognizing sexual relationships involving more than two partners.[29] For many gay rights activists, this was the goal all along. Marsha Gessen wrote in 2012:

> It's a no-brainer that [same-sex couples] should have the right to marry, but I also think equally that *it's a no-brainer that the institution of marriage should not exist* . . . . Fighting for gay marriage generally involves lying about what we are going to do with marriage when we get there—because we lie that the institution of marriage is not going to change, and that is a lie. The institution of marriage is going to change, and it should change. . . . I don't think it should exist (emphasis added).[30]

Consider the kind of world your children and grandchildren will inhabit if its most primal, elemental institution is effectively abandoned as a cultural good. What will that society look like? What will be lost? Will we, too late, realize that marriage is the essential foundation of a humane and civil society? When we, intentionally or unintentionally, subscribe to any other idea of marriage than the one God defines, the consequences will be destructive. Inevitably.

THE BITTER FRUIT OF A POST-MARRIAGE CULTURE

Chesterton once said, "This triangle of truisms, of father, mother and child, cannot be destroyed; it can only destroy those civilizations that disregard it."[31] We already know the bitter fruit issuing from the dissolution of this sacred institution. Much of our political and cultural dysfunction is produced by broken families and failed relationships, as mountains of sociological research demonstrate.

The massively increased divorce rates following the passage of "no fault divorce laws" in the 1970s have left two generations of emotionally traumatized children and adults. Little wonder that these people are reluctant to get married. Studies show that those who do take the plunge are more likely to get divorced than previous generations. It is a tragic downward spiral. As the number of divorced parents increases, so does the number of their children who get divorced.

Divorce, cohabitation, and the separation of sex and marriage have led to skyrocketing rates of out-of-wedlock births, and all the accompanying shattered lives and societal disorders. Today, of every one hundred children born in the United States, forty are born to single parents.[32] For Hispanics, 53 percent of children are born outside of marriage; for the African-American community, a heartbreaking 72 percent children are raised by single mothers.[33]

Before 1960, the African-American family was largely intact, strong, and resilient. For this community in particular, the Sexual Revolution has been catastrophic. As former president Barack Obama noted, "Children who grow up without a father are five times more likely to live in poverty and commit crime; nine times more likely to drop out of schools, and twenty times more likely to end up in prison. They are more likely to have behavior problems, or run away from home, or become teenage parents themselves."[34] Many scholars and policymakers say that America's *most pressing* societal problem is absentee fathers. (Of course, many, many single parents overcome these odds with the help of God, the church, and extended family.)

And yet, far too many of us prefer to ignore this inconvenient truth. Many choose a narrative that blames high rates of crime and incarceration among black youth on structural racism, while discounting the elephant in the room—skyrocketing rates of out-of-wedlock births. Rather than squarely facing the facts, we've now enshrined into law a definition of marriage that makes fathers optional and ultimately unnecessary. But there's no denying this reality: If you want to destroy a society, there is no more efficient way than to separate fathers from their families.

The breakdown of marriage also increases poverty and leads to ever-higher social welfare spending. If parents are unable or unwilling to care for their children, someone has to fill the void, and that someone is usually the government. A Brookings Institution study found that $229 billion in welfare expenditures in the United States between 1970 and 1996 can be attributed to the breakdown of marriage and the resulting social ills: teen pregnancy, poverty, crime, drug abuse, and health problems.[35] Another study in 2008 found that divorce and unwed childbearing cost taxpayers in the US $112 billion each year.[36]

Rising rates of suicide, drug abuse, and depression can all be traced to increased social fragmentation brought about by the dissolution of marriage and family. Since the 1980s, reported loneliness among adults in the US has increased from 20 percent to 40 percent. A 2017 article in *First Things* by Aaron Kheriaty paints a tragic picture:

The recently retired surgeon general announced last year that social isolation is a major public health crisis, on par with heart disease or cancer . . . Even where familial or other social connections remain intact, these ties are often weaker and the mutual obligations less binding today than in decades past. . . . Family is the first society in which we gain social identity and security, and its declining fortunes have left many Americans vulnerable to despair. . . . Sociologists have documented the close connection between the retreat from marriage and declining religious participation, especially among the working class. As a consequence of these changes, many Americans have "lost the narratives of their lives." . . . This leads to a loss of meaning and hope. . . . This is a condition that cannot be tolerated for long.[37]

Other bitter fruits are the moral chaos and injustice resulting from same-sex couples misusing reproductive technologies. Assisted by sperm and egg donors, and surrogate wombs, they are removing children from one or more of their biological parents to be raised absent a father or mother. According to Anderson, "[This trend is] *deliberately* increasing the number of children who grow up fatherless or motherless and subordinating children's needs to adult desires."[38] Peter Epps doesn't mince words:

It's not about the "right" of a man or a woman to "have a child" if that's the fashion accessory of the moment, or the satisfaction of some sentimental wish. Rather, every child just by existing has an insuperable claim on some man and some woman—on those who participate in the fundamental procreative act. Turning that act into commerce, turning "having a baby" into the province of

... services bought and sold. . . . [It] denies children their rights."[39]

We already know that the fast-growing assisted reproduction industry destroys massive numbers of human embryos. In the process of enabling same-sex couples to have children, more potential children will be destroyed than will be born. This is evil.

The breakdown in marriage is also leading to a sharp decline in family size and fertility rates. In the 1850s, it was common for US households to have six to nine children. Today, the norm is one or two. In August 2016, *The Week* published an article titled "America's Birth Rate is Now a National Emergency." Its author, Pascal-Emmanuel Gobry, wrote:

> The new birth rate numbers are out, and they're a disaster. There are now only 59.6 births per 1,000 women, the lowest rate ever recorded in the United States . . . most of it is due to people getting married later and choosing to have fewer children. And the worst part is, everyone is treating this news with a shrug. . . . It used to be taken for granted that the best indicator of a nation's health was its citizens' desire and capacity to reproduce. And it should still seem self-evident that people's willingness to have children is not only a sign of confidence in the future, but a sign of cultural health. It's a signal that people are willing to commit to the most enduring responsibility on earth, which is raising a child.[40]

Why are people getting married later and choosing to have fewer children? Part of the answer, of course, is the change from a primarily agricultural economy to an industrial, and post-industrial, society. More children used to mean more help on the farm or with household duties.

In the 1850s, children were viewed as a blessing, and as economic assets. No longer. Many view them as economic burdens.[41] This, in turn, reinforces changing attitudes toward motherhood. Mothers are increasingly leaving home and entering the workforce because child-raising and homemaking are not as valued by society. "Money is the marker of success in a market economy; it usually accompanies power, and it enables the bearer to wield power, including within the family," said Linda Hirshman of Brandeis University. Women who change their children's diapers have "voluntarily become untouchables."[42]

The rapid decline in fertility and household size is an underappreciated crisis for many Western nations. For a stable population, a nation needs a fertility rate of 2.1 births per woman. No society has ever recovered once the rate drops below 1.3. In 2015, the fertility rate in the United States was 1.8 and dropping. Today it is 1.786. Greece is now below 1.3, Italy is 1.2, Spain is 1.1. In thirty years, 60 percent of native-born Spaniards and Italians will have no brothers, sisters, cousins, aunts, or uncles. These cultures are literally committing suicide. In fifty years, countries named Spain, Italy, Norway, and Japan may still be on the map, but their former cultures will be nearly extinct, replaced by something else.

As a popular phrase goes: demography is destiny. So who is having children in the nations of Western Europe? Muslim immigrants. The number one name for baby boys in both England and Holland today is Mohammed. What will this mean for the future of these nations?

Dark days are ahead if we continue on this trajectory unimpeded. Who will provide the social capital to eventually pick up the pieces and start to rebuild? Might it be those of us on the losing side of the culture war—ordinary men and women who believe in, and live by, the true meaning of marriage? Followers of Jesus Christ must rediscover the truth—the magnificent reality of marriage—and build our own marriages and families on that foundation.

If demography is destiny, then those people who live this truth, have children, and teach it to them faithfully will one day outnumber those who are caught in a fading worldview that leads to demographic death. It won't be easy, of course. What took decades to deconstruct will take a long time to rebuild, but with God, all things are possible! Even in this dark hour, hope is stirring in unlikely places.

RETHINKING OUR VIEWS

Many of us have neglected to think carefully about marriage. We take its meaning for granted. Our notions of marriage draw from unexamined assumptions we've absorbed from our parents, our friends, teachers, the media, and the culture. Today, many are asking: "Why should I get married?" Perhaps they come from broken homes, or look around at friends who are now divorced. Why not just live together and avoid the hassle and expense of a wedding and the legal headaches if we decide to separate? When these questions come up, many Christians don't have an adequate response. If someone asked you, "Why should I get married?," how would you respond?

The hard truth is that Bible-believing Christians have tended to think about marriage, sex, birth control, and children in ways that align more with the prevailing culture than with Holy Scripture. T.M. Moore is right: Our focus now has to be "where we've strayed from the Lord's agenda and purpose. The way out of [this cultural crisis] is not, in the first instance, via political change, but by repentance, leading to revival and renewal."[43]

Perhaps we've absorbed the notion that marriage is *primarily* about romance and companionship—a deep, intimate relationship with another person. This image of marriage has been imprinted on our minds from the time we were children through music, films, and novels. Two people fall in love, find their "soul mate," and "live happily ever after." Certainly romance and companionship are *part* of any healthy marriage. The problem comes when this is all marriage is.

Marriage, according to God, is the formation of a new family, not just a couple's romantic feelings. Seeing marriage as nothing more than a perhaps temporary legal recognition of a romantic relationship isn't a minority view of some gay activists scattered here and there. It's the dominant view in the culture, and has been for some time. In essence, the church has unwittingly adopted this reductionist view of marriage. This helps explain why many Christians have struggled to answer homosexuals and lesbians who've been demanding "marriage equality."

This "romantic companion" approach is dependent on our evanescent emotions. What happens when strong feelings ebb, as they inevitably do? If I no longer "feel" in love with my spouse, and no-fault divorce is an option, no wonder the divorce rates in the church, while less than those in the society generally, are far too high.[44] Ultimately, the romantic companionship view of marriage abets our natural selfishness. It focuses on whether *my* needs for romance and companionship are being met. But marriage isn't about *my* emotional needs.

"The Bible has a richer, fuller, more robust understanding of marriage [that is] a whole lot more than our emotions," says Todd Wilson.[45] It is a union of heart, mind, spirit, and body. It's not just about the couple's happiness or emotional fulfillment, but about children, family, and future generations. It isn't about feeling "in love," but about fidelity to a lifelong covenant, regardless of the ebb and flow of emotions. It's a covenant that displays the steadfast love of Christ for His church.

But this richer meaning of marriage is rarely taught in the church. According to McDowell and Stonestreet, "For all the seminars and sermons offered by churches across America teaching how to have a 'happy' marriage, a 'fulfilled' marriage or a 'meaningful' marriage, there are precious few that disciple believers about God's intent and design for marriage."[46]

The romantic companionship view of marriage isn't the only area where the church has been discipled by the nation. The primary societal values of personal autonomy, choice, and materialism have also significantly shaped views of marriage within the church. The idea of an exclusive covenant relationship cuts against the grain of a society that elevates the "sovereign self." Marriage is cast as a loss of personal freedom—a "ball and chain." The good life, we're told, is filled with exciting adventures and material prosperity. Children are said to be a barrier to these goals because they limit freedom—and they cost a lot of money.

These attitudes are behind the growing trend of young people postponing marriage until their thirties, after they've gotten established in the workplace and secured a bank account large enough to fund their desired standard of living. Add to this mindset readily available, low-cost birth control, a growing hook-up culture, and pervasive pornography, and little wonder that birth control and abortion are viewed as holy sacraments in the West.

Sadly, the message communicated all too often, even in evangelical churches, is that sex is mainly for pleasure, and marriage is mainly for personal happiness. "The indissoluble link between sex, marriage, and children may be the single most-ignored, most obvious biblical principle in Christian circles," says Stonestreet. "Especially when I talk to young Christians, I can get them to acknowledge a link between sex and marriage, but the idea that sex, marriage, and children are–for the Christian–a package deal, is a really hard sell."[47]

Why is this such a "hard sell"? Largely because of Christian attitudes toward birth control—the use of which is simply assumed.

In all my years as a Christian in Bible-believing, evangelical churches, I've never once heard a sermon about birth control. Nor was it addressed in my pre-marriage counseling, other than being encouraged to agree with your spouse about the number and timing of your children.

Both in the broader culture and in the church, we tend to believe without question that children should come only when a couple is economically established. And then the maximum would be having two kids, or maybe three. Those couples who have more than three children are a minority. If children come shortly after the honeymoon, couples can expect some good-natured ribbing: "Didn't anyone teach you where kids come from?" A decision by a Christian couple *not* to use birth control is viewed as radical and extremist. The upshot is that there is almost no difference between the church and the culture when it comes to the age at which young people marry and the number of children they have.

McDowell and Stonestreet raise the alarm over this:

> As difficult as it may be for many Protestants to stomach, the birth control pill was not good for the institution of marriage . . . it furthers the destructive notion that marriage is just about furthering personal happiness. Plus, it obscures that one function of marriage [procreation] that clearly demonstrates why [it] requires a man and a woman.[48]

Pastors and church leaders must do far more to help Christians see the intrinsic connection between marriage, sex, *and* procreation, and why God-designed marriage is the necessary environment for raising godly children. Young Christians in particular should understand that marriage is intended to fulfill God's purposes in this world. His command to "be fruitful and multiply" is all about blessing the nations.

Christians need wisdom in how we think about birth control. We shouldn't passively accept it as an unquestioned cultural good. We must remember the history behind its creation and development, and its unwholesome fruits. While there may be legitimate reasons to limit family size, we dare not take our fears over personal cost or inconvenience as the final word.

Even entertaining the notion that Christians should welcome as many children as God chooses to give is frightening. Most of us feel inadequate to have one child, let alone five, six, or more. And the truth is, in our own strength, our fears are well-founded. But this is one of the great things about marriage. The whole endeavor is a faith-building exercise. There are no guarantees of successful outcomes, but God is ready and willing to provide the grace, strength, and resources (often from unlikely places) to do what seems impossible. My former pastor, Tom Garasha, aptly said, "Healthy things grow. Growing things change. Change requires risk. Risk requires faith, and faith makes you healthy."

The dissolution of marriage can be reversed, but only if that reversal first begins in the church. "There is no path forward to building a strong marriage culture that does not begin with a revival of God's people to His design for marriage," say Stonestreet and McDowell.[49] The dissolution of marriage, in the final analysis, isn't the work of sexual revolutionaries or LGBTQ activists. Our enemy is not flesh and blood. This is clearly Satan's strategy. If he can weaken and destroy marriage and family, he can significantly hinder God's plan to bless the nations. The good news is that this revival has already started. God is leading us there.

HOW SHOULD WE THEN LIVE?

The crying need of the moment is for the church to rediscover the true meaning of marriage, and repent of our uncritical acceptance of false cultural values and practices. While effecting God-honoring change in our communities, and indeed the whole world, will certainly be both daunting and time-consuming, planting the flag of marriage can begin in our homes this very day.

Jonathan Edwards (1703–1758) is among the finest theologians, pastors, and intellectuals America has ever produced. He played a central role in the First Great Awakening, authored many books, delivered countless sermons, and inspired generations of missionaries. But he shares his greatest legacy with his wife, Sarah—the amazing influence their eleven children had on shaping the destiny of the United States. In the span of 150 years, the successive generations of this one couple produced more than one hundred cross-cultural missionaries, thirteen college presidents, sixty-five college professors, one hundred lawyers, thirty judges, sixty-six medical doctors, three US senators, three state governors, three mayors of large cities, untold numbers of leaders in banking, commerce, and industry, and a vice president of the United States.[50]

This kind of culture-shaping influence did not happen by accident. It is the fruit of a marriage built upon the teachings of the Bible. What kind of legacy will *your* marriage and family produce? Very likely the most important work you will do in your lifetime is the work you will do in the home.

And this kind of influence with your children can start very simply. Kimberly Thornbury, formerly a vice president at The King's College in New York City, and her husband, Greg, started some family rituals to help their children begin applying their faith at an early age. They include starting a "house of prayer" using Christmas cards from friends and loved ones; setting aside a "first snowflake of the season" gift for each child; and having a "gratitude jar" with slips of paper on which are written reasons each family member has been thankful over the last year. These ideas are simple but can have a huge impact in time.

"I'm a firm believer that a few low cost household rituals, practiced faithfully, can have a disproportionate positive effect on the everyday busy family," she says. "Habits and layering, doing the same things every day, every month or every season are key to shaping individuals and families."[51]

As well, Christian marriages can and should be living depictions of Christ and His church (see Ephesians 5:22–32). Too often we hear of Christian marriages falling apart for one reason or another. Not only is this a tragedy for both husband and wife, it is a missed opportunity to show the beauty of Christ and faith in Him to a watching world that has almost despaired of ever finding selfless, sacrificial love and mutual delight.

While I can make no claim to having a perfect marriage, I can testify that God has been with me and my wife through decades of matrimonial challenge and delight. It isn't always easy, but it's more than worth the effort—for us, and those around us. I believe that our far from perfect example, powered by the grace of God, have made a difference in the lives of some of our unsaved friends and neighbors.

Beyond our own marriages and families, we need to courageously bear witness to the truth about marriage publicly. We need to tell the world: Marriage is God's creation, and we are not free to redefine it. Children are a blessing, and they deserve to be raised by the mother and father who gave them birth.

We'll be demonized for saying such things, but we need not let that silence us. Take the example of Washington state florist Baronelle Stutzman and Colorado baker Jack Phillips. Each routinely served homosexual customers, and even employed and befriended them. Yet when asked to use their creative talents to celebrate a same-sex marriage, they respectfully declined, knowing full well the likelihood of lawsuits, fines, and even death threats for their decision. But they stood firm, and their loving, courageous stance has kept the dam of religious liberty intact—at least for the moment.

Recovering the truth about marriage won't be easy. Many of us have been affected personally. We may be children of divorced parents—or we may be divorced ourselves. We may have done things that have deeply wounded our spouse or children. We may have aborted one or more children. We may be entangled in an illicit relationship. A growing number of young Christians have never seen a healthy, biblical marriage.

Christians must acknowledge our role in this brokenness. Rather than loving others as Jesus commanded (John 15:12), we have sinned against God and harmed those we are closest to—our own husbands, wives, parents, children, or siblings. Too often we have not understood or obeyed God's clear instruction for marriage. But thanks to God, forgiveness is available through Christ. God graciously offers each of us a second chance, or a third, or fourth. "If we confess our sins, He is faithful and just to forgive us our sins and to cleanse us from all unrighteousness" (1 John 1:9, ESV).

Do you need to confess to God and to those you have harmed? Do you have wrong beliefs and attitudes about marriage for which you need to repent? God is wonderfully gracious. He separates our sins from us as far as east is from west (Psalm 103:12), but first we must humbly acknowledge them. Once we have confessed and repented, we face a choice. Will we continue to be swept along by destructive cultural currents, or will we determine to follow God's way, no matter the cost? My prayer is that you will choose to follow God. If you do, then begin, as Joshua did, with this solemn commitment: "As for me and my house, we will serve the Lord" (Joshua 24:15, ESV).

All of us are either married, will be married, or know people who are married. We need to know the truth about marriage and consciously choose it. The broader culture seeks to strip marriage of its meaning, even define it out of existence. We must respectfully stand firm. Marriage is far too important, and far too central to God's character and good purposes for the nations.

Perhaps more than at any time in history, marriage cannot be taken for granted. It does not happen automatically. It must be passionately pursued. So choose this day!

CHAPTER 5

FREEDOM

Where the Spirit of the Lord is, there is freedom.

2 CORINTHIANS 3:17

You, my brothers and sisters, were called to be free.
But do not use your freedom to indulge the flesh;
rather, serve one another humbly in love.

GALATIANS 5:13

FREEDOM
The capacity to self-govern; to act according to one's choices within God's created order and under His moral law.

FREEDOM REDEFINED
The power or right to act, speak or think as one wants without hindrance or restraint.[1]

Just before Mao's Cultural Revolution, Lily was born to illiterate, working-class parents in China's western Sichuan province. Her earliest years, she says, were marked by "extremely poor living conditions, food rationing, social chaos, and communist indoctrination."

One day she met an American exchange student in Shanghai and heard for the first time the novel idea that individual rights come from God, who is the basis for freedom. The idea was life-changing for Lily.

Lily emigrated to America for graduate school in 1988 and left her life as a cog in the communist machine, building an entirely new life as an entrepreneur and educator. Now living in New Hampshire, Lily Tang Williams has decided to run for Congress, saying, "I fear that the country I love is becoming like the country I left."[2]

Lily's longing for freedom is something we all share. It is part of what makes us human. Another former communist turned Christian, Whittaker Chambers, expressed this beautifully:

> Freedom is a need of the soul . . . It is in striving toward God that the soul strives continually after a condition of freedom. God alone is the inciter and guarantor of freedom. He is the only guarantor. External freedom is only an aspect of interior freedom. Political freedom, as the western world has known it, is only a political reading of the Bible. Religion and freedom are indivisible.
>
> Without freedom the soul dies.[3]

FREEDOM DEFINED

Webster's 1828 American Dictionary of the English Language defines freedom as "a state of exemption from the power or control of another." The opposite of freedom is slavery, bondage, captivity, imprisonment, subjugation, and oppression. Freedom is synonymous with liberty, self-control, self-government, and self-determination.

FREEDOM
The capacity to self-govern; to act according to one's choices within God's created order and under His moral law.

At the center of freedom are choice and agency. Those fortunate enough to live in relatively free societies experience freedom in the countless choices they make daily. What will I eat for breakfast? Where will we go on our summer vacation? Where will we attend church? What home or apartment will we live in? What college will I attend? What occupation will I pursue? Who will I vote for to represent my values and preferred policies?

Freedom is often described in particular categories, including:

- *Religious liberty*, or the ability to act according to one's choices on matters of conscience and deeply held beliefs.
- *Civil liberty*, or the ability to act according to one's choices, with limited control, restraint, or interference by the government.
- *Political freedom*, or the ability to act according to one's choices regarding political life, including freedom of speech, freedom of assembly, and the freedom to elect representatives in the government.
- *Economic freedom*, or the ability to act according to one's choices in regard to the exchange of goods and services. This is often referred to as "the free market" or "free-market capitalism."
- *Spiritual freedom*, or the ability to choose the good, and to do it. To willingly act in ways that align with God's moral law. This is the deepest form of freedom and the precondition for all other freedoms.

TRUTH IS ESSENTIAL TO FREEDOM

Freedom, like a beautiful but a delicate flower, can thrive only in certain conditions. *Truth* is one. Jesus said in John 8:32: "And you will know the truth, and the *truth will set you free*" (italics added).

Why is truth essential to freedom? We all inhabit God's world, which operates according to an inviolable design, not only in the world around us but within our human nature and our conscience. If we exercise freedom in ways that contradict this order, we lose freedom.

Consider, for example, the law of gravity. Gravity is an objective reality. It is *true*, regardless of our subjective beliefs. We have the "freedom" to jump out of an airplane without a parachute, but that freedom will be short-lived.

Noah Webster carefully specified this idea in defining liberty as "the power of acting as one thinks fit, without any restraint or control, *except from the laws of nature*."[4] Freedom is rightly defined as the capacity to self-govern or to act according to one's choices *within God's created order and under His moral law.*

FREEDOM IS A UNIQUELY BIBLICAL IDEA

Freedom is inextricably linked to a biblical worldview, for it is the *only* worldview that supplies the two foundational truths needed to sustain freedom:

1.   All people are made by God, in His image, with God-granted rights to life and liberty.
2.   There is a moral law above all earthly law to which even the most powerful are under and accountable. The "rule of law" is predicated on the reality of the moral law.

Without these two essential biblical truths, a free society makes no sense. Said Jürgen Habermas, one of the most influential philosophers of the modern era:

> Christianity, and nothing else, is the ultimate foundation of liberty, conscience, human rights, and democracy, the benchmarks of Western civilization. To this day, we have no other options [than Christianity]. We continue to nourish ourselves from this source. Everything else is postmodern chatter."[5]

The view popular among institutional elites, however, is that freedom comes from *rejecting* the God of the universe as recognized by Judeo-Christian theism. Only then do we become free from God's arbitrary rules, limits, and constraints. But upon deeper reflection, we see that secularism isn't compatible with freedom, nor is a secular-materialist or Darwinian worldview able to support human freedom or free societies. Take, for example, the true observation of Darwinist Will Provine from Cornell University. He correctly observed that if Darwin was right regarding human origins, these are the logical conclusions: "There is no life after death; no ultimate foundation for ethics; no ultimate meaning for life; *no free will*" (italics added).[6]

If there is no God, all that exists is matter in motion. Every phenomenon must be attributed to random, purposeless material causes. Therefore, we are biologically determined creatures with no free will. Likewise, "there is . . . no ultimate foundation for ethics." Without God, there is no moral law, and no objective good or evil. In the secular-materialist Darwinian worldview, the only "law" is survival of the fittest. If the powerful are inclined to strip you of your freedom, and enslave you for their own benefit, what's to stop them?

Nor is there any basis for free choice or agency in an animistic worldview. We are merely hapless victims of powerful spiritual forces, including the spirits of deceased ancestors, that control all phenomena. In Hinduism, according to *National Geographic*, "More than 160 million people in India are considered 'Untouchable'— people tainted by their birth into a caste system that deems them impure, less than human."[7]

Meanwhile, in nations ruled by theocratic Islam, such as Saudi Arabia and Iran, there is little political freedom, and virtually no freedom of religion.

Only the Judeo-Christian worldview supplies the necessary ingredients for freedom. The idea of freedom is deeply rooted in the Bible, both the Old and New Testaments. Cultural essayist Rod Dreher writes about how Western, "liberal" societies are uniquely a product of a Judeo-Christian civilization. By liberal, he is referring to the original meaning of this word, which is derived from the word *liberty*, or freedom.

> Most of the things that proper liberals cherish in terms of political and social values come from Christianity. . . . There is a reason that liberalism emerged in the Christian West, and nowhere else.[8]

THE STORY OF FREEDOM

In *The Gift of the Jews: How a Tribe of Desert Nomads Changed the Way Everyone Thinks and Feels*, historian Thomas Cahill explains how the idea of freedom came into the world through the Bible. "The Jews gave us a whole new vocabulary. . . . Most of our best words . . . are the gifts of the Jews."[9] One of these words is freedom.

In the Bible, we learn what freedom is, starting with God Himself. *God is free.* He is the *freest* of all. In Psalm 115:3, ESV, we read, "Our God is in the heavens; He does all that he pleases." According to John Piper, "God always acts in freedom, according to his own 'good pleasure,' following the dictates of his own delights. God never becomes the victim of circumstance. He is never forced into a situation where he must do something [against His will] . . . He is not trapped or cornered or coerced."[10]

God is the sovereign King of heaven and earth. There is no higher authority. No one is more powerful. He is accountable to no one. As we will see, there is a relationship between authority and freedom. The greater the authority, the greater the freedom.

GOD'S FREEDOM, AND OURS

Because God is free, we are free, *for we are made in His image and likeness.*

To be sure, our freedom is not like God's. His is bound only by the moral perfection of His character. There is a mystery here, for God is also sovereign and omniscient. He knows what will happen in the future and guides history toward His chosen ends. Human choices don't constrain Him in any way. But if we are unable to alter God's providential plans by our free choices, are we truly free? Although difficult to understand, the Bible answers in the affirmative. It upholds *both* God's sovereignty and our freedom. God made us with the capacity to freely choose, and He holds us accountable and responsible for our moral choices. Yet He works out His sovereign purposes, nonetheless.

We see this mystery play out in the biblical story of Joseph, which begins in Genesis 37. Joseph's envious brothers *freely chose* to cast him into an empty well and leave him to die. Later, Joseph finds himself elevated to Pharaoh's court as second-in-command, and his brothers are stunned when Joseph reveals his identity to them:

> Then Joseph said to his brothers, "I am your brother Joseph, the one you sold into [slavery in] Egypt! And now, do not be distressed and do not be angry with yourselves for selling me here, because it was to save lives that God sent me ahead of you. For two years now there has been famine in the land, and for the next five years there will be no plowing and reaping. But God sent me ahead of you to preserve for you a remnant on earth and to save your lives by a great deliverance. (Genesis 45:5–7)

God worked His sovereign purpose through their free choices. God gives us freedom but works His will, nonetheless. Psalm 145:17

says, "The Lord is righteous in all his ways, and faithful in all He does." God is even able to use evil human choices for His good purposes.

MADE TO BE FREE

Have you ever wondered why God didn't create us as robots, programmed to respond to Him exactly as He wanted? Given our abuse of freedom, it would have saved Him a lot of heartaches. But as image-bearers of God, *we are free because God is free.* God made us free for many important reasons.

Freedom and love

Incredibly, God made us with the ability to relate to Him as a person, *in love.* Freedom is essential to this kind of relationship, for love, by its very nature, must be freely chosen. It can never be compelled or manipulated. Without choice, love makes no sense.

Freedom, dominion, and creativity

God rules over His creation as King, and He created us in His image to rule over creation as His vice-regents. With greater authority comes greater freedom, and God has given us incredible authority. We are created to rule—to govern ourselves and to govern His creation. Freedom is essential to both tasks.

God worked in creation to bring order, life, and beauty out of darkness and chaos. As His image-bearers, we too are created to work and apply our creativity to God's creation, bringing forth even greater order, innovation, and beauty. Freedom is essential to this task as well. It gives us the scope to dream, imagine, create, innovate, and build. To form businesses, invent useful products and resources, create beautiful buildings and landscapes, governing systems, and so on. No wonder political and economic systems that allow for greater personal freedom inevitably produce greater innovation, resources, and wealth.

Freedom a God-given human right

We possess freedom as a gift from God. To their everlasting credit, America's Founding Fathers acknowledged this powerful truth in the Declaration of Independence.

> We hold these truths to be self-evident, that all men are created equal, that they are endowed by their Creator with certain unalienable Rights, that among these are Life, *Liberty* and the pursuit of Happiness (italics added).

Because all people are created to be free, no person or government has the right to enslave them, no matter how powerless, uneducated, vulnerable, or impoverished they may be. "The mass of mankind has not been born with saddles on their backs," admitted the slaveholding Jefferson, "nor a favored few booted and spurred, ready to ride them legitimately, by the grace of God."[11]

Earthly tyrants fear this idea more than any other and will do almost anything to keep it from their subjects. In the words of Graham Shearer, "The ancient Christian insight that there is another king than Caesar . . . is the beginning of liberty."[12]

FREEDOM IN THE GARDEN OF EDEN

Let's take a brief survey of the biblical narrative of freedom, starting in Genesis.

> Now the Lord God had planted a garden in the east, in Eden; and there he put the man he had formed. The Lord God made all kinds of trees grow out of the ground— trees that were pleasing to the eye and good for food. In

the middle of the garden were the tree of life and the tree of the knowledge of good and evil.

The Lord God took the man and put him in the Garden of Eden to work it and take care of it. And the Lord God commanded the man, "You are free to eat from any tree in the garden; but you must not eat from the tree of the knowledge of good and evil, for when you eat from it you will certainly die. (Genesis 2:8–9; 15–17)

Note carefully God's words to Adam and Eve: *"You are free . . ."* God made us free. It is an essential aspect of our humanity. But as created beings, our freedom is not limitless. It thrives within set limits. We see these limits here: God says to Adam and Eve, you are free to eat from any tree in the garden . . . except one—the tree of the knowledge of good and evil. In the words of Christian essayist Bradford Littlejohn: "Human nature is constituted by limits, and true freedom is found in the recognition, not the imagined transcendence of, such limits."[13]

God established limits in the Garden in the form of the Tree of the Knowledge of Good and Evil and commanded Adam and Eve not to eat its fruit if they wished to live and remain free. He *commanded*, but significantly, He didn't force or compel. Instead, He allowed them the freedom to obey or disobey His command and face the consequences. He treated them according to their created nature—as free human beings.

Here, a new character enters the story—a mysterious serpent who tempted Adam and Eve to disobey God's command:

Now the serpent was more crafty than any of the wild animals the Lord God had made. He said to the woman, "Did God really say, 'You must not eat from any tree in the garden'?"

> The woman said to the serpent, "We may eat fruit from the trees in the garden, but God did say, 'You must not eat fruit from the tree that is in the middle of the garden, and you must not touch it, or you will die.'"
>
> "You will not certainly die," the serpent said to the woman. "For God knows that when you eat from it your eyes will be opened, and you will be like God, knowing good and evil. (Genesis 3:1–4)

This is the "big lie" that rolls down through the ages, tempting people in every generation who long for freedom without limits, and without accountability. But for created beings, limitless freedom is a delusion, and Satan knows it. When our first ancestors made their fateful decision, a transfer of allegiance occurred from God's kingdom to Satan's. Freedom is a great hallmark of God's kingdom, for "where the Spirit of the Lord is, there is freedom" (2 Corinthians 3:17), but in Satan's dark realm, there is no freedom, only bondage.

Our first ancestors foolishly used their freedom to transgress God's limits; consequently, they became slaves of Satan, and their enslavement was passed down to all subsequent generations. The apostle Paul vividly describes the horrible consequences:

> They have become filled with every kind of wickedness, evil, greed and depravity. They are full of envy, murder, strife, deceit and malice. They are gossips, slanderers, God-haters, insolent, arrogant and boastful; they invent ways of doing evil; they disobey their parents; they have no understanding, no fidelity, no love, no mercy. Although they know God's righteous decree that those who do such things deserve death, they not only continue to do these very things but also approve of those who practice them. (Romans 1:29–32)

Any society in which the mass of people act like this cannot be free for long. It will destroy itself, which is exactly what Satan wants. In rebelling against our Creator, we became slaves of Satan, ensnared by His evil scheme to enslave and destroy us, and the nations of the world.

Is there any hope that we can be liberated from this horrible bondage and regain our birthright of freedom? Yes, but not without help. Our captor is too powerful to overcome in our own strength. We need a powerful rescuer, which is exactly what God, in His mercy, provided. The story of this rescue operation is the greatest story ever told. It spans nearly the full length of human history, beginning in Genesis 3, reaching its consummation at the end of the age, as described in Revelation 21–22. The climax of this story is the life, death, and resurrection of Jesus Christ, the great Liberator. The Savior of the world.

THE STORY OF FREEDOM IN THE OLD TESTAMENT

Out of all the nations of the ancient world, God chose one man, Abraham, and made a remarkable covenant with him. Through Abraham's offspring, God would raise up a new nation, Israel. Unlike other nations, Israel would be a "holy nation" set apart as God's chosen people. But within a few short generations, Abraham's descendants find themselves enslaved in Egypt, one of the most powerful and ruthless empires of the age.

Had God abandoned His covenant with His people? Not at all. In miraculous fashion, He will set them free. The movement from slavery to freedom is a central theme in the Bible, and the dramatic story of the Jewish exodus from Egypt foreshadows the coming of Jesus the Messiah, who would make a way for the world to be set free from its enslavement to Satan.

Before they can live as free people, however, the Israelites must learn what freedom means. For four hundred years, all they had known was slavery. Their masters told them where to go and what to do. They were treated like animals—fed and watered and used as beasts of burden. And then, in the blink of an eye, they were free! This brought great joy but also a grim foreboding as they looked out on a desert wasteland. Their newfound freedom brought a new set of challenges. They began to complain, and even long for slavery again.

> In the desert, the whole community grumbled against Moses and Aaron. The Israelites said to them, "If only we had died by the Lord's hand in Egypt! There we sat around pots of meat and ate all the food we wanted, but you have brought us out into this desert to starve this entire assembly to death." (Exodus 16:2–3)

To suddenly shift from bondage to freedom can be incredibly daunting. Freedom requires the willingness to accept responsibility and own the consequences that come with choices. For those who have never known it, that responsibility can feel overwhelming.

FREEDOM REQUIRES VIRTUOUS SELF-GOVERNMENT UNDER GOD'S LAW

Many of the newly freed Israelites thought this way. They needed to exchange a slave mentality for a commitment to freedom, which requires a willingness to submit to God's authority and self-govern under His law. So God guided them into a season of preparation that began at Mount Sinai. There, God revealed Himself to them and renewed the covenant He made with Abraham, only this time with the descendants of Abraham, Isaac, and Jacob:

> Then Moses went up to God, and the Lord called to him from the mountain and said, "This is what you are to say to the descendants of Jacob and what you are to tell the people of Israel: 'You yourselves have seen what

I did to Egypt, and how I carried you on eagles' wings and brought you to myself. Now if you obey me fully and keep my covenant, then out of all nations you will be my treasured possession. Although the whole earth is mine, you will be for me a kingdom of priests and a holy nation.' These are the words you are to speak to the Israelites". (Exodus 19:3–6)

Here, God offers humanity a second chance. You disobeyed my command in the Garden of Eden, and the consequence was slavery. But because of my steadfast love for you, I've set you free again and offered you a fresh start: "Now, if you obey me fully and keep my covenant . . . then you will be my treasured possession." You will be my beloved people and once again experience true freedom and life.

But not *just* you. "The whole earth is mine," said the Lord. God's plan to emancipate the world started with one person, Abraham, and one nation, Israel. Through this lineage came Jesus, the Liberator of the world. God's plan is for Israel to be "a kingdom of priests." A model nation, revealing the kind of relationship God wants with all nations. A relationship in which He is worshiped and obeyed above all, and as a result, the nations thrive in freedom.

Like a marriage betrothal, the covenant God offers on Sinai must be *freely chosen*. Here again, God treats His people not as robots or slaves, but as free human beings.

So Moses went back and summoned the elders of [Israel] and set before them all the words the Lord had commanded him to speak. The people all responded together [freely], *"We will do everything the Lord has said."* So Moses brought their answer back to the Lord. (Exodus 19:7–8, italics added)

God then provides the terms of the covenant in the Ten Commandments. "I am the Lord your God, who brought you out of Egypt, out of the land of slavery. You shall have no other gods before me" (Exodus 20:2–3). A nation is most free when its people submit to God's moral law and interact peaceably with one another by choice. The great filmmaker Cecil B. DeMille, director of the Hollywood classic, *The 10 Commandments*, said it well:

> God . . . did not create man and then, as an afterthought, impose upon him a set of arbitrary, irritating, restrictive rules. *He made man free—and then gave him the commandments to keep him free* . . . We cannot break the Ten Commandments. We can only break ourselves against them—or else, by keeping them, rise through them to the fullness of freedom under God (italics added).[14]

Catholic Bishop Robert Barron observed similarly: "Freedom is the discipling of desire. In taking the law—God's law—into your heart, you become free."[15]

Years later, in the twilight of his life, Israel's faithful leader Moses made a final dramatic appeal to the Jewish people on the eve of their entering the Promised Land. In Deuteronomy 30:15–19, he restated God's law and challenged them to renew their commitment to it. The word "choose" is at the center of this famous passage, and choice is the essence of freedom.

> I call heaven and earth to witness against you today, that I have set before you life and death, blessing and curse. Therefore choose life, that you and your offspring may live. (Deuteronomy 30:19, ESV)

God sets before Israel, and all of us, two paths. One leads to life and to freedom under His rule and authority, in obedience to His law. The other leads to bondage and destruction through rejecting God and His law. God says to Israel, *"you choose"* which path you want, and the consequences that come with that choice.

Tragically, Israel chose to reject God and His law. Over and over, the people turned their back on God and disobeyed His commandments, and, as a result, they lost their freedom. They found themselves enslaved once again, this time in the Babylonian Empire, under the iron fist of another cruel tyrant.

THE STORY OF FREEDOM IN THE NEW TESTAMENT

During the darkest days of their Babylonian captivity, God comforted His chosen people through the Prophet Ezekiel. A day was coming when He would set them free once again. But this time, God would make a way for them to remain free by dealing with the root problem, their inability to keep the law due to their fallen, sinful hearts. To self-govern based on God's law, they would need to be remade. They would need nothing less than a new heart, and a new Spirit.

> "For I will take you out of the nations; I will gather you from all the countries and bring you back into your own land. I will sprinkle clean water on you, and you will be clean; I will cleanse you from all your impurities and from all your idols. I will give you a new heart and put a new spirit in you; I will remove from you your heart of stone and give you a heart of flesh. And I will put my Spirit in you and move you to follow my decrees and be careful to keep my laws. Then you will live in the land I gave your ancestors; you will be my people, and I will be your God". (Ezekiel 36:24–28)

Here is our dilemma. Freedom is unsustainable unless people keep God's law, and in our fallen, sinful nature, that is exactly what we are unable to do. As a result, we remain slaves to sin and Satan. The apostle Paul described this dilemma in his own life:

> I am unspiritual, sold as a slave to sin . . . I have the desire to do what is good, *but I cannot carry it out.* For I do not do the good I want to do, but the evil I do not want to do—this I keep on doing . . . What a wretched man I am! *Who will rescue me from this body that is subject to death?* (Romans 7:14; 18–19; 24, italics added)

We can all relate to Paul on some level. We've all felt trapped by various addictions, desires, and compulsions. Trapped by our own hatreds and bitterness. We see how they have power over us, holding us captive, leading to the destruction of our lives and relationships. We may deeply desire to be free from the power they wield over us, but are unable in own strength. We are under Satan's grip, enslaved by Him and destined for destruction. Unless we can be free from this inward bondage, we can never be free people or free citizens in a free society. Internal, spiritual freedom is the foundation of all other freedoms.

Who will rescue us? Who will make a way for us to escape this dilemma? God Himself, by sending His Son to do what we are unable to do. The Old Testament movements from slavery to freedom all foreshadowed the culmination of a future, and final, rescue operation. That moment came two thousand years ago in the person of Jesus, who announced that He was the long-awaited Liberator:

> [Jesus] went to Nazareth, where he had been brought up, and on the Sabbath day he went into the synagogue, as was his custom. He stood up to read, and the scroll of the prophet Isaiah was handed to him. Unrolling it, he found the place where it is written:

"The Spirit of the Lord is on me,
>   because he has anointed me
>   to proclaim good news to the poor.
> He has sent me to proclaim freedom for the prisoners
>   and recovery of sight for the blind,
> to set the oppressed free,
>   to proclaim the year of the Lord's favor."

Then he rolled up the scroll, gave it back to the attendant and sat down. The eyes of everyone in the synagogue were fastened on him. He began by saying to them, "Today this scripture is fulfilled in your hearing". (Luke 4:16–21)

Who are the oppressed, blind prisoners that Jesus came to set free? All of us. Jesus is the Great Emancipator who came to free us in the deepest, truest sense possible.

Jesus, as God in human flesh, lived a life of perfect freedom. Nobody compelled Him to do anything against His will. Everything He did, He did freely, including dying a horrible death on a Roman cross. "I lay down my life that I may take it up again. *No one takes it from me, but I lay it down of my own accord*" (John 10:17–18, ESV, italics added). This is freedom's ultimate goal. To freely choose sacrificial service, imprisonment, or even death for the good of another. How different this is from contemporary notions of freedom.

How did Jesus's sacrifice on the cross secure our freedom? The apostle Paul, in his letter to the Romans, explains how the cross secured our deepest freedom:

Therefore, there is now no condemnation for those who are in Christ Jesus, because through Christ Jesus the law of the Spirit who gives life has set you free . . . For what the law was powerless to do because it was weakened by the flesh, God did by sending his own Son in the likeness of sinful flesh to be a sin offering. (Romans 8:1–3)

For we know that our old self was crucified with him so
that the body ruled by sin might be done away with, *that
we should no longer be slaves to sin— because anyone who
has died has been set free from sin* . . . But thanks be to God
that, *though you used to be slaves to sin . . . you have been
set free from sin and have become slaves to righteousness.*
(Romans 6:6–7; 17–18, italics added)

Now, as God's beloved children and members of His family,
we are no longer enslaved by Satan. We have been ransomed, our
souls purchased at the price of Christ's blood on the cross. Because
Jesus died, was buried, and rose again to new life, we too have died
to our old, sinful nature and are remade. We have been given a new
heart and Spirit and the power to obey God and do what pleases
Him. God, in Christ, has given us new power to be virtuous, self-
governing people. In the immortal words of the apostle John: "if the
Son sets you free, you will be free indeed". (John 8:36)

We may live in a free, democratic society and enjoy civil and
political freedoms, but if we are not *spiritually* free, we remain slaves.
The opposite is true as well. We may be wrongfully imprisoned
or enslaved, and unjustly denied our external freedom, but if we
are inwardly free, we are "free indeed" and nobody can take that
freedom away.

Now, as free children of God, we face yet another choice. We
can live in the freedom Christ purchased for us by obeying God
and loving our neighbor as ourselves, or we can return to slavery
by rejecting God and living for our selfish desires and appetites.
This echoes the same choice Moses put before the Israelites in
Deuteronomy. It is a major theme throughout the New Testament:

It is for freedom that Christ has set us free. Stand firm,
then, and do not let yourselves be burdened again by a
yoke of slavery. (Galatians 5:1)

You, my brothers and sisters, were called to be free. But do not use your freedom to indulge the flesh; rather, serve one another humbly in love. (Galatians 5:13)

Live as free people, but do not use your freedom as a cover-up for evil; live as God's slaves. (1 Peter 2:16)

Reflecting on these New Testament passages, the great reformer Martin Luther wrote: "A Christian man is the most free lord of all, subject to none. A Christian man is most dutiful servant of all, and subject to everyone."

THE RISE OF FREE NATIONS

Over time, these powerful, biblical truths about freedom gave rise to free nations. In a fallen world, free nations are certainly not the norm. Historically, the default is tyranny. It wasn't until the Reformation that these biblical principles were uncovered. After the fall of the Roman Empire, the Roman church erroneously adopted much of the old imperial political order, with the pope replacing Caesar as not only a religious but also political authority. To keep the masses under its power, the hierarchy of this Christianized "Roman Empire" claimed sole authority to interpret the Scriptures.[16]

But all this changed when the German monk Martin Luther (1483 to 1546) and the French reformer John Calvin (1509 to 1564) sparked not only an ecclesiastical but a political revolution. They did so by opening up the Bible, translating it into the common language, and elevating it to a position of sole authority over every sphere of society—including the church. It was a cultural earthquake that continues to produce ripples and aftershocks in our present day.

As the peoples of northern Europe began to read the Bible in their heart languages, they discovered principles that give rise, not to political tyrannies, but to free nations in the pattern of ancient

Israel. They began to develop a theology of free, self-governing nations where:

- The law was king, and human law was legitimate only when grounded in God's moral law.
- Powerful rulers were subject to the same laws as everyone else.
- People were to be treated by those in authority as free human beings.
- Serfs, peasants, and slaves were elevated to the position of *citizens* who had the authority to self-govern under God's law.
- Political power was decentralized and separated into smaller units that could check and balance one another.
- Civil authorities became "civil *servants*" and were made accountable to citizens.

There is a reason that free nations emerged in the Christian West following the Reformation—and nowhere else. Freedom House has shown that nations that have roots in Judeo-Christian theism have been most free, while those that are based on non-biblical religions, or atheistic ideologies such as Marxism, are the least free.

THE GOLDEN TRIANGLE OF FREEDOM

These biblical truths took perhaps their deepest root in the North American colonies. In his masterful book *A Free People's Suicide*, Os Guinness describes the uniquely American formula for free nations as "The Golden Triangle of Freedom." At the apex of the triangle is freedom. But freedom requires *virtue*. Virtue requires *faith*, and faith, in turn, requires *freedom*.

Freedom requires virtue. Benjamin Franklin put it this way: "Only a virtuous people are capable of freedom. . . . As nations become corrupt and vicious they have more need of masters." People who are self-controlled and virtuous do not need a strong, centralized government to control them.

Virtue requires faith. By "faith," America's founding generation meant Christianity. This was their source of knowledge about virtue as well as their source of motivation and power to live virtuously. Through faith in Christ, we increasingly bear the "fruits" of the Spirit: love, joy, peace, patience, kindness, goodness, faithfulness, gentleness, and last, but not least, *self-control*, the supreme virtue needed to sustain freedom. As Edmund Burke prophetically said: "It is ordained in the eternal constitution of things, that men of intemperate minds cannot be free. Their passions forge their fetters."

America's founding generation was remarkably clear in its understanding that the inward, spiritual freedom that results from the Christian gospel is necessary for outward, civil, and political freedom. John Adams, who helped author the Declaration of Independence and the Constitution, and later served as the second president of the United States, spoke of the necessity of "religion" (by which he meant Christianity), for freedom:

> [I]t is religion and morality alone which can establish the principles upon which freedom can securely stand. The only foundation of a free constitution is pure virtue, and if this cannot be inspired into our People in a greater Measure, than they have it now, they may change their Rulers and the forms of Government, but they will not obtain a lasting liberty.

This was a bedrock belief for Adams, who also famously said:

> We have no government armed with power capable of contending with human passions unbridled by [virtue] and religion. Our Constitution was made only for a moral and religious people. It is wholly inadequate to the government of any other.

Faith requires freedom. This third and final part of the Golden Triangle is rooted in the truth that God created us as free human beings. We are not robots that can be programmed. We are not animals that operate from brute instinct. God made us with the capacity to make free choices regarding our deepest convictions. Genuine faith must be chosen. It can be taught and encouraged, not imposed.

THE IDEA OF FREEDOM IN EARLY AMERICA

This Golden Triangle of Freedom deeply shaped American thinking for decades. In 1831 Alexis de Tocqueville began traveling through America and wrote the magisterial work *Democracy in America*. He said: "The Americans combine the notions of religion and liberty so intimately in their minds, that it is impossible to make them conceive of one without the other."[17]

This conception of liberty eventually forced America into its bloody civil war over slavery. Human slavery is glaringly incompatible with the Declaration of Independence and its assertion that "all men are created equal" and endowed with unalienable rights to life and liberty.

The beloved American author Laura Ingalls Wilder set her *Little House on the Prairie* series in the years following the Civil War. In her novel *Little Town on the Prairie*, a youthful Laura visits the small farm town of DeSmet, South Dakota. Along with her father and little sister, Carrie, she is there to celebrate the Fourth of July. The celebration concludes with a public reading of the Declaration of Independence. After it is read, there is a stillness.

> Then Pa began to sing. All at once, everyone was singing, [and] Laura discovered what it means to be free.
>
> 'My country, 'tis of thee,
> Sweet land of liberty,
> Of thee, I sing. . . .
> Long may our land be bright
> With freedom's holy light.
> Protect us by Thy might,
> Great God, our King!'
>
> The crowd was scattering away then, but Laura stood stock still. Suddenly she had a completely new thought. The Declaration [of Independence] and the song came together in her mind, and she thought: God is America's king. She thought: Americans won't obey any king on earth. Americans are free. That means they have to obey their consciences. No king bosses Pa; he has to

boss himself. Why (she thought), when I'm a little older, Pa and Ma will stop telling me what to do, and there isn't anyone else who has a right to give me orders. I will have to make myself be good.

Her whole mind seemed to be lighted up by that thought. This is what it means to be free. It means you have to be good. 'Our father's God, author of liberty . . .' The laws of Nature and of Nature's God endow you with the right to life and liberty. Then you keep the laws of God, for God's law is the only thing that gives you a right to be free.[18]

The Golden Triangle of Freedom created perhaps the freest nation in history, a model for other nations to follow. It enshrined its freedoms in the Bill of Rights, including the freedoms of speech, religion, press, assembly, and the right to petition the government. But today, tragically, freedom is eroding in the United States and around the world. There is no guarantee that the United States or any nation can remain free.

Perhaps the greatest threat to freedom is its secular redefinition. Today, the vast majority of Americans, Christians included, understand freedom to be something very different from what the founding generation understood. The new understanding retains the element of choice but strips away the necessity of truth, virtue, and self-control, along with the Judeo-Christian worldview that undergirds it.

FREEDOM REDEFINED

Where earlier generations defined freedom as the capacity to self-govern within God's created order and under His moral law, redefined freedom means *"The power or right to act, speak, or think as one wants without hindrance or restraint."*[19] It rests on the assumption that humans are sovereign, autonomous individuals, no longer part of God's creation and under His law. We are a law unto ourselves. In the words of US Supreme Court Justice Anthony Kennedy in his majority opinion in the 1992 *Planned Parenthood v. Casey* decision:

> At the heart of liberty is the right to define one's own concept of existence, of meaning, of the universe, and of the mystery of human life.[20]

We commonly hear redefined freedom articulated this way: "Freedom is the right to do whatever you want, so long as it doesn't harm anyone else." But how does "not harming anyone" square with the fact that since 1973, in the US alone, more than sixty-three million unborn children have been destroyed by people who believed they had the freedom to do so?

It doesn't, unless you redefine the unborn as "non-persons." After all, at the heart of liberty is our "right" to define reality, including the "mystery of human life." And in the 1973 *Roe v. Wade* decision, this is exactly what Justice Harry Blackmun did, writing: "The word 'person' as used in the Fourteenth Amendment, *does not include the unborn*."[21] If the unborn is not a human person, then it can be destroyed without harming anyone. How convenient is that?

FREEDOM REDEFINED
The power or right to act, speak or think as one wants without hindrance or restraint.

The secularization of freedom can be traced back to the Age of Enlightenment (ca. 1620 to 1781), a time when Western civilization began to divide philosophically, a divide that continues into the present. The divide was (and is) over God, creation, and human nature. Each side in this great divide uses the word "freedom" but means vastly different things by it.

On one side of the divide are those who affirm the truth that God exists and we flourish within the limitations of His creation. Here, freedom is circumscribed. Within these boundaries, we thrive. On the other side of the divide, any talk of limits is intolerable. As Christopher Rufo explains: "The animating spirit of the [secular] Left's philosophy is the rejection of limits."[22]

The contemporary transgender movement exemplifies this rejection of limits. As Rufo explains,

> Human beings have a specific, fixed nature that includes human sexuality; there are inherent limits that cannot be surpassed through ideology or surgery . . . the attempt to surpass human nature always ends in human destruction.[23]

You see the divide clearly in the most consequential revolutions of the eighteenth century: The American and the French. As we have seen, the American revolutionaries of 1776 valued Christian morality as the foundation for human freedom and human rights. For them, the only alternative is a system where the strong rule the weak and might makes right.

That is what the French revolutionaries of 1789 ultimately discovered. Unlike the American Revolution, the French Revolution was violently anti-Christian. French revolutionaries famously established a "Cult of Reason" while desecrating the magnificent cathedral of Notre Dame in Paris and ultimately paving the way for dictatorship under Napoleon Bonaparte. If that were not bad enough, their secular redefinition of freedom inspired some of the bloodiest tyrannies of the twentieth century, in Russia, China, Vietnam, and Cambodia.

As British essayist Paul Kingsnorth explains: "Freedom is being destroyed primarily by those who scorn the idea that freedom comes from God . . . *Wherever God is delinked from freedom,*

freedom ultimately withers. When Christianity died in Europe, it was replaced by fascism, Nazism, and communism"[24] (italics added).

THREATS TO FREEDOM IN THE TWENTY-FIRST CENTURY

Today, freedom and free nations are under grave threat. As Kingsnorth rightly explains, when Christianity began to die in Europe, it was replaced by fascism, Nazism, and communism. All three ideologies are totalitarian, imperialistic, and virulently anti-freedom. Of these three, communism and fascism, closely related cousins, remain ongoing threats. Both are grounded in an atheistic worldview that asserts there is no God and no higher law to which humans are accountable. Both ideologies assume Darwin's theory of human origins. Consequently, people have no God-given right to life or liberty. Humans are highly evolved animals. As we have seen, the only "law" that applies is survival of the fittest. Might makes right. Everything is reduced to power.

In a fascinating interview, Canadian psychologist Jordan Peterson discussed the outworking of these destructive ideas with Indian scholar and philosopher Vishal Mangalwadi:

> Mangalwadi: If a woman is an animal as Darwinism presupposes, and if I can buy a cow and keep it chained up, and sell a cow, then why can't I buy girls, keep them locked up, and sell them? Is a girl different than an animal?
>
> Peterson: If power is the only real force, you can buy and sell humans if you have the power to do it.
>
> Mangalwadi: You can only *not* do this if a girl has inalienable rights to freedom because she is made in God's image.[25]

The ideology that underpins communism was developed by German philosopher and socialist revolutionary Karl Marx. His starting point was the same atheistic worldview just described, but with one significant, yet inconsistent, difference. He hijacked and bastardized the Judeo-Christian moral order by assuming categories of good and evil, along with a utopian vision for attaining a world cleansed of all evil. This moral vision separates Marxism from strict atheistic materialism and accounts for its ongoing appeal and astonishing resilience—despite its horrific, bloody track record.

In Marx's worldview, evil is defined as social inequality rooted in unjust social systems, predominantly capitalism. Its fight for "justice" focused on overthrowing the capitalist system. In true revolutionary fashion, capitalists were rounded up, imprisoned, and murdered in the millions, their property and wealth redistributed. "Heaven" for Marx was a this-worldly utopia of perfect social and material equality.

Any ideology whose primary goal is "equality of outcome" is, by its very nature, anti-freedom. It requires heavy-handed, often violent, top-down social engineering. In free nations, people's choices are respected, even though they invariably lead to different outcomes. But for Marx, different outcomes are the very definition of evil. Nations built on the foundation of Marxist principles, including Russia and China, devolved into bloody tyrannies with imperial ambitions and a track record of subjugating other nations.

Following the collapse of Soviet communism in 1990, Marxism has morphed and mutated into two closely related anti-freedom movements in the West. One is comprised of global business, big tech, and government elites under the banner of the World Economic Forum (WEF).

These globalist elites and plutocrats assume their immense wealth and connections to power give them the superior wisdom and virtue needed to socially engineer the world (and climate) to achieve their desired utopian vision. Their plan to realize this vision is called "The Great Reset." It's a scheme to leverage administrative and technocratic systems and structures needed to manipulate, coerce, and control the global population in ways that secure their own power and vast wealth while rendering everyone else as dependent serfs. There is no place for personal political and economic freedom in their system. Rather, the Great Reset is a push for a centrally managed global system. One that will render the individual subordinate to the collective will of the global community, which they speak for.

The WEF is an incredibly powerful network that includes senior government leaders from nations as powerful as the United States, Germany, Canada, and China, as well as the CEOs of massive corporations, including Amazon, Apple, Boeing, Facebook, Goldman Sachs, IBM, MasterCard, Microsoft, Visa, Walmart, and dozens more. According to political scholar Mark Mitchell, "It [represents] a consolidation of power unlike any other peace-time initiative in history. If every country from the United States to China joins forces with the world's most powerful corporations, the ability to effect change will be almost irresistible."[26]

A second, closely related threat freedom comes from the "woke" social justice ideology rooted in Marxist "critical theory" studies nurtured in Western universities since the 1950s. Like all Marxist-inspired ideologies, this one is incompatible with freedom. It sees a world with powerful oppressors who establish social and cultural systems (like free market capitalism, the American constitutional system of government, "whiteness," the "patriarchy," and biblical sexual morality). These "oppressors" determine outcomes for victim groups, defined within this framework primarily as "people of color" and gays, lesbians, the transgendered, homosexuals, and others in the LGBTQIA+ "community."

In the Darwinian worldview, there is no free will because human actions are biologically determined. In the "woke" worldview, there is also no free will because human actions are *socially* determined.

Victims' choices are not truly "free," but rather are determined by powerful social forces and systems. Consequently, so-called victims are not responsible for the consequences of their choices. Champions of the "woke" worldview scoff at the very idea of freedom, referring to it as a discredited notion introduced by white, European, and Christian oppressors to maintain their power.

Where the "woke" worldview takes root, freedoms are dramatically curtailed, including the freedoms of speech and religious liberty. These are replaced by growing calls for silencing, censorship, and even force.

The most outspoken and influential champions of the "woke" worldview, like the three young founders of the Black Lives Matter movement, are self-avowed Marxists who view free market capitalism as a source of great evil. Perhaps the preeminent spokesperson for the "woke" ideology, Ibram X. Kendi, famously said "capitalism is essentially racist; racism is essentially capitalist."

Oddly, given their antipathy toward free-market capitalism, these champions of "wokeness" have made common cause with the largest corporations on the planet, those most closely aligned with the WEF. Mark Mitchell explains why: "The leadership of both have much to gain by this seemingly bizarre arrangement. ['Woke corporations'] gain moral legitimacy [by claiming to stand for 'social justice'], and socialist leaders gain wealth, status, and power."[27]

Christianity recognized essential truths that gave rise to free people and free nations. We are now living through a social experiment to see if freedom can be sustained once these truths are rejected. According to Christian essayist Rod Dreher, "and the answer seems to be negative."[28]

Today's decadent, "woke" Western worldview is incompatible with freedom. It dissolves the Golden Triangle of freedom by replacing virtue with "if it feels good, do it" and self-control with self-indulgence. The Judeo-Christian religion that grounds virtue in the Golden Triangle is replaced by the "woke" neo-Marxist religion.

The results? On the personal level, ever-growing bondage to the flesh, appetites, and desires, along with unprecedented levels of depression, mental illness, and suicide. At the societal level, skyrocketing rates of drug addiction, soaring crime rates, family breakdown, and increasing social chaos. The social fabric is unraveling. The anti-Christian worldview at the center is incapable of holding a free society together. Social chaos, anarchy, and totalitarianism are on the march, and in many respects, are already here.

We are seeing in real-time that freedom is only possible when citizens are capable of virtuous self-government. In the powerful words of Robert Charles Winthrop (1809–1884), former speaker of the US House of Representatives, and a descendant of the great Puritan founding father of the Massachusetts Bay Colony, John Winthrop: "Men, in a word, must necessarily be controlled, either by a power within them, or by a power without them; either by the word of God, or by the strong arm of man; either by the Bible, or by the bayonet."[29]

It is only through an internally imposed order, or what the Bible calls "self-control" based on God's moral standard, that freedom can be recovered. Is it possible? The hour is late, but there is still time.

HOW SHOULD WE THEN LIVE?

We must not take freedom for granted, or we will lose it. In the prophetic words of American president Ronald Reagan:

> Freedom is never more than one generation away from extinction. . . . It must be fought for, protected, and handed on for [our children] to do the same, or one day we will spend our sunset years telling our children

and our children's children what it was once like in the United States where men were free.[30]

Freedom is a core characteristic of God's kingdom, and in the conflict between Satan's counterfeit kingdom of darkness and God's kingdom, we know the outcome. God's kingdom will ultimately prevail.

But freedom is also fragile and can flourish only under particular conditions. Because freedom is deeply rooted in the Judeo-Christian worldview, the recovery of freedom must be championed, first and foremost, by God-fearing Jews, and by followers of Jesus Christ. We are stewards of the truth, not for ourselves, but for the nations we are called to disciple, and to bless.

Rejecting the Sacred-Secular Mindset

But before the church can defend freedom, we must address something that continues to hinder our ability to be salt and light in an ever-darkening world. A false sacred-secular dualism has shaped our thinking for more than a century. According to this quasi-biblical worldview, God exists and the Bible is true and has authority, but only within a limited "spiritual" or sacred realm. This is the realm of the Bible, church life, personal holiness, heaven, and evangelism. The "lower" secular realm, however, includes nearly every area of culture and society apart from the church, including business, politics, education, sports, and the arts. Christ, according to this way of thinking, isn't Lord over all, but Lord over the higher realm only.

When Christians apply the sacred-secular way of thinking to the topic of freedom, they focus exclusively on spiritual freedom, while frequently ignoring political freedom, civil liberty, or the biblical principles that support free nations. Christian involvement in championing political, civil, or even religious freedom is viewed as either a waste of time, or disparaged as "politics," "culture-warring," or even "Christian nationalism." This involvement is seen as a distraction from the only work that ultimately matters: evangelism, personal holiness, and church growth.

Earlier generations of Christians, including the early Protestant reformers and America's Puritan founders, didn't think this way. They viewed Christ as Lord *over all*, not merely over a limited spiritual realm. They applied the teachings and principles of the Bible to *everything*, including politics, education, and business. They viewed their mission as broader than rescuing people out of the fallen world. Christians were called to bring God's truth into every sphere of culture and society for the good of the nations— for the blessing of the nations that God loves and died to redeem. They prioritized spiritual freedom, but they certainly didn't ignore or disparage political or civil liberty.

The sad fact that sacred-secular thinking has taken root in the evangelical church is largely why atheistic, redefined freedom has gained the cultural high ground. Far too many Christians didn't even try to defend true freedom. They simply walked off the cultural playing field. When followers of Jesus don't care about understanding the principles that undergird personal freedom or free nations, the inevitable outcome is a loss of freedom.

If we are to reverse this disastrous trajectory before freedom is lost, the church, and particularly teachers within the church, must abandon the false sacred-secular dualism and boldly proclaim Christ's lordship over all areas of life and society. We must be salt and light.

Recovering Biblical Marriage and Family

As we saw in the last chapter, commitment to biblical marriage and family will be critical to the defense of freedom. Freedom cannot exist without virtuous self-control best inculcated in the next generation by loving parents in the family. It is no wonder that freedom began to wither and die in the West while divorce rates skyrocketed in the early 1970s.

Christian parents should seek to raise virtuous, self-governing adults capable of living free. Who love and fear God, do what is right, are honest, hard-working, and take responsibility. These virtues are best learned in the home, with Christian parents as role models. Christian schools and churches can support parents by inculcating virtue in children and young adults.

Teaching the art of raising children to become virtuous, self-governing adults is beyond the scope of this chapter. But in broad terms, it is helpful to think of a funnel. When children are young, they are not capable of the self-control necessary for living free. They need loving parents to provide this control. To teach, train, and discipline them to know and fear the Lord and do what is right. This phase represents the narrow end of the funnel. As children grow and mature, wise parents widen the funnel by allowing greater freedom. By the time children reach adulthood and leave the authority of their parents, they should be capable of living freely, and passing the principles of freedom onto their children.

Today, this funnel is often inverted, with disastrous results. Parents give their young children far too much freedom before training them in self-control. Culture teaches us to see our children as sovereign, autonomous beings. When children have not been trained in virtuous self-government, heartbreak lies ahead. They will often abuse freedom to gratify selfish desires, leading to attempts by parents, teachers, or even civil authorities to constrict the funnel, often too late.

If you are just beginning your journey of raising children, take this lesson to heart. But if your children have already entered adulthood and you have regrets over past parenting choices, don't despair. There is still hope. God is gracious, and your adult children are never beyond His power. Your prayer on their behalf is a powerful resource. You can also influence your grandchildren when they are very young. Do so.

Other Ideas

Historically, free nations are not the norm. The default in our fallen world is totalitarianism and empire, where powerful oligarchs and tyrants selfishly exploit the powerless, and personal freedom is non-existent.

With the ominous rise of powerful totalitarian movements in the twenty-first century, we are moving back toward the default. These movements are leveraging the power of technology to control the masses. You see this most clearly in China, with a near-omnipresent video surveillance network combined with facial recognition software, artificial intelligence, and a burgeoning social credit system aimed at identifying and punishing those who stray from the control of the Party. The World Economic Forum is keen to develop similar systems of technocratic control in Western countries and alarmingly, used the Covid pandemic, and the fear it generated, to experiment with their own systems of social control, censorship, and penalties for those who failed to reinforce the narratives of the powerful.

Preserving individual freedom and free nations in the face of growing threats will require a willingness to face up to the threats and refuse to bury our heads in the sand. We need to learn the techniques for totalitarian control so we can avoid, as much as possible, falling prey to them.

One such technique is to separate and isolate people and keep them in a state of fear. Then they will be more willing to exchange their freedoms for promises of protection and provision. The "regime" will be more than happy to "take care of us" in exchange for our personal freedom. To the degree that we give in to their Faustian bargain, we demonstrate that we prefer slavery to freedom.

Countering this technique requires that we not allow ourselves to be isolated. Instead, let us move in the opposite direction by actively strengthening local relationships and support networks. The most vital such networks are families, local churches, and local organizations—what Edmund Burke famously called "little platoons." These relationships are perhaps the greatest threat to totalitarian powers, which is why virtually all communist regimes work hard to dismantle the family and other personal bonds. Seeking to strengthen those bonds is essential to preserving freedom.[31]

We must also beware of their methods to control us through emotional manipulation, particularly the weaponization of fear and hate. Fearful people who are dangerously divided and at each others' throats are easy to control. The Bible has a great deal to say about fear, knowing how powerful it is and how effectively our enemies can use it against us. The continued refrain in Scripture is "fear not." As beloved children of the King of kings, our lives are completely secure in His strong hands, no matter what men may do to us. We all understandably long for safety and security, but the Bible teaches that this will only be found in God's hands. Christian author and homeschool mother Katy Faust has excellent advice:

I will recommit myself daily to Christ, so I fear Him alone. Today, there are endless reasons . . . to fear—social ostracization, job threats, and being literally blacklisted, to name a few. Those legitimate fears will intensify in coming years, so courage is needed.

The only antidote I've found for my default posture of trembling is to fear God more. To do so, I must imbibe deeply the living Word, let the Psalms become my daily bread, and use 1 Peter as my field guide. Only then do I find the courage to become steadfast and immovable in the face of a [totalitarian] ideology that demands total fealty.

Everyone fears something. You will either fear God, or you will fear and bow down to something else. I choose God . . . every single day in small, faithful actions. You can, too.[32]

Another technique of totalitarian control is to take away the freedoms of marginalized groups first, followed by more mainstream groups. We must therefore be vigilant to protect the freedoms of all people, and to support, help, and encourage persecuted groups— never assuming that the loss of freedom will stop with them.

In recent years, we've seen the infringement of free speech on social media platforms. The censorship started with fringe, often controversial figures, but quickly expanded to more mainstream figures. It is tempting to passively ignore the loss of freedoms of negligible groups. But we must assume the attack will be pressed to everyone. Better to work to prevent it from gaining a foothold at the start. Learn the lesson of German pastor Martin Niemoller who regretted his passivity in the face of growing Nazi totalitarianism in the 1930s:

> First they came for the socialists, and I did not speak out— because I was not a socialist. Then they came for the trade unionists, and I did not speak out—because I was not a trade unionist. Then they came for the Jews, and I did not speak out—because I was not a Jew. Then they came for me—and there was no one left to speak for me.[33]

A simple way to do this is by supporting freedom advocacy organizations such as the Alliance Defending Freedom and others that provide legal defense to those whose liberties are under attack.

You can also support businesses and organizations that are pro-freedom, and not those that are actively working to curtail personal freedoms. Many of our large corporations, including big tech companies, are actively working in support of totalitarian movements in the United States and around the world. We must learn how they are doing this. Documentaries like *The Social Dilemma*[34] are indispensable in shining light on the tactics of these corporations. You should assume that anything you post on social media is being monitored. Again, Katy Faust offers advice:

> Big Tech has been collecting, selling, and profiting from your personal information for years, and you're getting nothing for it. Why continue to support them as if your lives depended on it? Why act like an addict that can't let go of social media platforms? Surveillance Capitalism is alive and well; let's not play into Big Tech's hands.[35]

The hour is late. The threats are growing, and the window of opportunity is closing. Free nations don't just fall from the sky— they are built. And by God's grace, they can be *rebuilt*.

Christians must have the courage of our convictions. Defending true freedom will not make us popular with cultural elites. We will be vilified, mischaracterized, and vehemently opposed. The enemies of Christ call true freedom tyranny, for what they desire above all else is to live in a world without limits.

But that world doesn't exist, and any attempt to live as if it does will end in disaster. This must be our warning, but a warning is not enough. We must call people back to true freedom and what it takes to sustain it. That necessarily includes freedom in Christ.

Many are ready to hear this message. They see the growing threats to freedom around the world. They don't want their children and grandchildren to live under a dictatorship. But they don't know how to begin to turn things around.

Let's be ready to answer and to show them. Let us choose freedom.

CHAPTER 6
AUTHORITY

Jesus came to them and said,
"All authority in heaven and on earth has been given to me."

MATTHEW 28:18

Jesus called them together and said, "You know that those who
are regarded as rulers of the Gentiles lord it over them, and
their high officials exercise authority over them. Not so with
you. Instead, whoever wants to become great among you must
be your servant, and whoever wants to be first must be slave
of all. For even the Son of Man did not come to be served, but
to serve, and to give his life as a ransom for many."

MARK 10:42-45

AUTHORITY

The power or right to issue commands, rules, or laws and to ensure they are carried out. Human authority is delegated from God, the supreme authority, and is accountable to Him. When properly exercised, authority creates conditions in which people thrive by providing wise leadership in a context of ordered liberty. Jesus, our model for authority in practice, sacrificially serves those under authority for their good.

AUTHORITY REDEFINED

An arbitrary, self-serving, and often harsh and oppressive use of power and control. A concentration of power in human government or rule that is unaccountable to God, constitutional limits, or the people under authority.

They had been to Jerusalem before, but this would be Jesus's final journey. He was fully aware of what lay before Him—betrayal, torture, and brutal death. That His spirit was deeply troubled was written all over his face.

Yet even now, His thoughts were not on Himself, but on His disciples. He wanted to prepare them for what they would face in the coming days. He stopped and gathered them around Himself. He had spoken to them before of His impending execution, but never in this detail.

> We are going up to Jerusalem, and the Son of Man will be betrayed to the chief priests and teachers of the law. They will condemn Him to death and will hand Him over to the Gentiles [the Roman authorities], who will mock Him and spit on Him, flog Him and kill Him. Three days later he will rise. (Mark 10:33–34)

Did His disciples seek to encourage Him with words of comfort? Did they pledge their loyalty no matter what? No, they were not thinking of Jesus at all.

When they resumed their journey, James and John caught up with Jesus and pulled Him aside. Lowering their voices, they said:

"Teacher, we want you to do for us whatever we ask."
"What do you want me to do for you?" Jesus replied.

In this exchange, James and John used the language of false authority. "Do for us *whatever we ask.*" How does Jesus respond to their utter insensitivity? We might expect Him to say something like, "Didn't you hear what I just said? Who do you think you are?" But instead, He shows grace and humility, using the words of a subordinate—a servant. *"What do you want me to do for you?"*

Their request: "Let one of us sit at your right hand and the other at your left in your glory." They ask for positions of worldly power and authority in what they imagine will be His imminent earthly kingdom, and they don't want to share that power with the other disciples.

Eventually, the other disciples notice Jesus, James, and John in a huddle, speaking in hushed voices. They become suspicious. Are they trying to cut a deal with Jesus without them? They "become indignant."

Jesus takes command. Raising His voice over their heated words, He utters one of the most extraordinary teachings in history. One that will revolutionize power and authority from that day forward.

> You know the way that those who are regarded as rulers
> of the Gentiles lord it over them, and their high officials
> exercise authority over them. (Mark 10:42)

You understand power and authority from the way it is commonly practiced by "rulers" and "high officials," Jesus says. They exercise authority by "lording it over" their subordinates, exercising power in harsh, arbitrary, and selfish ways, treating them as little more than slaves. Then come the all-important words: *"Not so with you."* Jesus takes this false understanding of authority and turns it on its head. True authority as practiced in His kingdom looks entirely different. If you desire power and authority in my Kingdom, Jesus says, you desire to be a servant.

> Whoever wants to become great among you [in a position
> of authority] *must be your servant*, and whoever wants to
> be first [highest in rank] must be slave of all. For even the
> Son of Man did not come to be served, but to serve, and to
> give His life as a ransom for many. (Mark 10:43–45)

Tragically, true authority is rarely practiced, much less understood. We've all been wounded by selfish authorities. Unsurprisingly, most people mistrust authority—so much so that the concept itself has an extremely negative connotation. Teachers and activists authoritatively counsel us to "question authority." Many Christians have allowed themselves to be carried along by the cultural current.

While understandable, this is a mistake. Authority, power, submission, and hierarchy are deeply biblical concepts, essential for human flourishing. Authority, like everything else, was distorted by the fall, but in Christ, the true nature of authority was restored. Rather than rejecting authority, our calling is to live out true authority and submission.

AUTHORITY DEFINED

Authority is commonly vested in a specific role or position. This is formal authority. But there is also informal authority that is often associated with advanced age, wisdom, experience, knowledge, or trustworthiness. This is often referred to as "moral authority." Ideally, formal authorities also possess moral authority.

Webster's 1828 Dictionary of the English Language defines authority as "legal power, or a right to command. . . . The power of him whose will and commands must be submitted to by others and obeyed." Think of a judge who issues binding rulings. Or the authority of parents to command, direct, and discipline their children in the home, or the authority of teachers to direct and discipline their students in the classroom.

AUTHORITY

The power or right to issue commands, rules, or laws and to ensure they are carried out. Human authority is delegated from God, the supreme authority, and is accountable to Him. When properly exercised, authority creates conditions in which people thrive by providing wise leadership in a context of ordered liberty. Jesus, our model for authority in practice, sacrificially serves those under authority for their good.

Authority is closely related to the concepts of power, dominion, rule, and government. Power, in fact, is central to the concept of authority. The New Testament Greek word *exousia* occurs 103 times, and it is translated into English as both power (sixty-nine times), and authority (twenty-nine times). We see one famous example in Matthew 28:18: "Then Jesus came to them and said, 'All *authority* (*exousia*) in heaven and on earth has been given to me.'"

AUTHORITY'S PURPOSE

Authority exists to create conditions in which free human beings can thrive and reach their fullest potential. There are three dimensions:

1. Authorities *provide leadership*. Leaders exist to envision a preferred future and take the initiative needed to move toward that vision in ways that maximize the gifts, talents, and strengths of those they are leading. In the Bible, Nehemiah is a great example of leadership authority. He envisioned a well-protected Jerusalem with a strong wall and organized the returned exiles into specific units based on families to build particular sections of the wall, maximizing the skills and labor of each person.

2. Authorities *create order*. Order is basic to human flourishing, through appropriate rules, policies, practices, and laws. A family, community, or nation thrives where these guardrails align with God's law. Order is cultivated when authorities reward lawful behavior and punish lawlessness. Those who don't reap chaos, crime, violence, and other injustices.

3. Authorities *serve those under authority*. As we have seen, authority exists for the good of others, and for society as a whole.

AUTHORITY'S PRACTICE

Human beings created in the image and likeness of God can learn the proper practice of authority by looking to His example. We see a beautiful example of how God exercises authority in Psalm 23. "The Lord [the supreme authority] is my shepherd," says David. A shepherd exists for the good of the sheep. He creates the conditions in which they are well-protected, provided for, and flourishing.

Authorities *provide* for the needs of those under their authority: "I lack nothing," says David. "He makes me lie down in green pastures. He refreshes my soul . . . my cup overflows." Authorities *lead*. "He leads me beside the still waters. He guides me along the right paths." Authorities *protect*. "Even though I walk through the darkest valley, I will fear no evil, for you are with me; your rod and your staff, they comfort me." Authorities *serve*. "You prepare a table before me in the presence of my enemies. You anoint my head with oil. Surely goodness and love will follow me all the days of my life, and I will dwell in the house of the Lord forever."

Jesus provides the most striking model for true authority. Though He is King of kings, He was born in the humblest of settings, in a barn, in a rural backwater, far from the centers of earthly power. His parents were simple laborers with no formal education.

From Jesus, we learn that authority need not be accompanied by wealth, prestige, or elite status. He taught His followers that the defining characteristic of true authority is humble, sacrificial service. He didn't lord His authority over His followers but treated them as friends (John 15:15). He washed their feet (John 13:4–5) and eventually sacrificed His life so that they might live (John 15:13).

All this wasn't contrary to His authority—it was *because* of it. This is what true authority looks like. Jesus did all this as the supreme authority, the all-powerful Lord, whose Name is above all names. Jesus didn't abolish the concepts of power, social rank, or hierarchy. He showed us their proper use and purpose. Wherever

His followers, down through the ages, have put His example into practice, the results have been utterly revolutionary.

Not only does God show us what true authority looks like. He delegates or shares His authority with people and establishes the pattern of people sharing authority with other humans in order to effect change. God delegates authority, for example, to parents regarding the education and upbringing of their children, or elders regarding leadership in a local church. Or think of Moses delegating authority for judging disputes to lower authorities accountable to him (Exodus 18:13–26).

In this model, authority is spread out over society, rather than concentrated in any single group or person. This system works through trust and accountability, with higher authorities entrusting lower authorities with power, and lower authorities accountable for their exercise of authority to higher authorities.

HIERARCHY AND AUTHORITY

To understand authority, we must understand the closely related concept of *hierarchy*, which refers to a system or organization of *ranking* based on authority.

In everyday life, we experience hierarchy in the workplace, where the highest authority belongs to the board of directors, followed by the president, the vice president, directors, managers, and so on. The military operates according to a highly organized and detailed hierarchy of authority. In the US Army, for example, generals are followed in rank by colonels, majors, captains, lieutenants, sergeants, corporals, and privates. Nearly every social organization has some system of authority and hierarchy, whether complex and formal, or loose and informal.

Today, many are critical of hierarchy. Marxist ideology, which continues to powerfully influence Western thought, is fundamentally opposed to hierarchy, at least in theory. Even many

Christians are wary of hierarchical systems. But authority, power, and hierarchy are biblical concepts. They are built into the nature of reality itself. God established a basic hierarchy of authority at the creation. God is the supreme authority, followed by human beings and the rest of creation.

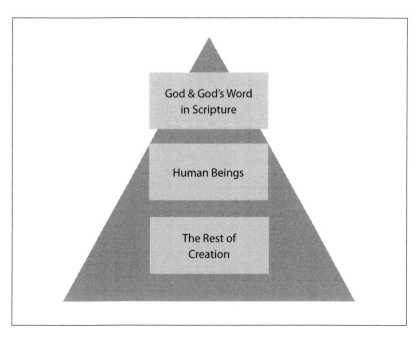

God, the supreme authority

There is no more basic or important truth than this: God is the supreme authority. He "has established his throne in heaven, and his kingdom rules over all" (Psalm 103:19). He is the supreme authority "the great King over all the earth" (Psalm 47:2).

When God took on human flesh in the person of Jesus Christ, those who heard Him speak recognized His unique authority. ". . . the crowds were amazed at his teaching, because he taught *as one who had authority*, and not as their teachers of the law" (Matthew 7:28–29). Once when Jesus was with His disciples in a boat in the Sea of Galilee, a violent storm arose. The terrified disciples cried out for Jesus to save them. So "he got up and rebuked the winds and the waves, and it was completely calm. The men were amazed and asked, 'What kind of man is this? *Even the winds and the waves obey him!*'" (Matthew 8:26–27, italics added). Jesus demonstrated authority not only over people but over creation itself.

On another occasion, Jesus was confronted by a Roman centurion who sought His help:

> "Lord," he said, "my servant lies at home paralyzed, suffering terribly."
>
> Jesus said to him, "Shall I come and heal him?"
>
> The centurion replied, 'Lord, I do not deserve to have you come under my roof. But just say the word, and my servant will be healed. For I myself am a man under authority, with soldiers under me. I tell this one, 'Go,' and he goes; and that one, 'Come,' and he comes. I say to my servant, 'Do this,' and he does it."
>
> When Jesus heard this, he was amazed and said to those following him, "Truly I tell you, I have not found anyone in Israel with such great faith" . . . Then Jesus said to the centurion, "Go! Let it be done just as you believed it would." And his servant was healed at that moment. (Matthew 8:7–10; 13)

This soldier impressed Jesus because he understood how authority and hierarchy operate and recognized Jesus's divine authority, even over disease. When questioned about the supremacy of His authority during His trial before the Jewish religious leaders, Jesus acknowledged it fearlessly.

> Again the high priest asked him, "Are you the Messiah, the Son of the Blessed One?"

"I am," said Jesus. "And you will see the Son of Man sitting at the right hand of the Mighty One and coming on the clouds of heaven." (Mark 14:61-62)

Yet these religious leaders were unwilling to acknowledge Jesus's divine authority and instead condemned Him to death on a Roman cross. He died, was buried, and three days later rose from the dead, demonstrating His authority over death itself. Jesus is alive and reigns forever as King of kings and Lord of lords. He is "exalted to the highest place" with a "name that is above every name" (Philippians 2:9–11).

The authority of God's Word

God established laws to govern the physical universe, providing order and predictability. Remarkably, with the aid of science, these laws are discernable to humans and can be expressed mathematically. He also established a moral law that establishes right from wrong, good from evil, and justice from injustice. This law was written down by God Himself, inscribed on stone tablets and given to Moses on Mount Sinai. Through Moses and the Jewish people, all of us have a written revelation of the moral law. The first law establishes God's supremacy in rank and authority. "You shall have no other gods before me" (Exodus 20:3).

The book that contains the moral law, the Bible, is God's revealed Word to mankind. In addition to God's written commands, it contains the writings of the Old Testament prophets, who spoke God's words. It also contains the words of Christ, God in human flesh, as well as of the apostles, Jesus's immediate followers in the New Testament.

God's Word in Scripture defines what is true, good, and beautiful, not just for Jews or Christians, but for all peoples, at all times. His commands in Scripture illumine the path for flourishing communities and nations. Jesus lived in perfect obedience to God's revealed Word in Scripture. The apostle Paul tells us that "All Scripture is God-breathed and is useful for teaching, rebuking, correcting and training in righteousness" (2 Timothy 3:16).

The etymology of the English word "authority" goes back to the old French word, *autorite*, meaning, an "authoritative book, or the Scriptures." The Reformers made this a point of emphasis in one of their famous "solas," Sola Scriptura, or *Scripture Alone*. The Bible is the highest in rank of authority.[1]

Humans: Subject to God, but with authority over creation

Returning to the basic "creational" hierarchy, God (and His Word in Scripture) is the supreme authority. Next are human beings. All people, both male and female, regardless of ethnicity or social status, are created by God, in His image and likeness (Genesis 1:26–27). God is the supreme authority. As image-bearers of God, we too possess authority—God granted authority over ourselves, and over the rest of creation.

Authority over self is referred to in the Bible as "self-control" (see, for example, 2 Timothy 1:7 and Galatians 5:22–23). Self-control is another way of saying "self-government" or authority over one's thoughts and actions. We have the God-given capacity to self-govern, to make choices and determine courses of action under God's ultimate authority. In this, we differ from the rest of the animal kingdom. Animals do not govern themselves but are governed by instinct, or by people, in the case of pets or livestock. Because God grants us authority to self-govern, no person has a right to enslave others or take away their authority to self-govern.

Self-government is the most basic form of authority, and is the foundation upon which all other authority rests. Unless a person can self-govern, they will be unable to rightly exercise authority over others. As Dutch humanist Hugo Grotius observed, "A man cannot govern a nation if he cannot govern a city; he cannot govern a city if he cannot govern a family; he cannot govern a family unless he can govern himself."

God also granted to all human beings authority or "dominion" over creation.

> Then God said, "Let us make mankind in our image, in our likeness, *so that they may rule over the fish in the sea and the birds in the sky, over the livestock and all the wild animals, and over all the creatures that move along the ground.*"
>
> So God created mankind in his own image,
> in the image of God he created them;
> male and female he created them.
>
> God blessed them and said to them, "Be fruitful and increase in number; fill the earth and subdue it. *Rule over the fish in the sea and the birds in the sky and over every living creature that moves on the ground.*" (Genesis 1:26–27, italics added)

"Rule over" indicates that mankind, every human being, is in a position of authority over creation. This same truth is expressed poetically in Psalm 8:

> You have made [human beings] a little lower than the angels
>   and crowned them with glory and honor.
> You made them rulers over the works of your hands;
>   you put everything under their feet:
> all flocks and herds,
>   and the animals of the wild,
> the birds in the sky,
>   and the fish in the sea,
>   all that swim the paths of the seas.

Human beings are subordinate to God in the creational hierarchy, but they are endowed with authority over themselves and over the rest of creation. Our positions of authority are God-granted, and we are both responsible and accountable to God for how we exercise our authority. It is a trust. A form of stewardship.

God delegates or shares authority with humans and establishes the pattern of humans sharing authority with other humans. The Bible establishes a model where human authority isn't to be selfishly hoarded but shared with those in positions most closely able to effect change. The Roman Catholic social doctrine of subsidiarity reflects this truth. It holds that responsibilities of authority should be handled by the person or entity nearest to those who are governed, and not by a distant, impersonal bureaucracy unfamiliar with local needs or issues.

EQUALITY AND AUTHORITY

Despite today's distaste for the concept of authority, the Bible, teaches that authority and equality are not contradictory. On both the divine and human levels we see both *equality of essence* and differing roles of authority and hierarchy. In our fallen world, where those in positions of authority often assume a proud sense of superiority and see those in roles of submission as inherently inferior, this pairing may seem impossible. But the Bible says this understanding misses the mark.

Equality of essence alongside roles of authority is possible; we see it within the Godhead. The Bible proclaims that God is "one" (Deuteronomy 6:4) and at the same time, three divine "persons": The Father, Son, and Holy Spirit. The three persons of the triune God are all *equally* God. In the words of theologian J.I. Packer, "The three personal "subsistences" (as they are called) are *coequal* . . . [with] each partaking of the full divine essence" (italics added).[2] The Father, Son, and Holy Spirit are co-equally God, and yet they willingly function in a relationship of authority and submission with one another. We see this clearly in Philippians 2:5–8:

> Have this mind among yourselves, which is yours in Christ Jesus, who, though he was in the form of God [coequal with God, the Father], did not count equality with God a thing to be grasped, but emptied himself, by taking the form of a servant, being born in the likeness of men. And being found in human form, he humbled himself by becoming obedient to the point of death, even death on a cross. (ESV)

Jesus Christ, the second person of the Trinity, is "in the form of God" or "in very nature God". That is, God the Father and God the Son *are co-equally God*. They share the same divine essence. In this, they are *equal*. But, though equal in essence, the Son willingly places Himself under the authority of the Father. This position of submission to the Father was evident throughout His earthly ministry. Before going to the cross, Jesus told His disciples:

> "the world may learn that I love the Father and that *I do exactly what my Father has commanded me.*" (John 14:31, italics added)

The Father is in a position of authority, and so He commands the Son. The Son submits to His authority and does "exactly what my Father has commanded," even to the point of death on a Roman cross. In this, He is our living example of what perfect submission to authority looks like. It is obedience motivated by love and a passion to glorify the Father.

How did the Father respond to the Son's perfect obedience? He exalted Him to "the highest place" and:

bestowed on him the name that is above every name, so that at the name of Jesus every knee should bow, in heaven and on earth and under the earth, and every tongue confess that Jesus Christ is Lord, to the glory of God the Father. (Philippians 2:9–11, ESV)

As the resurrected Jesus declared to His disciples on the shores of lake Galilee: "All authority in heaven and on earth has been given to me." Who gave Jesus "all authority"? God the Father. As the supreme authority, God the Father granted the Son executive authority to rule the cosmos on His behalf (Matthew 28:18).

As image-bearers of God, human beings also have equality of essence alongside roles of authority and subordination. Our equality of essence comes from the fact that we are created by God in His divine image. Therefore, we have equal worth. We are also equally stained by sin, and equally in need of redemption and forgiveness, which God offers to us all, *equally*.

Our basic relationship with other human beings is one of fundamental equality. There are no inherently superior or inferior people. Yet this does not foreclose roles of authority or systems of hierarchy. At different times each of us exercises and submits to authority, often simultaneously. But we should always remember, regardless of our position or role, that human beings are equal in God's sight. Equally valued. Equally loved. As Francis Schaeffer famously said, "there are no little people."[3] True authority, properly exercised, recognizes this fundamental truth and treats all people with equal dignity, as God's beloved image-bearers.

HUMAN AUTHORITY AND SUBMISSION

God has established roles of human authority. These include husbands in marriage, parents in the home, elders in the local church, and civil authorities in the state. Others include teachers in their classrooms and rightful authorities in businesses or organizations.

Authority over other human beings is always temporary. Parents have authority over their children only while they are under their direct supervision at home. Supervisors in the workplace have authority over their subordinates only as long as they hold their position of authority, and so on. Authority is not an innate, permanent role reserved for elite people. It is a temporary role, something for all of us. But it is a skill and a responsibility we must learn in order to exercise it rightly.

Submission, too, must be learned in order to be exercised rightly, and the Bible has much to teach on the subject. We will also submit to proper human authorities.

Proper, biblical submission means willingly coming under the rightful authority of another, delighting to follow his or her lead, and obeying any commands without grumbling. As Hebrews 13:17, ESV says, "Obey your leaders and submit to them, for they are keeping watch over your souls, as those who will have to give an account. Let them do this with joy and not with groaning, for that would be of no advantage to you."

Submission is of great value in Scripture—not only our submission to God as the supreme authority but to rightful human authorities. Wives are admonished to submit to their husbands (Ephesians 5:22–24), children to their parents (Ephesians 6:1–3), and citizens to civil authorities (Romans 13:1–7).

Our submission to legitimate human authorities is an act of obedience to God because He establishes human authority, which is accountable to Him for its proper exercise. In Romans 13:1, the apostle Paul writes: "Let everyone be subject to the governing authorities, for *there is no authority except that which God has established. The authorities that exist have been established by God*" (italics added).

Just because authorities have been established by God does not mean, of course, that they will exercise authority in God-honoring ways. Some reject God altogether. Yet, ultimately, they will answer to God for how they exercised authority. The Roman governor Pilate was granted civil authority by God but failed to exercise it properly. Remember the famous confrontation with Jesus after the Jewish authorities handed Him over to be crucified. Pilate questioned Jesus, but He remained silent. Pilate responded:

> "Do you refuse to speak to me? Don't you realize I have power [authority] either to free you or to crucify you?"
>
> Jesus answered, "You would have no power [authority] over me if it were not given to you from above. (John 19:10–11)

In a fallen world, rightful authorities often abuse authority for selfish ends, and there certainly are circumstances when *disobedience* to abusive, illegitimate authority is necessary (more on this later). But disobedience to authorities should be the exception, not the rule, only undertaken after careful prayer and discernment. Our default setting should be respectful submission to rightful human authorities "out of reverence for Christ" (Ephesians 5:21). We can rest in the knowledge that He will right all wrongs, including the abuse of authority, in His time.

Submission holds surprising power when exercised in ways that encourage God-ordained authorities to fulfill their responsibilities. In our times, it is common for those in rightful positions of authority to deny their responsibilities. Sometimes this is due to a false belief that any exercise of authority is a denial of our essential human equality. Sometimes it is due to apathy and passivity. Sometimes it is rooted in a fear of dominant cultural narratives. This is particularly true when it comes to the authority of the husband in marriage. This authority is demonized as "the patriarchy," a form of oppression. To live in ways that counter this narrative requires a strong backbone, a willingness to be vilified and misunderstood. Sometimes, it is due to the fact that the person in authority has less skill, education, or experience. But God-ordained roles of authority are not granted based on skill, age, personality type, or experience. They are granted by *God-ordained design*.

When skillfully and wisely exercised with care and gentleness, submission to rightful authorities can help those reluctant to fulfill their responsibilities to grow in their knowledge and practice of authority. Our exercise of submission should be marked by patience, gentleness, and trust in God, with a desire to help the person in authority grow and mature in their knowledge of the truth. When rightly exercised, true submission is anything but groveling subservience and subjugation. It is a position of true strength and deep trust in God.

THE LIMITS OF AUTHORITY

True authority is both temporary and limited, with boundaries that must be respected for the authority to be legitimate. True authority does not recognize any "presidents for life." First and foremost, authority must be exercised within the bounds of the law. "Law" includes legitimate manmade laws in alignment with the highest law, God's moral law as expressed in the Ten Commandments in the Old Testament and the Royal Law in the New Testament, "Love your neighbor as yourself" (Romans 13:9–10; James 2:8).

Martin Luther King Jr. in his famous "Letter from Birmingham Jail," written in 1963, argued that there are two types of laws: just and unjust. He wrote:

> I would be the first to advocate obeying just laws. One
> has not only a legal but a moral responsibility to obey

just laws. Conversely, one has a moral responsibility to disobey unjust laws. I would agree with St. Augustine that 'an unjust law is no law at all.'

According to the apostle Paul, "The one in authority is God's servant *for your good*" (Romans 13:4, italics added). Legitimate authority is limited to doing what is good for those under authority, and good is defined by God's character and His moral law. Even God Himself, the supreme authority, never violates the boundary of His moral law.

Authority used to compel what is clearly immoral or evil is illegitimate. For example, civil authorities in the Nazi regime in the 1930s promulgated laws that forbade German citizens from providing aid to Jews. Violators were shipped off to concentration camps. Because this manmade law contradicted God's moral law, which forbids murder (Exodus 20:13), it is both evil and illegitimate. German citizens had a moral duty to disobey it. For example, when the Jewish religious authorities commanded the apostle Peter not to teach others in Jerusalem about Jesus, he famously responded, "We must obey God rather than man" (Acts 5:29, ESV).

Authority is also limited by God-ordained spheres of authority, or what the Dutch theologian and statesman Abraham Kuyper called "Sphere Sovereignty." These "spheres" include personal authority (self-government), marriage, family, local churches, and the state.

This decentralization and delegation of authority is part of God's plan, and for good reason. History proves that in a fallen world, a concentration of power all too easily slips into tyranny. As Lord Acton famously said, "power tends to corrupt, and absolute power corrupts absolutely." To their credit, America's founders created a constitutional system where civil authority is separated into smaller, competing centers of authority. At the federal level, a separation of authority exists between the three branches of government—the executive, legislative, and judicial. At the national level, there is a separation of authority between the federal and state. And even at the state level, cities and counties exercise different areas of authority. The separation of authority into various spheres with distinct limits and boundaries provides a check against tyranny and preserves human freedom, which is the biblical ideal.

The most basic God-ordained sphere of authority is the self, or self-government. Many would say the sphere of self-government was grievously violated during the COVID pandemic by civil authorities around the world who compelled people to be vaccinated against their will. Civil authorities may encourage, persuade, or even incentivize people to make personal decisions with respect to their own bodies, but they must not *command* people.

The family is another God-ordained sphere, where parents have authority over their children while they are in the home. But their authority extends only to their children, and only while they are in the home. Those are the limits or boundaries. Within this sphere, parents must exercise authority in alignment with God's law and legitimate civil law, while protecting their rightful authority from encroachment by other authorities. Unfortunately, various civil authorities are increasingly doing just this, and many parents are letting them.

The local church is yet another God-ordained sphere of authority, with elders exercising legitimate authority over the affairs of their flock. But only their congregation, and only within the boundaries set by God's law, and legitimate civil law. Like parents, elders must guard their God-given role to govern their respective local churches against usurpation by civil authorities.

THE FRUIT OF TRUE AUTHORITY

Genuine authority is a form of service to those under authority for their good. Where authority's boundaries are respected, families, communities, businesses, churches, sports teams, and nations experience liberty and prosperity. They are well ordered, yet remarkably free. America's Founding Fathers called this the miracle of "ordered liberty": ordered, where a clear understanding and respect for the structures and spheres of authority exists; but free, in respecting each individual's responsibility to self-govern. True authority supports freedom and allows for maximum creativity, innovation, and prosperity. It creates environments where people are free to rise to their potential.

In our fallen world, false, destructive, and illegitimate authority is pervasive, but certainly not universal. God has revealed what true authority is and how it ought to be practiced. The fullest revelation of authority came in the person of Jesus Christ—God in human flesh—and for more than two thousand years, His faithful followers around the world have sought to follow His example.

When God's Word was opened to the common person during the Reformation and people could hear the truth about authority, entire nations began to change. Political freedom began to flourish for the first time in history. Documents like the Magna Carta placed limits on the authority of kings and sovereigns and expanded individual freedom.

In England, for example, civil authorities became civil "servants." Many other nations followed suit. In the United States, a "new order of the ages" was established based on the truth that all people are created by God, with a God-granted right to self-govern. The power and authority of the state were carefully defined, bounded, and limited. Many other nations have followed suit.

What is true for nations is true for society at any level, down to the most basic of all societies, the family. When parents follow Jesus's example of authority, marriages and children thrive. Moreover, the positive results ripple outward for many generations. When other authorities, including workplace supervisors, school or university teachers, coaches, or church elders do so, men and women, boys and girls can meet their potential.

Tragically, as the West has secularized since the Enlightenment and abandoned God and His Word, true authority has slowly been replaced by a false, worldly, and destructive "authority." The bitter fruit is already visible.

REDEFINED AUTHORITY

Without God, authority is shorn of all limits and is reduced to the exercise of raw power for self-serving ends. Those able to amass the most power set themselves up as absolute rulers or even as "gods," in the place of highest authority. This spirit of false authority animates the great empires of history: Egyptian, Babylonian, Persian, Greek, and Roman, all the way to the present, in grim places such as North Korea and China. This same spirit of arbitrary, unaccountable power and control isn't exercised only by the kings of great empires, but also by husbands over their wives, parents over their children, and supervisors in the workplace.

AUTHORITY REDEFINED

An arbitrary, self-serving, and often harsh and oppressive use of power and control. A concentration of power in human government or rule that is unaccountable to God, constitutional limits, or the people under authority.

False authorities exercise their power and control in oppressive ways, as Jesus said, "lording it over" subordinates (Matthew 20:25), who are reduced to little more than serfs, peasants, or slaves.

J. R. R. Tolkien portrayed this false authority as the "one ring" in his grand epic, *The Lord of the Rings*. Such power destroys those who possess it, along with all who are enslaved by their authority.

In one memorable passage, Frodo freely offers the ring to Gandalf, who refuses. "Understand, Frodo," the great wizard says, "I would use this Ring from a desire to do good. But through me, it would wield a power too great and terrible to imagine."[4]

In the same way, powerful people imagine that they can wield false authority and "do good." But in the end, it destroys them, and those under them.

False authority is simply the exercise of raw power, with all of the positive, constructive elements of true authority stripped away. False authority retains only one element of true authority: the power to issue commands, rules, or laws and to sanction violations. But consider all that is missing.

Gone is God Himself, the supreme authority and source of all authority, along with His example of how authority is rightly exercised as sacrificial service for the good of those under authority. Gone is the example of the God-man, Jesus Christ, who washed His disciples' feet—even those of the one who betrayed Him. False authority is rooted not in God's character or example, but in the character of fallen man.

Gone also is man, as created in God's image, with God-given dignity, worth, and rights, including the right to life and liberty. False authority views human beings as cosmic accidents with no inherent dignity, worth, or rights. Because the character of fallen man tends toward selfishness, authority is used for selfish ends. Gone is the element of sacrificial service to others for *their* good.

False authority creates a stifling, controlled order maintained by fear and threats. It rejects the inherent right to liberty that image-bearers of God possess. "Ordered liberty" is nowhere in sight. In fact, there is no basis for liberty at all. Whenever fallen authority is exercised, freedom dies. The order that results from false authority is the order of the gulag.

Gone as well is the tender balance of equality and authority. People are no longer equally image-bearers of God. False authority treats those in power as inherently superior, and those in submission as inherently inferior. The concept of submission becomes entirely negative. Because false authority is so common, even Christians reject the concept of submission, particularly in the areas of church, marriage, and family.

Gone as well is authority's creational hierarchy. God and His Word are no longer at the top, or even mentioned. False authority places human beings at the top, specifically, those able to amass the most power—the ruling elite, or the powerful, influential leaders in government, business, media, entertainment, and academia.

Another thing to keep in mind: false authority has none of the limits of true authority. The concept of God-ordained spheres of authority is entirely absent. As a result, the authority of people to self-govern, or the authority of parents in the home, or elders in the church are increasingly violated or usurped by secular civil authorities, who view these competing spheres as a threat to their ultimate power.

Authority stripped of God has no place for decentralized or delegated authority. Rather power becomes centralized, top-down, and tyrannical. Whoever can grasp the "ring of power" and force others to submit has authority.

FALSE AUTHORITY AROUND THE WORLD

Because God has revealed His truth to all people, both in creation and through the "law written on the heart" (Romans 2:15), all people have some sense of true authority and how it should be practiced, but throughout human history, the tragic norm has been false authority.

In Asian cultures shaped by Confucianism, such as China, Japan, and Korea, strong systems of authority and hierarchy exist. Seeking social harmony, Confucius (c. 551–479 B.C.) developed a system of strict hierarchy in five key relationships: the ruler to the subject, the parent to the child, the husband to the wife, the older brother to the younger brother, and the friend to the friend. Even within friendship, Confucius taught, a hierarchy must exist to ensure harmony. Authorities should treat those in submission with kindness, while those in submission should treat authorities with respect and reverence.

While this ancient philosophy established highly ordered societies, it lacks the biblical concept of equality of essence based on the inherent worth and dignity of the individual, along with God-granted rights to liberty and self-government. In most cultures shaped by Confucianism, little value is placed on individuals, so personal freedom and self-government are lacking. Also missing is the revolutionary biblical concept of the authority as a servant, working for the good of those under authority. In many Asian nations, authorities exercise power in a highly controlling, authoritarian manner.

Tragically, we see this in many Asian churches, too. Some pastors exercise control over nearly every aspect of their church members' lives. In addition, Confucianism is a stranger to the biblical concept of limited spheres of authority, leading to somewhat arbitrary and unbounded exercises of power.

In more traditional, animistic cultures, such as is in tribal communities, power is frequently exercised in authoritarian, highly controlling, and arbitrary manners. Every culture is shaped in the image of the God or gods that it worships. The "gods" of ancient animistic cultures are capricious, unpredictable, and often vengeful. These same characteristics shape the exercise of authority, contributing to a lack of ordered liberty, along with a variety of social dysfunctions.

FALSE AUTHORITY IN THE WEST

To understand how authority has been redefined in the West, we first must explore two momentous worldview shifts beginning in the early eighteenth century. At the core of any culture is a "cult," a deeply held religious belief system. A worldview shift involves replacing one "cult" with another.

The first shift happened during the Enlightenment when what I'll call "premodernism" was displaced by modernism. Premodern belief systems acknowledge a spiritual reality that transcends the universe. Though they are highly complex and sophisticated systems of belief that have built enduring civilizations, the great monotheistic religions—Judaism, Christianity, and Islam—are all premodern. Ultimate authority is vested in God and in His revealed will.

Modernism, however, dispensed with God and the spiritual realm, defining reality in material terms alone. For modern man, science is the final arbiter of truth. Now, scientific elites displaced God and the Bible as the supreme authority.

Then, starting in the mid-1900s, modernism began to give way to postmodernism. Postmodernism grounds reality, not in God or in the material universe, but in man himself—in the sovereign, autonomous individual. Where modernism left us with a purposeless world of matter in motion, the postmodern prophet Friedrich Nietzsche posited the Übermensch, the super man, who would courageously impose his will on reality.

Three Momentous Shifts in Western Worldviews[5]

Worldview	Dates	Reality	Supreme Authority
Premodern	Prior to the 17th century	Spiritual and material	God and His Word (e.g., the Ten Commandments)
Modernism	18th to 20th centuries	Material only	Science
Postmodernism	20th century to present	The human mind	The autonomous, sovereign self

Postmodernism views human beings as autonomous, self-determining agents. The word "autonomous" is derived from two Greek words, *autos*, meaning "self," and *nomos*, meaning "law." To be autonomous is to be a law unto oneself. In our postmodern world, the sovereign, autonomous self has supreme authority.

SOCIAL CHAOS

But there's an obvious problem. If each person is a law unto himself or herself (or *zheself*), on what basis can a society be ordered? Who has ultimate authority when we are our own little gods?

Postmodernism's grounding of reality in the autonomous, sovereign individual turns out to be unworkable. It leads to social chaos, with people no longer sure of their own sex, with vicious hatreds writ large on social media, in the streets, and in politics, with irreconcilable differences being the norm.

Postmodernism's grounding of authority in the autonomous individual is unsustainable. Society has to be ordered and its institutions established on *somebody's* view of reality. The question is whose? The answer: Whoever can amass the power to impose his or her view on everyone else. The radical autonomy of postmodernism is giving way to tyranny by a powerful group of elites.

At present, this new elite-imposed "reality" is based on Neo-Marxist critical theory in which people who can claim victim status are endowed with supreme authority. Powerful elites cynically claim to defend these victims as a way of justifying and ensuring their positions of authority. Let's look at this in more detail:

CULTURAL MARXISM AND AUTHORITY

In the worldview of Neo-Marxist critical theory, authority is conferred, not by wisdom, age, position, or experience—but by victim status. Claims of oppression and victimization based on a subjective "lived experience" must be believed without question. Victim groups include non-whites, females, and so-called "sexual minorities" or members of the LGBTQIA+ community. The more victim-boxes one can check, the greater the moral authority. This is what is known as intersectionality. The greater the authority, the greater the power.

The granting of power and authority to victim groups naturally (and perversely) results in an explosion in the demand for victim status. Some have called it a veritable victimhood Olympics. Would-be victims are constantly on the lookout for opportunities to claim offense or harm, searching out ever smaller "microaggressions" to claim victimization.

Authority is closely connected to power, so it is important to grasp how Marxist critical theory understands both. In a world without God, objective truth, or transcendent morality, all that remains is power, which explains why Marxist ideology is obsessed with power. Everything can be explained by power dynamics. The quest for power lurks behind all human interaction.

These core assumptions about authority and power are grounded in the postmodern academic discipline of *critical theory* or *grievance studies*, which gained prominence after World War II through the efforts of the neo-Marxist Frankfurt School social philosophers.[6]

A foundational belief in both the older Marxism and the newer ideology of critical theory is the conviction that power and authority exist for one purpose only: to gain advantage over those with less power. Power is zero-sum. The powerful are the privileged at the expense of the unprivileged and powerless. If one group gains, another must lose. In this framework, history is nothing more than an endless saga of power and domination, with each group working by any means necessary to wrest power from groups that possess it.

Marxist critical theory claims that historically, power was held *exclusively* by white, straight men who maintained their authority through a vast, often hidden, array of social systems: white supremacy, the patriarchy, capitalism, and traditionally Western notions of marriage, family, and sexuality. The goal of the contemporary "social justice" revolution is to dismantle these oppressive structures and transfer power and authority to victims. Victims only win when oppressors lose. That's how it works.

And how does the Bible respond to the social justice notion that ultimate authority resides with victims? Christians can agree that there are many victims of injustice and oppression in our fallen world, and they deserve justice and compassion. However, we disagree that we must confer moral authority on people who claim victim status, allowing them to define what is real, based on their subjective "lived experience."

Marxist ideology has no basis for limits on authority or respect for God-ordained spheres of authority. In particular, it despises authority in the home, disparaging it as "the patriarchy," a hegemonic, oppressive source of inequality. Gloria Steinem spoke for many when she asserted:

> Patriarchy requires violence or the subliminal threat of violence in order to maintain itself. . . . The most dangerous situation for a woman is not an unknown man in the street, or even the enemy in wartime, but a husband or lover in the isolation of their home.[7]

These same sentiments are shared by many evangelical feminists and egalitarian advocates, including the late, hugely influential blogger Rachel Held Evans, who wrote:

> Patriarchy is not God's dream for the world. Those who continue to perpetuate it perpetuate an injustice, which, of course, harms the Church internally and also its witness to the watching world.[8]

Like advocates of cultural Marxism, Held Evans described authority within the family in entirely negative terms. Yes, abusive authority exists, but rather than disparage all authority, Christians should discern between true and false authority.

When faithfully practiced, true authority's power to transform society is unparalleled.

HOW SHOULD WE THEN LIVE?

Jesus Christ came into the world to bring light, truth, and beauty into a world of darkness, lies, and despair. He came to bring His kingdom with its "right-side-up" value system, including true authority and hierarchy. After showing us what this looks like in practice, He commissioned and empowered us with His Holy Spirit to continue His mission of bringing light into dark places, and this includes living out the reality of true authority.

Over the centuries, many millions of Christians have faithfully, though imperfectly, followed the Lord's example. Entire cultures have been created on the foundation of true authority; entire nations have been shaped by it. Hope comes as followers of Jesus Christ seek to exercise true authority and submission. The power this holds to shape cultures in positive ways is immense.

Where to begin? Reflect on your own thinking and practice regarding authority, submission, and power. Here are some helpful questions to ponder.

In your positions of authority:

- Are you aware of and fulfilling your God-given responsibilities, or are you denying, neglecting, or shirking your responsibilities?
- Are you fully submitting to God, the supreme authority, seeking first His Kingdom and His righteousness, and seeking to do His will above all?

- Are you fully submitted to the authority of God's Word in Scripture, allowing it to guide all that you do, in every area of your life?
- Are you taking ownership of your own thoughts and actions?
- Are you rightly caring for God's creation, including the property, resources, and animals under your direct care? Are you helping these things to thrive and become all that God desires?
- Are you providing effective leadership? Do you have a future vision, and are you taking initiative to reach that vision? Are you maximizing the gifts of the people under your leadership, getting everyone involved and working together?
- Do you treat your subordinates as equal in dignity and worth as fellow image-bearers of God? Do you regularly honor and encourage them?
- Are you creating order by establishing and upholding effective rules and boundaries that align with God's moral law? Are you maintaining order by rewarding those who uphold those rules while consistently and fairly disciplining violators?
- Are you lovingly and sacrificially serving those under your authority for their good? Are you helping them grow, mature, and become all God wants them to be? Do you seek to honor them above yourself (Romans 12:10)?
- Do you understand and respect the God-ordained spheres, limits, and boundaries of authority? Do you respect the rightful authority of others, while guarding and protecting your rightful spheres of authority from encroachment and usurpation by others?

In your roles of submission:

- Are you resentful and begrudging toward authority, or do you willingly submit to the rightful authority of others, delighting to follow their lead and obey their commands?
- Do you willingly and proactively place yourself under God-ordained authorities who are reluctant to acknowledge and fulfill their responsibilities, out of a desire to help them grow and mature in their knowledge of the truth?
- Do you submit first to God as your supreme authority, and are you willing to disobey authorities when they overstep their bounds or issue rules or commands that violate God's law and harm others?

Authority applies to all of us: as individuals, in our relationships, and with creation itself. When we determine to understand and live out the revolutionary definition of authority that comes to us through God's Word and the example of Jesus, hope comes crashing in. What steps will you take to apply the truth of authority in your life?

CHAPTER 7

JUSTICE

Your throne, O God, will last for ever and ever;
a scepter of justice will be the scepter of your kingdom;
You love righteousness and hate wickedness.

PSALM 45:6-7

JUSTICE

Conformity to God's moral standard as revealed in the Ten Commandments and the Royal Law: "love your neighbor as yourself." Communitive justice: living in right relationship with God and others; giving people their due as image-bearers of God. Distributive justice: impartially rendering judgment, righting wrongs, and meting out punishment for lawbreaking. Reserved for God and God-ordained authorities including parents in the home, elders in the church, teachers in the school, and civil authorities in the state.[1]

JUSTICE REDEFINED

Deconstructing traditional systems and structures deemed to be oppressive, and redistributing power and resources from oppressors to their victims in the pursuit of equality of outcome.

Toward the end of the State of the Union address in 2019, President Trump challenged Americans to "work together to build a culture that cherishes innocent life" and to "reaffirm a fundamental truth: All children, born and unborn, are made in the holy image of God."[2]

Stacey Abrams, a former gubernatorial candidate from Georgia, defended the right to a legal abortion by saying, "America achieved a measure of reproductive justice in *Roe v. Wade*."[3] Just what did she mean by "reproductive justice"?

The phrase wasn't hers. It was coined in 1994 by a group called "Women of African Descent for Reproductive Justice." They defined it as "the human right to maintain personal bodily autonomy, have children, not have children, and parent the children we have in safe and sustainable communities."[4]

The irony here is painful. In the days of slavery, the moral reasoning went something like this: Black slaves are not fully human but are the powerless, voiceless property of powerful slave owners to dispose of as they choose. Today, this kind of moral reasoning has made abortion the leading cause of death for black lives in America today.[5] Every year, well in excess of *a quarter of a million* unborn black children are lost through abortion.[6] In New York City, more black babies are aborted than are born alive.[7] *This is justice?*

BIBLICAL JUSTICE

The Latin word *justus*, according to Webster's 1828 Dictionary of the American Language,[8] means "straight, or close." Like a plumb line, *justus* refers to a standard or basis *for morality*. Justice is alignment to a standard of goodness. In fact, goodness, or righteousness, is synonymous with justice. Antonyms are injustice or evil. An action can be said to be unjust if it is out of alignment with a moral standard.[9]

A moral standard is commonly referred to as a law, which is why justice is equated with lawfulness, and injustice with lawbreaking or lawlessness. For most of us, "law" brings to mind legal codes enacted by politicians and upheld by civil authorities. But justice isn't merely obeying manmade laws. In fact, sometimes justice demands that we *disobey* manmade laws.

JUSTICE

Conformity to God's moral standard as revealed in the Ten Commandments and the Royal Law: "love your neighbor as yourself." Communitive justice: living in right relationship with God and others; giving people their due as image-bearers of God. Distributive justice: impartially rendering judgment, righting wrongs, and meting out punishment for lawbreaking. Reserved for God and God-ordained authorities including parents in the home, elders in the church, teachers in the school, and civil authorities in the state.

So how do we determine *which* manmade laws are just, and which are not? According to the great medieval theologian Thomas Aquinas, an unjust law is a human law that is not rooted in eternal and natural law, or "the law of God." Christian apologist Greg Koukl calls this "the Law-over-everything-and-everyone."[10]

How do finite and fallible human beings discover this transcendent moral standard? We find it in God, the Creator of the universe, whose character is goodness, righteousness, and holiness (or moral perfection). As John Calvin said, the law reveals God's character.[11] *He* is the moral plumb line who determines what is good and right for all peoples, for all eras. And because God doesn't change, this standard doesn't change. God is the immovable "Rock" whose "work is perfect, for all his ways are justice. A God of faithfulness and without iniquity, just and upright is he" (Deuteronomy 32:4, ESV).

In the Bible, we translate the Hebrew words *tsedek* and *mishpat* as either "righteousness" or "justice," depending on the context. The Bible has more than thirty examples of "righteousness" and "justice" being used interchangeably. For example, "I walk in the way of righteousness, along the paths of justice" (Proverbs 8:20), or "The LORD works righteousness and justice for all the oppressed" (Psalm 103:6).[12]

God is both righteous and just. If He were not righteous, He would not be just. If He were not just, He would not be righteous. Yet He is both! And He, not the changing consensus of elite opinion, is the plumb line by which we measure all claims of justice.

WHAT WE CANNOT *NOT* KNOW

If God's character and His law provide the only sure plumb line by which we can decide the merit of any claims of justice, it raises the question: Can we really know Him and His law? This question is urgent if we are to rightly respond to the moral chaos around us (and in our own hearts). If such a transcendent moral standard exists, it wouldn't be of any use if we had no knowledge of it. But God *has* made it known to us. Here's how.

First, He communicates it to us *inwardly.* As image-bearers of God, all people have a built-in sense of this law "imprinted on our heart," so to speak. The apostle Paul wrote about this in his epistle to the Romans: "When Gentiles, who do not have the law, do by nature things required by the law . . . they show that the requirements of *the law are written on their hearts*, their *consciences* also bearing witness, and their thoughts sometimes accusing them and at other times even defending them" (Romans 2:14–15, italics added). Natural law theory says that human beings can apprehend God's moral law through their God-given reason.[13]

Paul makes the audacious claim that *all people*—not only the Jews—know tacitly what God's eternal moral standard is, because they "do by nature things required by the law." They show that God has written it "on their hearts" because their consciences convict them of wrongdoing.

Second, when Paul says that Gentiles "do not have the law," he is referring to the *other* way God communicates His transcendent law to us, that is, through the Ten Commandments—the legal code handed down from God to humankind three and a half millennia ago. The Ten Commandments were "inscribed by the finger of God" (Exodus 31:18), delivered to Moses and the Jewish people, and through them, to all of us. This summary of God's moral law is one of His greatest gifts to humanity, because it provides the only true, unchanging foundation for justice in human history. This is why the image of the stone tablets is engraved at the apex of the United States Supreme Court building.

JUSTICE IN EVERYDAY LIFE

Justice essentially is living out the Ten Commandments in our everyday relationships. It defines how we *ought* to treat others—what kind of behavior is good and right, and what is not. Gary Breshears, a theology professor at Western Seminary in Portland, Oregon, explains what the Hebrew word *tsedek* (translated into English as "justice") means: "a life in which all relationships—human to human, human to God, and human to creation—are well-ordered and harmonious."[14]

Practically, justice means "following the rule of law, showing impartiality, paying what you promised, not stealing, not swindling, not taking bribes, and not taking advantage of the weak because they are too uninformed or unconnected to stop you," according to pastor Kevin DeYoung.[15]

"We do justice when we give all human beings their due as creations of God," Tim Keller says,[16] paraphrasing Aristotle. The last part of this sentence is key: "as creations of God." Justice requires recognizing what it means to be human—that we all possess inherent dignity and worth, with (in the Declaration's immortal phrasing) "unalienable rights."[17] To "do justice" is to treat others as uniquely valuable, and to respect their God-given rights. It is "loving your neighbor as yourself."[18] This is the duty of every human being.

JUSTICE AS FAIR, IMPARTIAL JUDGMENT

But there is another kind of justice that is reserved for God-ordained authorities—including parents in the home, pastors in the church, and civil authorities in the state. This aspect of justice demands that authorities punish injustice, render judgments fairly, and treat everyone equally before the law, because that is how God— the supreme authority in the universe—treats us. He impartially rewards good and punishes evil. He does not ignore the sins of any. He does not take bribes (Deuteronomy 10:17).

Why does justice require injustice to be punished? Because if evil goes unpunished, injustice multiplies. "Justice means exacting an appropriate payment for a crime," Koukl says. "No payment, no justice."[19] We commonly say that lawbreakers must be held "to account" for their crimes, bringing to mind accounting concepts such as debts, payments, and balance sheets. Proper accounting requires that the books be balanced. So does justice.

INJUSTICE AND THE FALL

If justice means treating others in conformity with God's perfect moral standard, then we must admit that *injustice* is pervasive in our fallen world. Because of our fallen nature, we are double-minded when it comes to justice. We cry out for justice when we, our friends, or our loved ones have been mistreated, but we find it inconvenient when we are doing the mistreating. We make excuses for our bad behavior, or we brush it aside. We claim our innocence in the face of all evidence.

It gets worse. We've not merely wronged other people. We've wronged God Himself. We have *sinned*. To sin is to violate God's law. Because God is the ultimate standard for goodness, He is ultimately the offended party. God isn't indifferent to injustice. It is abhorrent to Him. "For the wrath of God is revealed from heaven against all ungodliness and unrighteousness of men" (Romans 1:18, ESV). Today Christians are uncomfortable talking about God's wrath. We prefer to dwell on His love, mercy, and forgiveness. Those are all wonderfully true, but if we fail to reckon with God's hatred of injustice, our picture of Him is incomplete.

God's compassion stirs in Him a hatred for injustice. He is tenderhearted toward its victims. He sees their tears, storing them in a bottle (Psalm 56:8). He will deliver the needy who cry out, the afflicted who have no one to help. He will take pity on the weak and the needy and save the needy from death. He will rescue them from oppression and violence, for precious is their blood in his sight (Psalm 72:12–14).

God rises up in anger against those who oppress the weak, the marginalized, and the poor. He will hold every oppressor accountable. But there is good news. God provides a way of escaping

the punishment and wrath that our rebellion has earned us—a way
that displays God's glory in all its radiant splendor.

THE GREAT DILEMMA

God's justice is tied, like all of His attributes, to His goodness or
righteousness. But His goodness shows itself in other qualities as
well, such as His love and mercy. These qualities come together in
one of the most important passages of Scripture: Exodus 34:6–7, the
account of God appearing to Moses on Mount Sinai and proclaiming
His name. "The Lord passed before [Moses] and proclaimed,

> 'The Lord, the Lord, a God merciful and gracious, slow
> to anger, and abounding in steadfast love and faithfulness,
> keeping steadfast love for thousands, forgiving iniquity
> and transgression and sin, but who will by no means
> clear the guilty, visiting the iniquity of the fathers on the
> children and the children's children, to the third and the
> fourth generation.'" (ESV)

Notice how love, mercy, and justice are central to God's
character. He is "merciful, gracious, abounding in steadfast love."
And yet He "will by no means clear the guilty." This presents
a seeming dilemma, for mercy is the act of withholding justly
deserved punishment.

What if God were just but not merciful? Would He still be
good? No. He'd be like the infamous Inspector Javert in Victor
Hugo's *Les Miserables*, a man ruthlessly committed to justice, yet
without a shred of mercy. And yet, what if He were merciful but not
just? If God overlooked evil, He would likewise not be good. Such a
God would be culpable in the proliferation of evil.

We find the resolution of this dilemma at the apex of God's
extraordinary story of redemption—the life, death, and resurrection

of Jesus Christ. God incarnate, in an act of sheer love, took upon Himself the punishment we deserved for our transgressions. "For Christ also died for sins once for all, the just for the unjust, so that He might bring us to God" (1 Peter 3:18 NASB).

This is the good news at the heart of the biblical redemption story. God's mercy and justice meet at the cross. This indescribable gift of forgiveness in Jesus Christ is available to all, no matter how great our sins.

JUSTICE AND MERCY IN THE SHADOW OF THE CROSS

The cross is God's ultimate solution for dealing with the evil and injustice in this world. Calvary made achieving this goal possible, but it won't happen fully until Jesus returns. God delays the final judgment for the moment, knowing full well that evil and injustice will continue. He delays His ultimate judgment, not because He is powerless over evil nor because He lacks compassion for its victims. He delays it for the sake of mercy, for God is "patient . . . not wanting anyone to perish, but everyone to come to repentance" (2 Peter 3:9).

But His patience won't last forever. When Jesus returns, He will be the Judge. On that day, perfect justice will be done. Evil will be punished, wounds will be mended, tears will be wiped away, and the world will be made right again.[20] All will stand before Christ's judgment seat, and books will be opened. One will contain a record of everything we've ever done. Every one of our thoughts and actions will be judged against God's perfect moral standard. Nothing will be hidden. There will be no escaping justice.

But mercifully, there is another book—the Book of Life. It too contains a record. It lists the names of those who, though guilty, have received mercy simply by requesting it. How? The punishment for their lawbreaking was paid for on the cross. In this judgment on the last day, it won't matter if you are male or female, black or white, rich or poor. The only divide that will matter will be the one between the "poor in spirit" who cry out for mercy, and the proud who do not.

A CULTURE BUILT ON JUSTICE AND MERCY

Those of us who grew up in cultures profoundly shaped by a Judeo-Christian worldview often fail to appreciate the unique inheritance of our relatively just societies. We take for granted that human beings have inalienable rights and deserve respect, and that those accused of wrongdoing are entitled to due process. We forget that in the broad sweep of history, relatively just societies are the exception, not the rule.

On this side of Christ's return, there will be no perfectly just societies, yet some will be more just than others. What are some of the hallmarks that set these societies apart?

Respect for the rule of law

Just societies acknowledge a moral law higher than themselves and a supreme lawgiver to whom even the most powerful are accountable. America's founders acknowledged both in the first sentence of the Declaration of Independence:

> When in the Course of human events it becomes necessary for one people to dissolve the political bands which have connected them with another and to assume among the powers of the earth, the separate and equal station to which *the Laws of Nature and of Nature's God* entitle them, a decent respect to the opinions of mankind requires that they should declare the causes which impel them to the separation. [italics added]

Just societies are built upon the rule of law, the understanding that the law applies equally to everyone. The rule of law says that those who create laws and administer justice are under, and must themselves adhere to, the law.

Human dignity and God-granted human rights

Just societies are built upon the truth that all human beings are God's image-bearers and, as such, have equal dignity, incalculable worth, and rights that cannot be taken away. "All men are created equal, [and] . . . are endowed by their Creator with certain unalienable Rights." Injustice results when certain groups are dehumanized. In early America, slaves were viewed as less than fully human by many. Today, the unborn are as well.

A check on corruption

One of the greatest blights on any nation is corruption—the abuse of power for personal (usually financial) gain. Transparency International's Corruption Perceptions Index[21] reveals that, with few exceptions, the countries with the lowest levels of corruption were born out of a Judeo-Christian framework. Those without this advantage tend to have higher perceived levels of public sector corruption, according to experts and businesspeople.

The reason is straightforward. Societies are built in the image of the God, or gods, that they collectively worship. If the gods are selfish, capricious, and unpredictable—if they can be bribed for special treatment—then the culture will follow along with high levels of bribery and corruption. But if the culture is formed by the worship of the true, living God who "love[s] righteousness and hate[s] wickedness" (Psalm 45:7) and "is not partial, and takes no bribes" (Deuteronomy 10:17), corruption will be significantly checked.

Establishing due process

Due process describes the kind of respectful treatment that the accused are due as image-bearers of God. It includes (1) the right to a timely trial by an unbiased judge and jury; (2) the presumption of innocence until guilt has been established by the testimony of multiple witnesses, and the presentation of corroborating evidence;

(3) the right of the accused to be informed of the charges against him or her; (4) the right of the accused to confront his or her accusers, and to cross-examine opposing witnesses; (5) the right of the accused to be represented by legal counsel; and (6) the right of the accused to defend himself or herself, including the calling of witnesses.[22]

Due process is another fruit of Judeo-Christian civilization. Its biblical roots go back to passages such as Deuteronomy 19:15, which says, "One witness is not enough to convict anyone accused of any crime or offense they may have committed. A matter must be established by the testimony of two or three witnesses." Likewise, in the New Testament, God is described as one who "judges each person's work impartially" (1 Peter 1:17).

Entrusting final judgment to God

Just societies understand that not every wrong will be righted on this side of Christ's return. They remember that ultimate justice is to be dispensed thoroughly and perfectly only by God's Son, Jesus Christ (John 5:22), and that a day of final accounting is coming.

This is not the case with those who deny God and the final judgment, who dismiss religion as the "opiate of the masses." Believing in no ultimate Judge who will separate the sheep from the goats, they take it upon themselves to mete out perfect justice.

JUSTICE REDEFINED

Today, an ideology (and accompanying movement) described by its adherents as "social justice" has radically redefined the popular understanding of justice. This new ideology is characterized by its:

- obsession with power, oppression, and victimization.
- use of tactics reminiscent of Mao's Cultural Revolution and an "ends justifies the means" methodology

- fixation on class, race, gender, and sexual orientation as defining characteristics of personal identity.[23]
- hostility toward Judeo-Christian religion, particularly in its beliefs about family and sexuality
- antipathy toward the natural family
- fixation on redistributing wealth and power by an ever-larger state

For millennia, the Judeo-Christian worldview gave the West an overarching narrative, a framework and basis for justice, and sufficient grounding for human dignity. Today, all this has been cast aside. Karl Marx (1818–1883) created a new narrative, *a new worldview*—a new religion, in fact—to replace the Judeo-Christian worldview.

Throughout the twentieth century, Marx's religious metanarrative was put to the test, first in Russia under Lenin and Stalin, then in China under Mao, and later in North Korea, Vietnam, Cambodia, and Cuba. These vast social experiments produced prison states, gulags, and genocides that killed hundreds of millions.

JUSTICE REDEFINED
Deconstructing traditional systems and structures deemed to be oppressive, and redistributing power and resources from oppressors to their victims in the pursuit of equality of outcome.

And yet Marxism remains with us. As communist states were beginning to collapse in the mid-twentieth century, a new generation of Marxist theorists arose in Europe to rescue the movement. These included Antonio Gramsci (1891–1937), Herbert Marcuse (1898–1979), and Max Horkheimer (1895–1973). Their reboot of Marxism (which they referred to as "cultural Marxism") was incubated in universities in the United States under the broad heading of "critical social theory."

By utilizing a cultural strategy that some have called "the long march through the institutions,"[24] the champions of cultural Marxism achieved stunning success at embedding their presuppositions into Western public education, academia, the media, entertainment, big business, and politics. Today, ideological social justice dominates the commanding heights of Western culture. It has even made significant inroads into mainstream evangelicalism.

Ideological social justice is perhaps best understood as a postmodern religious alternative (a "successor ideology") to Christianity. Essayist Andrew Sullivan explains its appeal:

> For many, especially the young, discovering a new meaning [for life] . . . is thrilling. Social justice ideology does everything a religion should. It offers an account of the whole: that human life and society . . . must be seen entirely as a function of social power structures, in which various groups have spent all human existence oppressing other groups, and it provides a set of principles to resist and reverse this interlocking web of oppression.[25]

A COMPREHENSIVE WORLDVIEW

To rightly comprehend the new ideology of social justice, we must see it for what it is: a comprehensive worldview. All worldviews have, at their core, a set of presuppositions that frame everything else. These presuppositions typically answer the big questions. What is ultimately real? Who are we? What is our fundamental problem as human beings? What is the solution to that problem? What's our purpose in life?

Ideological social justice answers each of these questions and many more, giving shape to a comprehensive worldview. See the contrast with biblical justice.

	Ideological Social Justice	Biblical Worldview
Who are we?	Creatures whose identity is *wholly* socially determined. We are products of our race, sex, and gender identity.	Creations and image-bearers of a good, holy, and loving God with inherent dignity and immeasurable worth.
What is our fundamental problem as human beings?	Oppression: White, heteronormative males have established and maintain hegemonic power structures to oppress and subjugate women, people of color, and sexual minorities (LGBTQ+) and others.	Rebellion: *All have sinned*, and fallen short of the glory of God. Our rebellion against God has resulted in *broken relationships*—between God and man, between man and his fellow man, and between man and creation.
What is the solution to our problem?	Revolution: Oppressed victims and their allies must unite to unmask, deconstruct, and overthrow these oppressive power structures, systems, and institutions.	The gospel: On the cross, God incarnate bore the punishment we deserved for sinful rebellion in order to show us a mercy we could never deserve. His death on the cross and His resurrection opened the way for the reconciliation of all of our broken relationships.
How can we be saved?	Victims are morally innocent and do not require salvation. Oppressors can never be fully pardoned, but partial salvation is available if they confess their complicity in oppression and support the revolution.	"If you declare with your mouth, 'Jesus is Lord,' and believe in your heart that God raised him from the dead, you will be saved. . . . Everyone who calls on the name of the Lord will be saved." (Romans 10:9, 13)

	Ideological Social Justice	Biblical Worldview
What is our primary moral duty?	To stand in solidarity with, protect, and defend the oppressed: women, people of color, sexual minorities (LGBTQ+), etc.	To love God with all our heart, soul, mind, and strength (which involves living in obedience to all that Christ commanded) and to love our neighbors as ourselves.
Is there a future, final judgment?	No. There is no god who will return to punish the wicked and reward the upright. Rather, injustice must be rooted out here and now by those with the power to do so.	Yes. Jesus will return and accomplish perfect justice. He will preserve all that is good and rid the world of all that is evil. Until then, He extends mercy and forgiveness to sinful people.

Neil Shenvi says that these are two distinct and incompatible worldviews. He notes that ideological social justice and Christianity conflict regarding basic questions of epistemology, identity, morality, and authority. The core principles of each are diametrically opposed. The false worldview of ideological social justice has, at its core, a counterfeit definition of justice. It redefines justice to mean deconstructing traditional systems and structures deemed to be oppressive, and redistributing power and resources from oppressors to their victims in the pursuit of equality of outcome.

Let's explore more deeply some of the basic worldview assumptions that support this false definition and how they differ from the biblical worldview.

WHAT IS OUR FUNDAMENTAL PROBLEM?

For believers in social justice, the answer can be expressed in one word: "Oppression." In this worldview, evil doesn't originate in the human heart. There is no doctrine of the fall or human depravity.

Rather, evil is sourced outside of man, in society, and specifically in social structures, systems, institutions, laws, and cultural *norms that perpetuate inequalities* and grant one group power and privileges at the expense of others.

How different all of this is from the biblical worldview. What is our fundamental problem as human beings? Our one-word answer isn't "oppression" but "rebellion." "All have sinned and fall short of the glory of God" (Romans 3:23). Our fundamental problem is that we—*all of us*—are in a state of open rebellion against our Creator.

Our fundamental problem is not "out there" in oppressive societal structures. Our problem is "in here," in our foolish, darkened hearts. All of us are implicated. In the immortal words of Aleksandr Solzhenitsyn: "The line separating good and evil passes not through states, nor between classes, nor between political parties either—*but right through every human heart*" (emphasis added).[26]

WHAT IS THE SOLUTION?

"Revolution" is the answer of ideological social justice. Oppressed victims and their allies must unite in an intersectional coalition to unmask, deconstruct, and ultimately overthrow oppressive power structures.

In the zero-sum world of social justice power struggles, there is no "live and let live" tolerance. No win-win, or even compromise. No place for forgiveness, or grace. No "love your enemy." No "first get the log out of your own eye" introspection. There is only grievance, condemnation, and retribution. Bigots, haters, and oppressors must be destroyed.

Those who uphold the biblical worldview agree with social justice revolutionaries on this: our societies are broken and need to change! With all the injustice in the world, all the suffering, pain, and heartbreak, we need cultural transformation. Yes, there are oppressive systems, structures, and institutions. We cannot stand idly by while these things continue destroying people and despoiling God's magnificent creation. But we differ on how this change should come about.

The problem is broken relationships and, fundamentally, alienation from our Creator. Until this root problem is addressed, there is no possibility for lasting social change. The breathtakingly good news is that hope for forgiveness and reconciliation with God is available! God Himself has taken the initiative in reconciling with His rebellious children.

> For God so loved the world, that he gave his only Son, that whoever believes in him should not perish but have eternal life. For God did not send his Son into the world to condemn the world, but in order that the world might be saved through him. (John 3:16–17)

Ultimately, injustice isn't a social problem. It is a sin problem. The only solution is a personal, heart-level transformation, not just for a particular group of so-called "oppressors," but for everyone. Biblical transformation encompasses both the inward and the outward, the personal and the societal, the regeneration of fallen human hearts and minds and the reformation of society.

Biblical social change is an *inside-out* process that begins with inward transformation. First John 1:9 (NASB) says that "If we confess our sins, He is faithful and righteous to forgive us our sins and to cleanse us from all unrighteousness." This divine act of heart-level regeneration is followed by God's work of sanctification, leading to a transformed character. Certainly, institutional evils such as slavery, abortion, corruption, pornography, and sex trafficking are real and must be opposed. But we have no hope for lasting social change apart from the gospel and new life in Christ.

WHAT IS OUR PRIMARY MORAL DUTY?

Social justice, like Marxism, rejects the idea of an objective, transcendent, universal morality. It asserts that human beings are autonomous—laws unto themselves. Morality in this system doesn't vanish. As image-bearers of God, a moral sense is deeply embedded in our human nature. But a morality that is untethered from God is continually in flux and utterly arbitrary.

Over the past decade, we've experienced nothing short of a moral revolution. Things that were formerly understood to be good—such as freedom of speech; freedom of religion; reserving sex until marriage; marriage as the exclusive, lifelong union of a man and a woman; and even the male-female binary itself—are increasingly understood to be bigoted, hateful, discriminatory—tools of oppression.

Because people are not responsible moral agents, but victims or beneficiaries of oppressive systems, guilt or innocence is not a function of individual choices, but group identity. If you are a victim, you are morally innocent. If you are an oppressor, you are morally guilty, regardless of your actions.

The false system of moral guilt and innocence at the heart of social justice morality makes it incompatible with the gospel. It is a false gospel. While the consequences of sin may be passed down from one generation to another (Jeremiah 32:18), the guilt of sin is earned individually (Ezekiel 18:20). Though God loves people of every ethnic group (Revelation 7:9), He is no respecter of persons (Acts 10:34), and no one will get a pass from Him based upon membership in any particular group (Galatians 3:28). Salvation is by grace through faith (Ephesians 2:8–9).

As followers of Jesus Christ, we should react the same way to social justice morality that the apostle Paul reacted to the false gospels in his day: "But even if we or an angel from heaven should preach to you a gospel contrary to the one we preached to you, let him be accursed" (Galatians 1:8, ESV).

What is our primary moral duty, according to the biblical worldview? To love God with all our heart, soul, mind, and strength, and to love our neighbors as ourselves (Matthew 22:37–40). Loving God means obeying His commands (John 14:15), and loving our neighbors certainly involves caring for the plight of oppressed people. This was Jesus's point in the parable of the good Samaritan. We are morally obligated to care for truly oppressed and victimized people. However, the Bible doesn't define victims or oppressors as ideological social justice does. Oppressors are certainly not exclusively white men, nor are victims exclusively people of color, women, or LGBTQ members. In the Bible, victims look a lot more like the man beaten up, robbed, and left to die alongside the road in the parable of the good Samaritan.

Yes, we have a moral duty to care for oppressed and victimized people, but we have to understand who these people are biblically— not according to the presuppositions of ideological social justice. We also must not categorically view representatives of powerful, often oppressive, systems as irredeemably evil. God shows His love to such people throughout the Scripture. Zacchaeus, a hated tax collector for the oppressive Roman Empire; Nicodemus, a member of the Sanhedrin that eventually condemned Jesus to death; and Cornelius, a Roman soldier, were among the first Christians.

Finally, as Christ-followers, we must uphold the biblical idea of morality as objective and rooted in God's character and His Word, which is the final authority. Any form of justice not grounded in God's moral law will result in injustice, for it is based on fallen human reason.

IS THERE A FUTURE, FINAL JUDGMENT?

The social justice worldview has no place for a final judgment. What is deemed "evil" must be rooted out here and now, by men and women, using any means necessary. In the former Soviet Union, "capitalists" were rounded up and shipped off to gulags or starved to death by the millions. Cambodia's Khmer Rouge had its killing fields. Red China slaughtered millions of undesirables during its horrific Cultural Revolution. We see a similar, but not yet fully developed, dynamic in the West.

This is not the Christian vision of justice. Only a perfect judge can execute perfect justice, and only Christ can perfectly fulfill that awesome responsibility. As the Judge of all, He *will* preserve all that is good while ridding the world of all that is evil.

Only a perfect, holy, and righteous God is able to do this task. Only He can build the better world that all of us, in our best moments, desire. He will have the final say, but ultimate justice will have to await His return. Until that day, God extends the possibility of mercy and forgiveness to sinful people, and so do His followers, pointing to Him while we practice biblical justice along the way.

With these building blocks in place, we can grasp how ideological social justice is no longer seen as mere personal or societal conformity to God's law. It is all about "unmasking" and overthrowing oppressive systems. And what makes these structures oppressive? They perpetuate disparities, or "inequity."

EQUITY VS. EQUALITY

The word "equity" has an almost sacred connotation in the worldview of ideological social justice. Equality is a deeply biblical idea, but the social justice understanding differs greatly from what is revealed in Scripture. In the Bible, equality refers to the equality that all human beings possess as image-bearers of God. In the classical Marxist worldview, however, equity means *equality of outcome—* in other words, sameness, uniformity, and interchangeability. Ironically, despite its proclaimed commitment to "diversity," the actual outworking of ideological social justice is to make diverse people the same.

Social justice ideology conflates disparities with injustice and oppression. Wherever disparities exist between groups, social justice assumes that the cause *must* lie with systemic or institutional oppression of one sort or another. For example, if 80 percent of Google's software engineers are male and 20 percent are female, the disparity, *ipso facto*, *proves* systemic male privilege and sexism. Because justice equals sameness, Google must change its hiring policies to ensure an equal number of male and female engineers.

But is this disparity *really* caused by institutional sexism? Or could men and women have different psychologies or life experiences that contribute to their being more or less inclined to become software engineers? These are dangerous questions to ask where ideological social justice holds sway. Just ask former Google software engineer James Damore, who was fired for asking them.[27]

This demand for sameness appears nearly everywhere. Norms and civic ordinances that exclude transgendered people from using the bathrooms and locker facilities of their choice are said to be unjust because they treat people differently. The laws and regulations excluding gays and lesbians from the institution of marriage must be scrapped because "same-sex" couples are to be treated the same as "opposite-sex" couples. Social justice demands it.

Even families are suspect in this worldview. According to John Stonestreet of the Colson Center for Christian Worldview:

> Social scientists have long known that loving families with two parents confer an enormous advantage on children. Evidence shows that these kids are more likely to attend college, less likely to suffer or perpetuate abuse, less likely to do drugs or cross the law, and have a higher likelihood of passing these advantages on to their own children.[28]

But if social justice requires equality of outcome—sameness— then loving families are unjust! Justice requires sameness. The solution? According to professors Adam Swift of the University of Warwick and Harry Brighouse of the University of Wisconsin Madison, "If the family is the source of unfairness [inequality] in society, then it looks plausible to think that if we abolished the family there would be a more level playing field."[29] This illogic is the beating heart of ideological social justice.

DIVERSITY

Along with equity, the other supreme value of ideological social justice is "diversity." The phrase "diversity, equity, and inclusion" or "DEI" is the beating heart of the social justice movement. Countless schools, organizations, and institutions loudly champion their core commitment to these goals.

The Bible also affirms diversity. But as with justice and equality, the biblical value of diversity is very different from what ideological social justice champions. Diversity simply means difference or variety. The Bible presents diversity as a blessing. God created a world of tremendous diversity. There is not one kind of flower or tree or insect or person but a great diversity of each. Of the billions of people to have walked this earth, no two are the same. God clearly loves diversity. He also loves unity. All people share a deep unity as image-bearers of God. In this most profound sense, we are all equal. We have a unity, *but not a uniformity*.

Diversity without unity leads to chaos and conflict. Unity without diversity leads to stifling, totalitarian conformity. Human flourishing requires both, which is why the Bible affirms both.

Ideological social justice actually values uniformity, paradoxically, in the name of diversity. There is no unity-diversity balance in this worldview. The affirmation and value of "diversity" is actually strictly limited to only a few select categories. Beyond these, there is stifling pressure to conform. The diversity that is affirmed is *group* difference, not *individual* difference, and even among groups, not all group differences are equally celebrated—or even tolerated.

Ideological social justice has no place for human beings as individuals. It reduces people to mouthpieces for the groups they belong to. They are expected to think just like everyone else in their group. If you are black, you are expected to think, speak, and act like a "black" person, and the same is true for women, LGBTQ+ people, and everyone else. There is no room to celebrate individual differences of belief inside these groups. Representative Ayanna Pressley, a black, female US congresswoman from Michigan, put words to this presupposition in comments she made at the *Netroots Nation* Conference in 2019:

> "We don't need any more brown faces that don't want to be a brown voice. We don't need black faces that don't want to be a black voice. We don't need Muslims that don't want to be a Muslim voice. We don't need queers that don't want to be a queer voice."[30]

Her point was clear. If you are brown, black, Muslim, or "queer" and you don't think or speak like your group, you are not needed. Conform to the group, or get out! Is this a celebration of diversity? No, it is oppressive conformity.

Social justice champions speak of their "respect for differences and tolerance for all people, cultures, identities, and perspectives," but this is disingenuous. Their value of diversity isn't for "all people." The most oppressive intersectional group—straight, white males— are certainly *not* celebrated. "Diversity" doesn't apply to it.

LGBTQ+ activist organizations, for example, are increasingly targeting Bible-believing Christians for exclusion because of their beliefs. Take the case of Christian baker Jack Philips. He has been repeatedly harassed and fined by the State of Colorado, which sought to drum him out of business for his respectful refusal to make a custom-designed cake for a same-sex wedding. For social justice activists, there certainly is no celebration of diversity, no "inclusion," no "respect for differences" or "toleration for all people and perspectives" when it comes to Philips and people like him.

So much for a celebration of equality, diversity, and inclusion. This is a push to get in line with the new orthodoxy *or else!* It is rank intolerance masquerading as tolerance. It is uniformity disguised as "diversity."

WHAT IS LOST?

What do we lose if ideological social justice continues to eclipse biblical justice? We are already seeing change and can expect to see much more:

- Less gratitude and more grievance
- Less personal responsibility and more claims of victimhood, hostility, division, and blame casting
- Continued erosion of the rule of law, with moral norms and laws becoming arbitrary, constantly changing, conforming to the whims of whatever group can marshal power to sway popular opinion
- The loss of due process; no more "innocent until proven guilty"
- The loss of free speech and the ability to debate and discuss challenging topics openly (By shutting down debate, the door opens ever wider to violent extremism)
- The loss of any basis for civility, social unity, cohesion, or tolerance; no more "live and let live"; no more "love your enemy"

HOW SHOULD WE THEN LIVE?

The false religion of ideological social justice lures people by providing them with a source of identity, community, and purpose. But like any cult, once you are in, it is very hard to escape. According to former social justice advocate Barrett Wilson (not his real name): "The people giving me these stars, hearts and thumbs-up [on social media] were engaging in their own cynical game: A fear of being targeted by the mob induces us to [virtue] signal publicly that we are part of it."[31]

How tragic that so many of our prominent evangelical leaders have abdicated their responsibility to be salt and light by promoting many of the central tenets of this dangerous, unbiblical worldview. Rather than proclaiming the truth that sets people free, they are pushing ideas that are destroying lives, fracturing relationships, and dividing our nations.

People like Barrett don't need the church to validate their beliefs in ideological social justice. They need to hear a story that defines what justice really is. In the counterfeit story they've absorbed, justice is the uprooting of traditional structures and systems, with the goal of redistributing power and money from so-called oppressor groups to victim groups. The goal is a utopian equality of outcome. This is a secular perversion of justice, however. In our story—the true story—justice is conformity to God's perfect moral law as found in the Ten Commandments and the royal law: "Love your neighbor as yourself" (James 2:8).

Thankfully, many Christians are waking up to the dangers of ideological social justice. There are growing numbers of organized resistance movements. These efforts are to be commended and supported. But as they speak out against this destructive worldview, it is important that they not merely oppose it, but instead uphold, defend, and proclaim the biblical worldview. Let's not be *anti*-ideological social justice. Let's be *pro*biblical justice.

Here are some areas where opponents of ideological social justice need to be cautious.

CULTURAL TRANSFORMATION

Ideological social justice is revolutionary, calling the oppressed to overthrow their oppressors. That battle is carried out in the social, cultural, and political arenas. Tactically, the ends justify the means.

In reaction, the temptation for opponents is to write-off Christian efforts to "engage the culture" or "transform the culture" as an unbiblical distraction from our spiritual purpose and mission—to save souls for heaven. This world is going to hell, so why bother trying to reform or change it for the better?

The biblical worldview, however, sees this world as God's handiwork, and He loves His creation. His death on the cross isn't merely to save human souls out of the world, but to redeem all things broken through the fall. See Colossians 1:15–20.

The biblical worldview sees evangelism and spiritual regeneration not as an end, but rather as a means to a larger end: the reconciliation of all things. Here's how New Testament theologian N. T. Wright puts it:

> The great emphasis in the New Testament is that the gospel is not how to escape the world; the gospel is that the crucified and risen Jesus is the Lord of the world. And that his death and Resurrection transform the world, and that transformation can happen to you. You, in turn, can be part of the transforming work.[32]

Christians committed to the biblical worldview are passionate about working to transform this world—to see positive social and cultural change. But change must first be inward and spiritual before it can manifest itself externally in society and culture. The problems with the world are not "out there" in society; rather, they are "in here" in our fallen hearts and minds. All positive cultural change includes gospel proclamation and inward spiritual regeneration by the Holy Spirit.[33]

RACISM

Ideological social justice sees racism (and sexism, and homo/trans-phobia) as widespread, systemic, and pervasive. For its adherents, America is so deeply stained by racism that the only hope is revolutionary change. In response, the temptation for the antisocial justice camp is to downplay racism or deny that it remains a significant problem in America. This is a mistake. While incredible progress has been made, and while America today is one of the most ethnically diverse and tolerant societies in the world, racism remains a real problem, and Christians are duty-bound to fight genuine racism where it exists, in their own hearts and in society.

STRUCTURAL, SYSTEMIC INJUSTICE

Because ideological social justice sees brokenness and injustice as rooted in social systems and structures, the temptation will be for opponents to deny or downplay the very idea of structural or systemic evil. This would be *anti*social justice but not *pro*biblical worldview.

The biblical worldview provides a comprehensive view of the fall. It not only affects individuals, it disorders all of creation, including human-formed organizations, systems, and structures. God wants to redeem it all. We can agree with proponents that structural or systemic evil exists. We need look no further than the pornography industry, which in the United States alone generates more than $2.5 billion in annual revenue and drives the evil of sex trafficking.

The fight against systemic social evil is not a distraction luring the church away from her central mission. No, this fight is fundamental to our calling. However, Christians don't ignore what causes the fallen systems in the first place. If you want to reform evil structures and systems, you have to reform—or rather transform—fallen human hearts.

WESTERN CIVILIZATION AND THE UNITED STATES OF AMERICA

The advocates of ideological social justice see Western civilization and the United States as irredeemably corrupted by systemic racism, sexism, greed, and injustice. The temptation will be for opponents to swing to the opposite extreme. But Christians need to uphold the truth about our nation's history, both good and bad.

Our attitude toward America, or Western civilization, shouldn't be marked by a negative, critical, and ungrateful spirit. Nor should it be marked by hubris or superiority. Instead, let us approach the topic with humble gratitude. Ultimately, our blessings come from God Himself.

TACTICS

Advocates of ideological social justice increasingly use power tactics to advance their narrative. Tactics like political correctness, bullying, shaming, threatening, deplatforming, silencing, and more. Cancel culture doesn't believe in free speech, dialogue, or debate with ideological adversaries. Let's not attempt the same power tactics. But neither let us be cowed into silence or submission.

Instead, we are called to love those who oppose us and pray for them (Matthew 5:44). Christ's kingdom advances as truth is lovingly proclaimed and demonstrated (Ephesians 4:15). "Do not be overcome by evil, but overcome evil with good" (Romans 12:21).

LET'S MOVE BEYOND CRITICIZING CULTURE, TO CREATING CULTURE

Ideological social justice is dangerous because it is false. There is no "love your neighbors," much less "love your enemies." There is no grace. No forgiveness. No humility. Don't we want to live in a culture where truth, justice, and love are the highest goods? A culture where God is honored as King, and all people, regardless of their race, sex, or class are respected and loved as His beloved children? A culture in which people are judged by "the content of their character, not the color of their skin"?

This culture still exists in America today.

In June 2015, the world saw the worst that human beings can do to one another. One evening, white supremacist Dylann Roof, age 21, walked into the Emanuel African Methodist Episcopal Church in Charleston, South Carolina, and gunned down nine African American men and women who were participating in a Bible study. The authorities quickly caught up with Roof, eventually convicting him of murder.

At Roof's sentencing hearing, many of the surviving family members stood up in court, not merely to list their justified grievances, but to forgive him. Nadine Collier, the daughter of Ethel Lance, one of the victims, told Roof, "I will never be able to hold her again, but I forgive you and [God] have mercy on your soul. You hurt me. You hurt a lot of people, but God forgives you, and I forgive you."

Anthony Thompson told his wife's killer, "I forgive you, and my family forgives you. But we would like you to take this opportunity to repent. Change your ways."[34]

That kind of supernatural love and forgiveness is a true revolution. These people amaze us because they forgive their enemies. That power came, in part, from a recognition that they too are sinners forgiven by God and objects of His amazing, extraordinary grace.

These kinds of stories are possible only in cultures that have been deeply shaped by the Transforming Story—the truth of the biblical worldview. It is powerful. It is deeply beautiful. It is good. It is true.

How do Christians respond to ideological social justice? Do we merely react against it, or do we offer a better way? Nancy Pearcey is exactly right:

> The best way to drive out a bad worldview is by offering a good one, and Christians need to move beyond criticizing culture to creating culture. That is the task God originally created humans to do, and in the process of sanctification we are meant to recover that task. . . . In every calling we are culture-creators, offering up our work as service to God.[35]

This is a dangerous moment for evangelicals in the West. Our confusion over justice needs to be replaced by careful discernment. If we continue to allow the yeast of social justice to contaminate our theology at a time when the culture desperately needs to see true, biblical justice advocated and lived out, the losses will be incalculable, both in time and in eternity.

That need not be our fate if we, followers of Jesus Christ, reject the false presuppositions of social justice and unapologetically embrace and advocate for true, biblical justice, not only in the home and in the church, but in every sphere of society where we have influence.

CHAPTER 8

FAITH

Without faith it is impossible to please God,
for whoever would draw near to Him must believe that
He exists and that He rewards those who seek Him.

HEBREWS 11:6, ESV

FAITH

To assent to the weight of evidence; to trust in the truthfulness and reliability of something or someone based on a careful search of available evidence and personal experience.

FAITH REDEFINED

Affirming the truthfulness of something without regard to evidence, or even despite a lack of evidence.

When Judge Amy Coney Barrett was nominated for the Seventh US Circuit Court of Appeals in 2017, this woman of significant professional accomplishment was, in many respects, an ideal candidate who checked all the boxes. A graduate of Notre Dame Law School with the highest honors, she clerked for Justice Antonin Scalia at the Supreme Court before returning to her alma mater to teach in the areas of the federal courts, constitutional law, and statutory interpretation. Plus, Barrett was relatively young, with a sterling reputation.

By any reasonable standard, Barrett should have been a shoo-in for the position, putting her on the fast track to the Supreme Court. "She is exactly the kind of person you want serving on the Court of Appeals," cultural commentator and author John Stonestreet noted, "if we lived in more reasonable times."

Of course, we don't live in reasonable times—far from it. At Barrett's confirmation hearings in the Senate, several senators latched onto the fact that Barrett is a practicing Catholic—no surprise, given her Notre Dame pedigree.

Diane Feinstein of California scolded, "When you read your speeches, the conclusion one draws is that the dogma lives loudly within you." (Barrett had said in a speech "Your legal career is but a means to an end, and . . . that end is building the kingdom of God. . . . [I]f you can keep in mind that your fundamental purpose in life is not to be a lawyer, but to know, love, and serve God, you truly will be a different kind of lawyer.")[1]

Feinstein was upset that Barrett was so open and public about her Catholic faith, and how it influenced her work as a lawyer. This was a violation of an immutable principle for Feinstein: Faith is personal and private, not public. You may practice it in your home, church, synagogue, or mosque, but you must never allow it to influence your work in public.

Behind this is a false conception of faith that now dominates Western society. The idea is that faith is a personal, subjective religious belief that has no grounding in facts or evidence. Therefore, it has no place in public life. In private, we may trust whatever God or gods we happen to have faith in, but in public, we are all taught to "trust the science."

Many people, including many Christians, have absorbed this understanding of faith, but it is true? Is faith a "blind leap" into the unknown? Or is it the magical power of belief—that if you truly believe with all your heart, you can make your dreams come true?

Faith is one of the Bible's most important words, so Christians must understand it accurately. And while we tend to think about faith in terms of "religion," faith isn't limited to religion. It is something that everyone practices all the time, even without fully realizing it.

TRUE FAITH

Faith means to put your trust in someone or something based on the weight of evidence. It means to trust in the truthfulness and reliability of something or someone based on personal experience and a careful search of available evidence.

Faith is synonymous with trust, trustworthiness, and truth. Words that express the opposite of faith include distrust, doubt, anxiety, fear, insecurity, skepticism, unsureness, and indecision.

The Old Testament Hebrew word for faith is *emet*, the same as the Hebrew word for truth. Emet refers to faithfulness, reliability, trustworthiness, and dependability. *Emet* relates to something that is real and entirely truthful.

The New Testament Greek word for faith is *pistis*, connoting evidence and moral conviction. It comes from *pietho*, which means convincing by argument and assenting to the evidence.

FAITH

To put your trust in someone or something based on the weight of evidence. To trust in the truthfulness and reliability of something or someone based on personal experience and a careful search of available evidence.

While some today speak of the "power of belief" and suggest that faith is an end in itself, this is not the case with genuine faith, which is always faith in something or someone. To exercise faith, you begin with questions like these: Is that person trustworthy and dependable? Did that historical event actually happen? Is that thing safe or reliable? Can I trust it? You then seek answers to such questions by honestly searching for the truth. You observe carefully. You gather evidence. You listen carefully and analyze the evidence by applying reason and logic. This is exactly what the New Testament (Greek) word for faith (pistis) means.

Next, you begin to form tentative conclusions and, in an all-important final step, you *assent* to the evidence and take action based on those conclusions. This final step in the process is the essence of faith.

Here's a humorous example of what assent means, borrowed from Eric Metaxas:

Let's imagine a high-wire artist who has affixed a cable across a dangerous waterfall and then proceeds to walk back and forth across it. A crowd gathers, of course, and upon returning from his jaunt across the taut wire, the man points to a wheelbarrow and asks the crowd whether they believe he can push it all the way across to the other side. Most people believe that he can, so they nod, or even shout "Yes!" The hire-wire artist singles out a man in the front of the crowd, who seemed most confident in answering affirmatively. "You, sir!" the high-wire artist says to the man. "You say you believe that I can wheel the barrow across the cataract. Is that true? Do you really believe it?

"I do!" the man says.

"Even with a heavy load inside the barrow?"

"Why not? Certainly!"

"Very well," the high-wire artist says, "I'm glad to hear it. So please help me show everyone else that I can do it by getting into the barrow."[2]

At this point in the story, for the man, it is no longer merely an intellectual exercise but has become very personal. If the man gets in, he will indeed have exercised faith. If not, he won't. *Your faith is proven by what you do and how you act.* In other words, I can tell what you truly trust by how you behave.

Here are a few simple examples of faith in practice.

You're in a friend's house, and he invites you to sit in a chair. If that chair looks old or rickety, you may ask, "Will it support me?" You then "gather evidence" by quickly looking for prominent broken parts or screws loose. Finding none, you then turn to your experience sitting in other chairs, concluding that nearly all of them supported you. So, you conclude that the chair will support you based on experience and the best available evidence. Next is the all-important step. You *assent* to your conclusion by actually sitting down in the chair. If the chair supports you, then faith in the chair is well-founded, and your faith in chairs grows ever stronger. You realize the chair is trustworthy, dependable, and reliable. This whole process plays itself out in a matter of seconds, and because you do it all the time, you may not even realize you are exercising faith.

You plan to visit a family member in another state by traveling on a commercial airline. You've never flown before, so there is a question: Is flying in a commercial airliner safe? You then seek to answer the question by carefully observing and gathering available evidence. You might look at the safety track record of airline travel. You might talk to people you trust who travel frequently and trust airline safety. You might question pilots or others who fly for a living.

Then, after careful, logical thought and reasoning, you conclude that airline travel appears safe. You've convinced yourself intellectually. You believe it is safe. But for that belief to become faith, you must assent to the evidence by purchasing a ticket, getting on an airplane, and taking the trip. The turning point is this final step of faith: getting on the aircraft.

Once you do this, you have evidence and personal experience. Your faith grows stronger the more personal experience you have. Your trust in the reliability and dependability of airline travel grows as you exercise faith with each subsequent trip.

These examples apply to things, but the same basic process applies to people.

Let's say your car is broken. You find an auto repair shop nearby and ask, "Is the mechanic trustworthy? Will he repair my car for a reasonable price?" You gather available information and evidence. You look at reviews on Yelp and Google. You seek information from a trusted friend who has used the mechanic. You then conclude that the mechanic is trustworthy and has integrity, and you assent to the evidence by dropping off the car for repairs. If the vehicle is repaired for a reasonable price, you conclude that your faith in the mechanic was well-grounded.

You can see from these simple, everyday examples that faith isn't exclusive to religious people. *It is a basic necessity of life for everyone.* We exercise faith in hundreds of ways in our everyday lives, often without even realizing it. Without faith, getting out of bed each morning would be virtually impossible.

Christian faith

Now, let's look at what faith means for a Christian. Christian faith starts by asking some of the most important questions anyone can ever ask. Does God exist? Is the Bible God's Word? Has it been passed down through history reliably? Is Jesus who He claimed to be?

These are huge questions, and a lot (in fact, everything!) hangs in the balance, so it is important not to approach them lightly but seriously and soberly.

A person who seeks honest answers to these questions through careful reasoning, observation, and textual and historical evidence analysis, with the Holy Spirit's enlightening, and concludes affirmatively is well on his way to becoming a Christian. One final step is required, however. A person must assent to the evidence by bending his knee and *fully committing himself to Christ.* Christian faith goes beyond intellectual *belief* into *active trust, expressed by surrender and obedience.*

Faith is a central theme in the Bible. While this chapter can't allow for an in-depth study, it will help to look at a few of the key Bible passages on faith, starting with the famous definition of faith in Hebrews 11:1-2.

Faith is confidence in what we hope for and assurance about what we do not see. This is what the ancients were commended for.

What is the object of faith in this verse? God—and specifically God's promises in Scripture. It refers to those with complete confidence and assurance that God will do as He promised. Those with such faith were "the ancients" listed in Hebrews 11, including Abel, Enoch, Noah, Jacob, Joseph, Moses, Rahab, and many others. However, one couple, Abraham and Sarah, is worth looking at in more detail because they are an excellent example of what Hebrew 11:1 means by faith.

God chose Abraham and, through Him, promised to fulfill His grand redemptive plan for the ages. We read this great promise in Genesis 12:1–3.

> The Lord had said to [Abraham], "Go from your country, your people and your father's household to the land I will show you.
>
> "I will make you into a great nation,
>   and I will bless you;
> I will make your name great,
>   and you will be a blessing . . .
> and all peoples on earth
>   will be blessed through you."

God promised to make Abraham "into a great nation." But there was a problem. Abraham and Sarah were childless and were too old to bear children. How could he become the father of a great nation with no offspring?

But Abraham and Sarah had walked with God for many years, and that relational experience had proven to them, beyond any doubt, that God was utterly trustworthy. If He promised it, it would come to pass. As it says in Hebrews 11:11:

> By faith, even Sarah, who was past childbearing age, was enabled to bear children *because she considered [God] faithful who had made the promise.* (italics added)

God's trustworthy nature was the object of Abraham and Sarah's faith. Abraham and Sarah's faith in God's promise wasn't "a blind leap." It was based on years of intimate experience walking with God, and He had proven Himself trustworthy every step of the way.

Romans 4:19–22 picks up the story:

> Without weakening in his faith, [Abraham] faced the fact that his body was as good as dead—since he was about a hundred years old—and that Sarah's womb was also dead. Yet *he did not waver through unbelief regarding the promise of God*, but *was strengthened in his faith* and gave glory to God, *being fully persuaded that God had power to do what he had promised.* (italics added)

In the words of Hebrews 11:1, Abraham had complete confidence in what he hoped for and assurance about what he did not see—that he would be the father of a great nation.

As one Christian writer helpfully said, "Biblical faith is not a vague hope grounded in imaginary, wishful thinking. Instead, faith is a settled confidence that something in the future—something that is not yet seen but has been promised by God—will actually come to pass because God will bring it about."[3]

In the end, God once again proved himself faithful, and Isaac was born. Then, God chose to test Abraham and Sarah's faith. We read about it in Genesis 22:1–2:

Sometime later God tested Abraham. He said to him, "Abraham!"

"Here I am," he replied.

Then God said, "Take your son, your only son, whom you love—Isaac—and go to the region of Moriah. Sacrifice him there as a burnt offering on a mountain I will show you."

Sacrifice Isaac? He was the promised child who would grow into a mighty nation just as God had promised. This command must have been deeply confusing and distressing for Abraham and Sarah, yet they did as God instructed, even to the point of binding Isaac's hands and feet and laying him atop a stone altar with a knife ready to complete the sacrifice. Hebrews 11:17–19 reveals Abraham's profound faith in God that enabled him to do this:

> By faith Abraham, when God tested him, offered Isaac as a sacrifice. *He who had embraced the promises* was about to sacrifice his one and only son, even though God had said to him, "It is through Isaac that your offspring will be reckoned." *Abraham reasoned that God could even raise the dead,* and so in a manner of speaking he did receive Isaac back from death. (italics added)

As we know in hindsight, God provided a substitute sacrifice, a ram, at the last possible moment, and Isaac's life was spared. Abraham had complete faith that God would be true to His promise that Isaac would be the forefather of a great nation. Somehow, in some way, Isaac would be spared for this promise to be fulfilled, even if God had to raise him from the dead.

Through true biblical stories like these and many others, we, too, can have faith in God and His promises. He never lies. He never deceives. He doesn't change like the shifting sands. His word is rock solid. All the evidence we could ever need is in the historical record of God's work in the Bible.

As we trust in God ourselves, our experience of God's faithfulness in our lives strengthens our faith. It isn't an overstatement to say that we can boil the entire message of the Bible down to this simple idea: *Trust God.* Trust His promises. He will never let you down.

As one Christian writer helpfully put it, "Biblical faith is a confident trust in the eternal God who is all-powerful, infinitely wise, eternally trustworthy—the God who has revealed himself in His Word and in the person of Jesus Christ, whose promises have proven true from generation to generation."[4]

Saving faith

We read much about "saving faith" in the New Testament. The ground of saving faith is the finished work of Christ on the cross. It begins with questions like these: "Is Jesus Christ who He claimed to be?" "Did he actually die on a Roman cross, exchanging His perfect righteousness for my sins and paying the penalty I deserved?" "Could this incredible good news be true?"

To seek honest answers and to conclude that "yes, these things are true" is to come right to the doorstep of salvation. But saving faith requires that you (with the indispensable help of the Holy Spirit) step through the door. That final step involves more than belief in facts, but complete trust in Jesus, expressed through total surrender to Jesus as King and Lord. Saving faith is not mere belief or intellectual assent but complete trust in, and total surrender to, the risen and living Christ, the Savior of the world and the King of heaven and earth.

This complete faith, marked by repentance, submission, and obedience, is what saves us. We can't earn our salvation through "good works." Our sin runs too deep. We can only accept the free gift of salvation through faith. Here's how the apostle Paul explains this in Romans 3:21–25, ESV:

> But now the righteousness of God has been manifested apart from the law, although the Law and the Prophets bear witness to it—the righteousness of God *through faith in Jesus Christ for all who believe.* For there is no distinction: for all have sinned and fall short of the glory of God, and are justified by his grace as a gift, through the redemption that is in Christ Jesus, whom God put forward as a propitiation by his blood, *to be received by faith.* (italics added)

Similarly, Paul says in Ephesians 2:8–9:

> For *it is by grace you have been saved, through faith*—and this is not from yourselves, it is the gift of God—not by works, so that no one can boast. (italics added)

This is saving faith. It is the faith of the famous Reformation cry *"Sola Fide."* By faith alone are we saved—faith in the finished work of Jesus Christ on the cross on our behalf.

Contrary to the false definitions in our modern dictionaries, saving faith for the Christian isn't believing in a beautiful myth or fairy tale because I want it to be true. It isn't a "blind leap" without regard to the evidence—just the opposite. Saving faith is taking actions based on the weight of the evidence—based on what is historically true.

As the apostle Paul said in 1 Corinthians 15:17: "If Christ has not been raised from the dead, your faith is futile." In other words, our faith is worthless if these are not historical realities but made-up fairy tales. There is more than enough historical and textual evidence to back up the truth of the gospel.[5] Don't take my word for it. Do the research yourself. Ask the hard questions. Seek honest answers. If the evidence points overwhelmingly to the truth of the gospel, then be willing to humble yourself and assent to the evidence by placing your faith in Jesus Christ.

There is nothing wrong with being skeptical and doubting at the beginning of a process of honest examination, particularly of claims as audacious as the gospel makes. But once you reach the point where you are convinced that all the evidence points overwhelmingly to the truthfulness of the gospel, continuing to doubt is counterproductive. It reflects a proud, rebellious heart. This is why Jesus often asked of those He healed, "Do you believe I am able to do this?" (Matthew 9:28). Do you genuinely believe I am who I say I am? Do you trust me completely, or are you still in doubt?

As it says in Hebrews 11:6, ESV: "Without faith [that is, complete trust in Jesus] it is impossible to please [God], for whoever would draw near to [Him] must believe that He exists and that he rewards those who seek Him."

And while we don't earn our salvation through "good works," but instead by faith in the finished work of Jesus on the cross, that faith, if it is genuine, has to show itself in a life of faithful obedience to Jesus Christ and His commands.

God doesn't save us so that we can go on living the same kind of sinful and disobedient lives we did before, but now with "fire insurance" to prevent us from going to hell after we die. The great German pastor and Bible scholar Dietrich Bonhoeffer called this "cheap grace." This attitude reveals that we lack genuine faith in Jesus Christ. Here's what genuine faith looks like:

> What good is it, my brothers, if someone says he has faith but does not have works? Can that faith save him? If a brother or sister is poorly clothed and lacking in daily food, and one of you says to them, "Go in peace, be warmed and filled," without giving them the things

needed for the body, what good is that? So also faith by itself, if it does not have works, is dead.

But someone will say, "You have faith and I have works." Show me your faith apart from your works, and I will show you my faith by my works. You believe that God is one; you do well. Even the demons believe—and shudder! Do you want to be shown, you foolish person, that faith apart from works is useless? . . . For as the body apart from the spirit is dead, so also faith apart from works is dead.(James 2:14–26, ESV)

Saving faith involves complete surrender, which involves a changed way of living that will show itself in our actions. Will we trust Jesus with our income? With our career? With our life? With our family? How we behave will reveal to the watching world whether our faith is genuine.

THE POSITIVE CULTURAL CONSEQUENCES OF TRUTH FAITH

Trustworthiness, dependability. These are the glue that hold society together. Without faith and trust in people or institutions, societies can't function.

You can't even do science without faith.

The scientific endeavor is grounded on faith in natural laws that are so precise, orderly, and regular that it's possible to communicate them mathematically. In the famous words of Albert Einstein, "[God] does not play dice with the universe." This is why the apostle Paul could claim that the reality of God's existence is manifestly known to all people who observe His creation (Romans 1:19–20). Creation reflects beauty, order, purpose, and intricate design precisely because it is "created" by a good and all-wise God. It makes no sense otherwise.

So much depends on faith. In any well-ordered, well-functioning, and flourishing society, people must have a high degree of faith in each other and their institutions. That faith can only exist where there is trust. Trust in the dependability of natural laws. Trust in people's honesty and reliability and the legal, governmental, and civil institutions they create.

But where does a society's trust and reliability come from? They don't spring out of thin air. They grow in the rich soil of a deep faith in a God who Himself is entirely true, honest, trustworthy, reliable, and dependable.

As Darrow Miller is fond of saying, "We build societies in the image of the God (or gods) that we worship." Or as it says in Psalm 115:8: "Those who make [idols and false gods] *will be like them*, and so will all who trust in them (italics added).

Societies grounded in the worship of pagan "gods" who are erratic, unpredictable, and vengeful see that reflected in low levels of trust in people or institutions, leading to all manner of dysfunction, corruption, and brokenness.

Societies that reject God and only see a material universe formed by a chaotic, unguided, purposeless process of evolution with only one immutable law—the "survival of the fittest"—also have no basis for trust or faith. How can you trust a purposeless universe? How can you trust your brain to understand it if it is the product of a mindless process of evolution? It turns out that science is incompatible with a materialistic worldview. How can we trust people and the institutions they create when all human relationships devolve into contests for power and domination?

Societies that reject God as the supreme authority end up in a never-ending competition for earthly power and authority, with different groups working to stealthily rig the system to their sole advantage. Here, too, trust breaks down. People become highly critical and suspicious of each other, always looking for ways that those with power have manipulated systems and institutions to oppress them. This is the worldview of "neo-Marxist" critical theories that now dominate our Western institutions, from education to big business, to law and government.

Faith and trust erode when societies hold these false worldviews. And when you can't trust anyone, relationships fall apart—and then everything falls apart. That is what we are seeing in the West today. Marriages are fracturing, and people are choosing not to marry at all, leading to plummeting birth rates. Suspicion and open hatred between various groups are on the rise, and there are historically low levels of trust in our institutions.[6]

To rebuild our societies, we must recover faith. Faith in God and faith in each other. We must start by recognizing and discarding the current false definition.

FAITH REDEFINED

Mark Twain once quipped, "Having faith is believing in something you just know ain't true." Tragically, this misconception about faith is now fully institutionalized in the West. The Oxford Dictionary of the English Language defines faith this way: "A strong belief in God or the doctrines of a religion, based on spiritual apprehension rather than proof."[7]

In his book *The Selfish Gene*, celebrity atheist Richard Dawkins states without fear of pushback that faith is "blind trust, in the absence of evidence, even in the teeth of evidence," while Bertrand Russell defines faith as "a firm belief in something for which there is no evidence."[8]

In other words, faith is a "blind leap."

These definitions are precisely the opposite of how the Bible defines faith. How did we reach the point where the true meaning of faith could be completely inverted?

FAITH REDEFINED
Affirming the truthfulness of something without regard to
evidence, or even despite a lack of evidence.

The answer lies in the creation of what some have called the Enlightenment Myth. According to this false narrative, science and religion are at war with each other. Science tells us what is true and, therefore, publicly authoritative, serving as the basis for public policy, law, and education. Things that science cannot study—spiritual reality, God, morals, and ethics—are deemed matters of "faith" and private belief.

According to the Enlightenment Myth, Christianity is a clever fairy tale. If you want to believe in it despite the lack of evidence, that is your business, but you must keep that belief private. The public realm must be guided by facts and science, not religion.

Today, many people, sadly including many Christians, have entirely accepted this narrative. Under the influence of public figures such as Dawkins, they see religion, including Christianity, as anti-reason and anti-science. They have relegated faith to the realm of myth and fairytale. In their thinking, faith makes us feel good, but it is not real. As science advances, faith necessarily retreats.

This false, destructive narrative has been the main driver behind the secularization of the West over the past century. It traces its roots back to fifteenth century Europe, and while we covered some of this historical ground in our chapter on Truth, it will be helpful to review it again briefly.

During this so-called "Age of Enlightenment," modern science was in full bloom, with great mysteries of the universe yielding their secrets one after another. Alongside the excitement of discovery, an ancient pride began to grow in the hearts of many Enlightenment philosophers: Through science and human reason *alone*, we will come to know everything. We no longer need to appeal to a supernatural realm—to God, angels, or demons—to explain various natural phenomena, as people did during the former "Dark Ages."

The late theoretical physicist Stephen Hawking perfectly captures the Enlightenment Myth's essence: "Before we understood science, it was natural to believe that God created the universe, but now science offers a more convincing explanation."[9]

This myth elevates science but is actually a quasi-religious worldview. The proper name for it is materialism, naturalism, or scientism. Today, it is the reigning worldview in the post-Christian West and underpins all of the dominant ideologies of the twenty-first century, including postmodernism and neo-Marxism.

As discussed in chapter one, the Enlightenment Myth created what Bible scholar Nancy Pearcey calls "The Fact/Value divide." It can also be viewed as a "Faith/Facts Divide."

"Faith"
Religion, ethics, morality
Private beliefs, not publicly authoritative
Unreal, fantasy, not based on evidence

"Facts"
Known through science, based on evidence
Publicly authoritative
Real, true

According to the Faith/Facts Divide, Christianity is something people believe in, not because it is grounded on historical facts, evidence, and reason, but because they want it to be true, regardless of facts or evidence. Christianity is anti-science and anti-reason. It is so-called "faith."

The Faith/Fact Divide and the Enlightenment Myth that it springs from are both false. There is no conflict between Christianity and science. Both require faith. Science is grounded on faith in unchanging natural laws and the orderliness and predictability of Creation.

The irony today is that many prominent scientists exercise false faith. They "affirm the truthfulness of something without regard to evidence, or even the lack of evidence." Take the example of the aforementioned Richard Dawkins, an Evolutionary Biologist at Oxford University. He once said: "Biology is the study of complicated things that have the appearance of having been designed with a purpose."[10] He readily admits that biological organisms, such as a DNA molecule, the human eye, or a hummingbird's wings, show overwhelming evidence of design and purpose. But then he makes a "blind leap" against the clear evidence, concluding that these things are, in fact, not designed but arose purely by chance through a purposeless process of material evolution.

Neither true faith nor science takes this kind of "blind leap." Rather, they follow the evidence wherever it leads in an honest search for truth.

The amount of evidence for God's existence is overwhelming and grows with each passing day. Consider what we now know about how "finely tuned" the universe has to be for life to exist. If the mass of the electron, the strength of gravity, the lifetime of the neutron, or hundreds of other similar factors were altered even slightly, complex life could not exist anywhere in the universe. Here's how Eric Metaxas described this in a 2014 Wall Street Journal article:

> Today there are more than 200 known parameters necessary for a planet to support life—every single one

of which must be perfectly met, or the whole thing falls apart. Without a massive planet like Jupiter nearby, whose gravity will draw away asteroids, a thousand times as many would hit Earth's surface. The odds against life in the universe are simply astonishing.

Yet here we are, not only existing, but talking about existing. What can account for it? Can every one of those many parameters have been perfect by accident? At what point is it fair to admit that science suggests that we cannot be the result of random forces?

Metaxas concludes: "Doesn't assuming that [God] created these perfect conditions require far less faith than believing that a life-sustaining Earth just happened to beat the inconceivable odds to come into being?"[11]

Scientists who persist in claiming that the universe burst into existence by chance can only do so by making the most extravagant leap of blind faith. Why do they do it? Because in their rebellious hearts, they don't want to acknowledge God's existence, for that would mean that they are under and accountable to a higher authority.

Richard Lewontin, an evolutionary biologist from Harvard University, is a perfect example:

Our willingness to accept scientific claims that are against common sense is the key to an understanding of the real struggle between science and the supernatural. We take the side of science in spite of the patent absurdity of some of its constructs . . . *because we have a prior commitment, a commitment to materialism.*

He says that for scientists like him, "Materialism is absolute, *for we cannot allow a Divine Foot in the door.*"[12]

Here, again, we see a prominent scientist exercising false faith by affirming a materialist worldview without regard to evidence— even despite a lack of evidence. Why? Lewontin is admirably honest: Because "we cannot allow a Divine Foot in the door." Materialism is true, not because that is where the scientific evidence leads, but because *we want it to be true.* We refuse to acknowledge God's existence. This, of course, isn't science. This is a false religion masquerading as science. It is scientism.

Where does this leave genuine science? Christians today have a wonderful opportunity to reclaim not only true faith but true science as well. Let's take up the mantle of right reason, clear, logical thinking, and a commitment to follow the evidence wherever it leads with complete conviction that "all truth is God's truth, and right reason cannot endanger sound faith."

But to do this, we must firmly reject the Enlightenment Myth and the Facts/Faith Divide. Sadly, far too many Christians continue to accept the false assertion that Christianity and science are at war with each other, or else they operate in entirely different and wholly disconnected spheres.

In some Christian circles, asking hard questions about the Bible is frowned on, if not explicitly, then implicitly. There are certain questions you just don't ask. The implication that many, particularly young people, take away is this: Don't ask hard questions. Don't doubt. Don't think or trust in reason. *Just believe.*

Faith *requires* asking hard questions. How can you place your faith in something or someone without evidence that they are trustworthy? If the Bible is what it claims to be, the absolute truth I can place my whole trust in, then that should be proved under the most intense scrutiny.

Tragically, many Christians still believe, as Darrow Miller did in the story told in chapter one, the strange idea that their so-called "faith" somehow makes Christianity true. The object of their faith isn't the objective reality of God or the truthfulness of the Bible, but *faith itself*. They believe in the so-called "power of belief." This idea is, in part, fueled by the rise of postmodernism in Western culture during the late twentieth century. As we have seen, postmodernism rejects objective truth in favor of personal and private views of "truth." This has had an equally disastrous impact on the concept of faith.

In our postmodern world, faith becomes personal and subjective. "If your faith works for you, fine." It can be "true" for you. Such a subjective faith doesn't require reason or evidence. It might even be opposed to reason or evidence. Subjective faith lives only in the mind of the "believer." It is a private faith, not a public reality.

This tragic redefinition of faith based on the modernist myth and the Faith/Fact Divide has led many Christians (and non-Christians as well) to a view of faith as a magical incantation. According to this view, if you want something, just believe in it hard enough, and *your faith will make it come true*. This false view is not faith *in God* but in faith itself. So many people believe in the magical, mystical power of belief to make their dreams come true, to have whatever they want out of life. You see it in the growing movement in which people seek to "manifest" their goals into reality. The power here doesn't come from God but from "belief" itself.

The chorus of the theme song "When You Believe" from the 1998 DreamWorks film *The Prince of Egypt*, performed by Mariah Carey and Whitney Houston, provides a good example of this false view of faith.

> There can be miracles
> When you believe
> Though hope is frail, it's hard to kill
> Who knows what miracles you can achieve?
> When you believe, somehow you will
> You will when you believe[13]

Who knows what miracles *you* can achieve when you *just believe*. Believe what? There is no object to the faith or "belief" in this song other than "belief" itself. "Belief" has magical powers to accomplish the miraculous.

But our faith isn't what makes mountains move (Matthew 17:20) or heals people from cancer. Only the object of true faith, namely God, can do these things because nothing is impossible for Him (Luke 1:37). God can do these things, and He invites us to trust that He can. We can express that trust actively in prayer, asking Him to do the miraculous. And He invites us to do just that! (Mark 11:24).

We are not passive bystanders, waiting for God to do the miraculous. He graciously invites us to join Him in accomplishing His good purposes. When we pray, we should pray *in faith*, that is, in complete trust in God and in the full realization that there is nothing too hard for Him to accomplish. If He answers our prayer, we give Him the credit, honor, and glory. *He* did it, not our "belief" apart from Him.

HOW SHOULD WE THEN LIVE?

As we close this chapter on faith, take time to reflect on your own faith in God and the Bible. Have you absorbed the Enlightenment Myth and the Faith/Fact Divide? If so, you are certainly not alone. This sadly remains a deeply entrenched false view of faith in the church. It has done more damage to Christianity than almost any other false idea. It has led directly to the secularization of Europe and the Americas for more than a century, leaving empty church buildings and a rapidly declining number of Christians in its wake.

If your view of faith is closer to the false faith discussed in this chapter than what genuine faith is, I invite you to repent. To repent simply means to change your mind. Have your mind transformed, by intentionally casting aside a belief that you now know is false, and replace it with what is true.

This may mean that you will need to "own" your faith, perhaps for the first time. Many Christians believe Christianity is true because of someone else's faith—usually their parents. Or, like Darrow, they've been taught the lie that faith is what makes Christianity true and that you shouldn't ask hard questions. "Just believe." They believe the lie that faith is separate from reason, facts, and evidence.

Your faith in God and the Bible needs to be grounded on *your own conviction* that both are utterly true and trustworthy. If you have questions or doubts about that, don't bury or ignore them. Express them in the form of questions, and then honestly seek answers to those questions, and commit to follow the evidence wherever it leads. If you do, I'm convinced you will find Jesus Himself at the journey's end. As He said, "I am the truth" (see John 14:6).

There is no substitute for having a personal "full assurance" in the truthfulness of what you believe. You will need that when trials come, when your faith is tested. In the fire, you need the personal conviction that God is trustworthy and that you can fully rely on His promises. You can't get there without making that determination for yourself.[14]

And if you claim to have faith in Jesus, does that faith go beyond "saving faith"?" Does it make a difference in this world? Does it change the way you actually live? Yes, Jesus is our Savior, but He is also our Lord and King. It's very common in the church for Christians to say they have faith in Jesus as their personal Savior but not as their supreme authority. The truth is, Jesus doesn't give us this choice.

If He is your Savior, He also demands your total allegiance. Our right response to faith in Jesus the King is total surrender. To have faith in Jesus is to surrender to Him all of our relationships. All of our finances and resources. Our work. Our plans, hopes, and dreams. All of it. Our attitude must be "not my will, but Yours be done," just as Jesus Himself modeled for us (Luke 22:42).

Anything short of this is not genuine faith in Jesus. It is a kind of quasi-Christianity, where we have faith in Jesus to save us for heaven, but we don't trust Him in a host of other areas of life. When it comes to our work, our family, our money, or our future, we trust and seek wisdom from sources other than the Bible. We assume the Bible's message is limited to personal salvation and has nothing to teach us about marriage, finances, relationships, farming, medicine, law, government, business, or a host of other topics.

Frankly, you may prefer this. You don't want Jesus to interfere in certain areas of your life. You want to do what pleases you or what will win the favor and plaudits of powerful or influential people. Again, this is a false faith because it isn't faith in Jesus, the Lord and King.

Everything has to be surrendered to Him. He demands it all. As some have said, He is either King over all or He is not King at all. His Word, the Bible, is our supreme authority, not just over spiritual issues, such as salvation and church matters, but over everything. The principles, laws, precepts, and ordinances of God's Word have to underpin every endeavor, every part of life and work.

Your choices and actions will prove what you place your ultimate trust in. People will see the difference between putting your total trust in Jesus, or putting it in your spouse, or children, or finances, or future plans. You can't serve two Kings. It doesn't work. As Jesus said, you will hate one and love the other, or vice versa (Matthew 6:24). Ultimately, anything short of fully trusting in Jesus will lead to heartbreak and misery, for nothing else can fulfill your deepest desires and needs for meaning and purpose. Only Jesus can.

So take time and examine your faith in Jesus. If you uncover areas you are withholding from Him, name them specifically and surrender them to Him with open hands. You won't regret it! As you trust in Him completely in every area of your life, you will begin to see Him work. You will experience His power in ways you never have before. With this life change will come a joy and sense of purpose that simply isn't available to people who haven't fully surrendered.

Finally, examine your *own* trustworthiness. A society built on the worship of the One True God of the Bible has high levels of personal trust because God is utterly trustworthy and true, and when we worship Him, we become "like Him" (1 John 3:2).

So examine your relationships with friends, family members, business relationships, and co-workers, and ask yourself, "Am I trustworthy? Do I keep my word, even when it hurts?" (Psalm 15:4). "Do I keep my vows, particularly in marriage? Do I have personal integrity? Do my words and actions align?" If not, you may not have placed your full faith and trust in Jesus but in something or someone else.

This is an opportunity to repent. Yes, we see a profound breakdown of trust in our culture right now, reflected in everything from high divorce rates to soaring levels of cynicism in our institutions. Many people can't name a single person in their lives they can genuinely trust. This sorry state of affairs is disastrous, and if we don't change course, our civilization is headed for destruction.

Rebuilding trust must begin with each of us. We may not be able to change the culture at large, but we can change our relationships. We can change our family, our church, our sports team, and our office. This is where it begins. You really can start to rebuild trust in our society by being a faithful, trustworthy person in your circles of influence. How? Not in your own strength, but by trusting fully in Jesus Christ. He will give you the power to do this because you will see that He is fully trustworthy.

And committing to God in genuine faith is not so much a task to be completed but a joyous privilege to embrace as we consider how matchlessly beautiful that He is.

CHAPTER 9

BEAUTY

Out of Zion, the perfection of beauty, God shines forth.

BEAUTY

A combination of qualities present in a thing or person, both externally and internally, that gives joy and deep satisfaction. Beauty can move us deeply and fill us with awe and wonder. Because God is its ultimate source, beauty has an objective reality that transcends personal tastes. Along with truth and goodness, it is considered one of three such "transcendentals."

BEAUTY REDEFINED

A combination of aesthetic qualities that appeal to one's personal, subjective senses or tastes. Beauty is entirely a matter of personal preference and individual expression.

Christian author Os Guinness tells a fascinating story of how his great-great-grandmother approached the brink of suicide and then stepped back.

Her name was Jane Lucrietia D'Esterre, and the year was 1815. At that time, she was eighteen years old and living in Scotland. She was young, talented, and beautiful, but her husband had recently died in a dueling match, leaving her alone and impoverished with two small children to raise by herself.

Given such sad circumstances, we can understand Jane's dark thoughts as she stood on the edge of a bridge and contemplated the cold waters of the small river far below. As Jane prepared to jump, her eyes momentarily lifted to a small field beyond the river. She saw a young farmer at work with his plow and horse. He looked about her age and was focused on his task. Meticulous and skilled, the young man's newly turned furrows looked as finely executed as the paint strokes on a master artist's canvas. As he plowed, she could hear his distant voice, quietly singing hymns.

Jane was fascinated despite herself, and a deep sense of wonder and admiration welled within her. Then, slowly, her admiration turned into rebuke. What was she doing on this bridge, wallowing in self-pity? How could she be so self-absorbed when she had two small children who needed her? With a renewed sense of determination, she returned to her home—saved from death by the simple sight of a beautiful field and a skillful farmer's work well done.[1]

Although nothing more is known about this farmer, he was most likely a Christian. He brought beauty into his farming and sought to live his life—including his menial work plowing fields—to the glory of God. The mere witness of his devotion to God, expressed in the beauty of his well-tended field, was enough to renew hope within Jane and pull her back from despair.

This simple story illustrates the power of beauty. In the words of Elizabeth Lev, "Beauty is the gateway to goodness and truth."[2] The artistry of a farmer's field provided a window through which Jane could recognize the goodness in the world and the truth that her life mattered.

TRUE BEAUTY

But what exactly is beauty? Is it purely a subjective experience—a matter of personal taste—as in the statement, "Beauty is in the eye of the beholder"? Or is it sourced in some kind of objective reality beyond us, even beyond this world?

Beauty can be challenging to define. It touches our senses and emotions in a way that bypasses our thinking and reasoning. We experience beauty but rarely think about it or define it. That doesn't mean that we shouldn't, however.

When correctly defined, beauty is a combination of qualities present in a thing or person, both externally and internally, that gives joy and deep satisfaction. Beauty can move us deeply and fill us with awe and wonder. Because God is its ultimate source, beauty has an objective reality that transcends personal tastes.

Words synonymous with beauty include delightful, sublime, radiant, perfection, glorious, flawless, and exquisite. Antonyms include hideous, unsightly, repulsive, foul, vile, ghastly, and loathsome. To begin to think about beauty, it helps to reflect on questions like these: What is the most beautiful thing you've ever experienced? What makes it beautiful? What is the most hideous or repulsive thing you've ever experienced? What makes something hideous?

> ### BEAUTY
> A combination of qualities present in a thing or person, both externally and internally, that gives joy and deep satisfaction. Beauty can move us deeply and fill us with awe and wonder. Because God is its ultimate source, beauty has an objective reality that transcends personal tastes. Along with truth and goodness, it is considered one of three such "transcendentals."

Human beings are drawn naturally to beauty. There is a strong relationship between beauty and delight, joy, or enjoyment. In the words of English poet John Keats, "A thing of beauty is a joy forever." The beautiful, sublime, and flawless draw us, while the ugly, foul, and vile repulse us.

Beauty is a "common grace" in every culture, in its fabrics, music, food, dance, and architecture. People everywhere experience beauty in ways big and small, in shapes, colors, sounds, forms, designs, and patterns. In mountain vistas and the brilliant colors of a sunrise. In a snow crystal's intricate, delicate pattern. In a child's eye. In the incredible order and symmetry of the DNA molecule or a distant galaxy. Even in something as simple as a carefully tilled field or a well-tended garden.

We also experience beauty in cleanness, order, and purity. We recognize beauty in a well-kept and tastefully decorated room in a way we don't when that room is dirty and disheveled. We recognize beauty in a crystal clear mountain stream in a way that we don't when that stream is clogged with trash. At a more complex level, we experience beauty in the exquisite order and design of God's creation—an order so precise it can be described mathematically. As Richard Feynman, Nobel laureate in physics, stated, "You can recognize the truth [of a law of physics] *by its beauty* and simplicity." [3]

Not all beauty is external and experienced through our senses. There is also an invisible, inward beauty we experience in moral virtues such as kindness, compassion, love, sacrifice, courage, or inner strength. There is a deep connection between beauty and goodness, or moral virtue. Psalm 96:9, for example, describes God's moral perfection as "beautiful."

> O worship the Lord in *the beauty of holiness*: fear before Him, all the earth." (KJV, italics added)

Similarly, the apostle Peter refers to moral virtue as "inner beauty" in 1 Peter 3:3:

> Your beauty should not come from outward adornments, such as elaborate hairstyles and the wearing of gold jewelry and fine clothes. Rather, it should be that of your inner self, the unfading beauty of a gentle and quiet spirit, which is of great worth in God's sight.

We experience beauty in all of these ways and many more. "It is hardly possible to define all the properties which constitute beauty," said Daniel Webster in his definition of beauty in the 1828 Dictionary of the American Language.

Ultimately, beauty finds its source in God, the "perfection of beauty" (Psalm 50:2). He is glorious, flawless, and morally perfect. We see the perfection of His beauty in His holiness, lovingkindness, and mercy. We see it in Jesus's tender compassion when He touched a man with leprosy, healing him. Most sublimely, we see it in Jesus's breathtaking love, displayed in His sacrificial death on the cross, giving Himself completely so that we might live.

We also experience the perfection of God's beauty in the magnificent artistry of creation. God is the First Artist.

- He is the First Composer creating the sound of waves and the wind, the silences of the heavens, the music of the spheres, and the choir of birds in the morning's dawn.
- He is the First Painter, creating spectacular sunrises and sunsets and colorful gardens filled with flowers, plants, birds, and trees—trees that are *pleasing to the eye* and good for food" (Genesis 2:9, italics added).
- He is the First Sculptor forming the Grand Canyon, the mighty Rocky Mountains, the Alps, and the Himalayas.
- He is the First Choreographer, creating the dances of the porpoise, the dove's mating ritual, the hummingbird's flight, the snowflake's floating, and the falling of leaves.
- He is the First Author, giving us the first words, writing the Bible, and the hymns of the Psalms. [4]

Beauty is also sourced in the human spirit. We, too, can create beauty because we bear God's image. In the words of the great novelist J. R. R. Tolkien:

Beginning with what God has provided, man can actually make new things. A composer can create a symphony that no one has ever heard. A painter can create a painting that no eye has ever seen. A poet can write a poem that no one has ever read.[5]

To experience, delight in, and create beauty are significant parts of what it means to be human. As my friend Darrow Miller says, "Beauty is a necessity for life." It is essential for human flourishing.

The Three Transcendentals

Because beauty is sourced in God—in His character and creation—it is an objective reality regardless of our subjective feelings about it. In this way, beauty is the same as truth and goodness, which are also universal, objective realities rooted in God's character.

These three, Truth, Goodness, and Beauty, are sometimes referred to as "The Three Transcendentals" because they are objective, transcendent realities rooted in God. They exist in harmony with each other and help to define one another. They reflect the integration of the life-giving dance of the three Persons of the Holy Trinity. "They define the culture of God's Kingdom," says Miller.

As image-bearers of God, human beings have the unique capacity to relate deeply with all three Transcendentals. The ancient Greeks described these capacities by using the words *Logos, Ethos,* and *Pathos.* Logos describes our ability to think and reason. It corresponds with Truth. Ethos describes our innate moral sense or our conscience. It corresponds with Good. Pathos describes our feelings and emotions, often experienced in a bodily or sensory way, through sight, sound, and touch. It corresponds with Beauty.

Truth	Logos	Our ability to think and reason using words, language, the rules of logic, and mathematics.
Goodness	Ethos	Our conscience, or "the law written on the heart," guiding us in doing what is right or good (Romans 2:14–15).
Beauty	Pathos	Our feelings and emotions.

All three—Logos, Ethos, and Pathos—are essential aspects of human nature. They exist in harmony with each other and are essential for human flourishing. But tragically, in today's secularized, materialistic West, beauty is often overlooked or minimized. We think of beauty as nice but not necessary.

M. Thomas Seaman challenges this modernist, secular way of thinking.

> We are so accustomed to thinking of beauty as merely decorative and ornamental that we forget that beauty is a moral necessity. God wrought beauty in the structure of the universe. Beauty is the highest form of righteousness. Beauty and truth are not separated in God's world, and they ought not to be in human thought. God, who gave as much care to painting a lily as to forming the eternal hills, joined truth and beauty in holy union; and what God has joined together, man ought not attempt to put asunder, because beauty has a moral value for truth.[6]

When God communicates and relates to us as human beings, He does so through all three—Logos, Ethos, and Pathos—because that is how He made us. He doesn't only use speech and language (Logos) but communicates to us in ways that speak to our moral sense (Ethos) and our feelings and emotions (Pathos).

When God revealed the Law to Moses, for example, He not only used the words inscribed on the stone tablets, but he also used a lofty mountain, lightning, thunder, and dark clouds. The rich sensory experience filled the Israelites with powerful emotions, including fear and awe. When God commanded the building of the Tabernacle, He gave instructions for it to be built with exquisite artistry and craftsmanship using costly materials. The physical beauty (pathos) of the Tabernacle (and later of God's Temple) complemented God's written communication (logos) on the stone tablets, all to communicate a universal standard of moral goodness (ethos).

All three are essential. They complement and define each other. We need all three. Contrary to much modern thinking,[7] human beings are not disembodied brains, like some kind of mechanistic Artificial Intelligence system, but embodied human beings made to experience and engage in the full range of God's created order. Beauty isn't an optional, decorative "add-on" for human flourishing and knowledge of truth and goodness. It is a moral necessity.

Consider the power of beauty. It communicates to us deeply, touching the depths of our soul. In the words of Hans Urs von Balthaser, "The beautiful ceases you, it changes you, and then it calls you and sends you."[8]

Father Thomas Dubay understands the power of beauty. Here, he highlights the power of music:

> We human beings are moved by music as no other animal is. Stranger still [music] moves us . . . apart from whether we can play it, read it, or even much understand it. *Music reaches the passions without passing through the mind* (italics added).[9]

Dubay understands that beauty speaks to us in ways that words, reasoning, and logic alone cannot. All of us know this at some level. We've all been touched deeply by the beauty of God's creation. We've all stood in silent awe, looking up into the night sky, observing the countless stars, planets, and distant galaxies. Their beauty, order, and regularity touch our emotions. Their magnificence and vast grandeur "speak" to us in a way that words alone cannot. "Creation is a book proclaiming the Creator," says Dubay. "It is a book of beauty that our intellect reads, but through the passageways of our five senses."[10]

The Psalmist puts it this way.

> The heavens declare the glory of God;
>   the skies proclaim the work of his hands.
> Day after day they pour forth speech;
>   night after night they reveal knowledge.
> They have no speech, they use no words;
>   no sound is heard from them.
> Yet their voice goes out into all the earth,
>   their words to the ends of the world. (Psalm 19:1–4)

Father Dubay correctly states that beauty draws people to God, like moths to a flame. Jerry Root and Stan Guthrie agree:

> Beauty is God's first, last, and most effective messenger. We learn that the world is good and orderly because of the beauty of [Creation], which we only later come to understand intellectually . . . we come to know God through His divine artistry.[11]

Consider the example of Whittaker Chambers (1901–1961). A former Communist Party member, Chambers was a hard-bitten atheist and Soviet spy during the Cold War. However, one morning in 1938, he was feeding his young daughter, and his gaze landed on her tiny ear. At that moment, he "concluded that the shape of her ear could not be explained by Marxist materialism. Something this beautiful and unique implied design, which implied the existence of God."[12] God spoke to Chambers through something as ordinary as the beauty and purposeful design of his daughter's ear in a way that words or arguments could not. Days later, he surrendered His life to Jesus Christ. As David Taylor says, beauty has a unique power "to do something that only it can do: generate longing, a longing that is satisfied supremely in the Source of all created beauties, Jesus Christ."[13]

Creating beauty

Beauty finds its source in God. In His character, His revealed word in Scripture, and His magnificent creation. As image-bearers of God, we, too, can be a source of beauty in this world through our character, actions, and creativity. Some of history's most beautiful human creations are expressions of worship of the living God.

The beauty we create begins with God, the source of all that is beautiful, and our discovery and imitation of His character and creative genius. As we carefully and deeply reflect on God's character, revealed Word, and creation, we can discover or derive ideas and principles that we apply to our creative work. In doing so, we imitate God in our creative endeavors and create more beauty, which pleases God and is a form of worship. The process begins and ends with God.

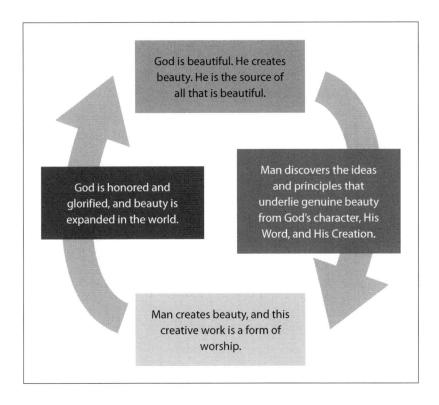

Let's explore this process further. What ideas and principles from God, His character, and His Word allow us to create what is beautiful? Here are a few:

God's Character

- Holiness, or moral perfection
- Love, compassion, grace
- Justice
- Faithful commitment
- Kindness, gentleness
- Patience, forgiveness
- Power, strength
- Courage
- Work, creativity

God's Creation

- **God loves unity and diversity.** For example, there is a unity to "flowers"; they all have certain core elements in common. Yet there is an incredible, almost infinite diversity of sizes, colors, designs, and more. We see this same unity and diversity everywhere in creation.
- **God creates with excellence of skill and craftsmanship.** Flawless perfection is the hallmark of God's creative work.
- **Human beings are uniquely beautiful.** Man (male and female) is the high point of God's creation and the only creature created in His image. Therefore, even though marred by the fall, we catch glimpses of humans' beauty and dignity.
- **God creates with great artistry.** His handiwork deeply stirs our emotions and speaks to us in a language that transcends words.
- **God's creation touches all of our senses.** We experience beauty in creation in a fully embodied way with our sight, hearing, touch, smell, and taste, as well as our spirit and emotions.
- **God creates order, not chaos.** His creation reflects deep purpose, order, and fine-tuned precision. We see it everywhere, from DNA molecules to the movements of stars to various scientific constants, including natural laws.
- **God communicates to us through His Creation.** God's creation speaks to us of His existence and His character. It points us back to Him (Romans 1:19–20, Psalm 19:1–4).

God's Word

- The Bible is the most powerful story ever told. It reveals the true story of reality—a love story of God and image-bearers that runs from creation to fall, redemption, and consummation. Redemption is the central theme, and the cross and resurrection are the climax.
- It is written in exquisite poetry, prose, and historical narrative, using a rich vocabulary and words that God alone defines.
- God is a master storyteller who uses a wide array of literary elements to teach us truth.

These are a few ideas and principles that underlie the genuine beauty derived from God and His creation. They form the basis for our creative endeavors and allow us to create beauty, imitating God and His work.

The beauty we manifest is a proper form of worship. Many evangelicals have a shriveled, incomplete view of work and creativity. As image-bearers of a beautiful, creative, working God, we honor and glorify Him through our creative work. Work is not a necessary evil that resulted from the fall, and worship is not accomplished primarily at a once-a-week church worship service.

The Hebrew word *Avodah* can be translated as either "work" or "worship." When done in imitation of God's beauty, our handiwork gives God honor and glory. It is a pleasing form of worship. It draws people to Him, just as Jane Lucretia D'Esterre was drawn powerfully to God through observing the artistry and excellence of a Scottish farmer.

In his short book *Tree and Leaf*, the great twentieth-century writer J. R. R. Tolkien describes some of the ideas and principles he derived from God, His Word, and His creation that He sought to imitate in the writing of his epic fantasy *The Lord of the Rings*. Here, he speaks about his "discovery" that the Bible has all the elements of a great fantasy or "fairy story," except that it is true.

> It is not difficult to imagine that the peculiar excitement and joy that one would feel, if any specially beautiful fairy-story were found to be . . . true, its narrative to be history, without thereby necessarily losing the mythical allegorical significance that it had possessed. . . . But this story [the Bible] is supreme, and it is true. Art has been verified. God is the Lord, of angels, and of men—and of elves. Legend and History have met and fused.[14]

So many biblical themes and ideas are expressed in Tolkien's masterpiece: good overcoming evil in unexpected ways (what he called "eucatastrophe," or a catastrophe that runs in reverse), sacrifice, death and resurrection, courage, friendship, providence, mercy (or "pity"), and the idea that even small, insignificant people can change the course of history.

He discovered all of these themes and ideas in the Holy Scriptures and, in a work of imitation, applied his human creativity, life experiences, and mastery of writing to bring them to life in his novels. Here, Tolkien talks about how he sought to imitate God through writing in the areas of excellence and artistry.

> It is because of who and what God is, it is because of the beauty and truth manifest in his Son, it is because of the perfection of his redeeming work, that evangelicals can never be content with the mediocre in aesthetics. Here, as in all else, the call is to the unremitting pursuit of excellence to the glory of the God of all truth.[15]

The result of Tolkien's imitation of God was the creation of a masterpiece. *The Lord of the Rings* is the third best-selling novel of all time.[16] As a work of great beauty, it moves people worldwide deeply and draws them to God.

Tolkien's friend and fellow writer C. S. Lewis also sought to imitate God in his writing. Here, he describes God as the source of all beauty and wisdom and how our greatest human creations are merely imitations and "reflections."

> . . . an author should never conceive of himself as bringing into existence beauty or wisdom which did not exist before, but simply and solely as trying to embody in terms of his own art some reflection of that eternal Beauty and Wisdom.[17]

This same understanding has inspired many of history's greatest artists. Consider Michelangelo and his priceless masterpiece, *David*, imitating God in near-flawless perfection and breathtaking artistry. The *David* displays the glory and beauty of man as God's image-bearer. Michelangelo draws us back to God by making the great Old Testament king his subject matter. Here, we see David in the prime of his life, from whose line Jesus, God incarnate, would take on human form to become King of kings and Lord of lords.

We can also think of Johann Sebastian Bach's musical works. He, too, sought to imitate God in the near-flawless perfection of his compositions and concertos. He composed with exquisite artistry, and his music still moves people deeply worldwide. He dedicated all of his works *Soli Deo Gloria*. To God alone be the glory. He was far from alone in his devotion to God, as expressed in his artistic endeavors.

The great theologian R. C. Sproul reminds us that about 85 percent of the work of two of the greatest painters of all time, Michelangelo and Rembrandt, centered on biblical themes.

Now consider some of the greatest writers of all time—Milton, Shakespeare, Dickens, Donne, Dostoyevsky, and Tolstoy. Out of those six, many would say that Shakespeare was the greatest. His work is filled with biblical allusions and imagery. The same is true of Milton, Dostoyevsky, and Donne.[18]

As the Bible transformed the West over the centuries, it produced one of the most beautiful cultures the world has ever known. Not only great artists but ordinary people have sought to imitate God as farmers, artisans, scientists, educators, and designers. You see the results as you travel through Europe and are stunned by its pristine landscape, beautiful farmlands, magnificent cathedrals, breathtaking architecture, and priceless works of art. Nearly all of it made to point beyond itself, to God.

And we find exquisite beauty, not only in cultures profoundly shaped by the Bible, like those in Europe and the West. Through careful observation of God's creation, many ideas and principles that underlie true beauty are available to people everywhere. As Romans 1:19–20 says,

> What may be known about God is plain to [people everywhere], because God has made it plain to them. For since the creation of the world God's invisible qualities—his eternal power and divine nature—have been clearly seen, being understood from what has been made.

From God's general revelation in creation, people worldwide have discovered and applied the principles of beauty. You see it in the masterful and profoundly moving artistry of a Japanese garden, in the vibrant colors and exquisite designs of West African fabrics, in the soaring architecture of the Taj Mahal in India, as well as in the sublime architecture of Oxford University.

These ideas and principles, rooted in God, are the basis for genuine, objective beauty. But, like all principles, they can be applied in various ways—in musical composition, architecture, sculpture, the culinary arts, sports, dance, gardening, writing, interior design, landscape design, agriculture, etc. The people who discover and apply them come from various cultural backgrounds and influences and have different gifts and personalities.

The result is a great variety of artistic styles and forms that are all genuinely beautiful. True beauty isn't one thing. It is *many* things. Naturally, some people will prefer some styles and forms to others, which is where personal aesthetic taste comes into play. However, to say that beauty is merely "in the eye of the beholder" ignores the objective reality that underlies all true beauty.

Many today, including lots of Christians, struggle with the idea of universal, objective standards of beauty. We have all absorbed, to some degree, the contemporary notion that beauty is entirely personal and subjective. In the words of Robert Florczak:

> The idea of a universal standard of quality in art is now usually met with strong resistance if not open ridicule . . . "And who will determine quality?" I often hear.

To this, he has a helpful rejoinder:

> If we are intellectually honest, we all know of situations where professional expertise are acknowledged and depended upon. Take figure skating in the Olympics, where experts in the field judge artistic excellence. Surely, we would flinch at the contestant who indiscriminately threw himself across the ice and demanded that his routine be accepted as being as worthy of value as that of the most disciplined skater.[19]

And yet, in the area of beauty and artistic endeavor, this kind of universal standard has been rejected.

COUNTERFEIT BEAUTY

Today, most people think of beauty as something entirely personal and subjective. We've reduced beauty to an outlet for individual expression or aesthetic tastes, with many contemporary artists "merely using their art to make statements, often for nothing more than shock value."[20]

We no longer believe beauty is an objective, transcendent reality; instead, *we* decide what is beautiful. As the British philosopher David Hume said: "Beauty in things exists merely in the mind which contemplates them."[21] We no longer see beauty as a moral necessity; instead, we see it as an optional decoration, ornament, or accessory. In the United States, in particular, the priority is on the pragmatic. The essential questions are "Does it work?" and "Is it functional?" Seldom do we ask, "Is it beautiful?"

BEAUTY REDEFINED

A combination of aesthetic qualities that appeal to one's personal, subjective senses or tastes. Beauty is entirely a matter of personal preference and individual expression.

HOW DID WE GET HERE?

We must go back to modernism and postmodernism's birth in eighteenth-century Europe, during what came to be known as the Enlightenment. As we've discussed in previous chapters, this period witnessed incredible scientific breakthroughs. Great mysteries of the physical world were being revealed one after the other.

These great discoveries stirred within certain leaders a proud rebellion against God. "We don't need to rely on God or turn to

Him to explain how things work, as our ancestors did in the former 'Dark Ages.' We don't need to appeal to myths and fairy tales to explain the universe's workings and human nature. Through science and human reason, we can know everything."

The tragic truth is a different story. Our ancient foe used these rapid advances in human knowledge to deceive us with his oldest lie:

> God knows that when you eat [the fruit of the forbidden tree] your eyes will be opened, and *you will be like God*, knowing good and evil. (Genesis 3:5, italics added)

That same lie rolls down through history into the present. It still says that we no longer need God. We can be God, determining good and evil, truth, beauty, and everything else.

The Enlightenment marked a significant turning point in Western history. While intellectual elites retained a notion of "God" as the creator or "first cause" for some decades, He was increasingly seen as distant, removed, and uninvolved in creation. However, even this limited role of God as "creator" was abandoned in the mid-1800s due to Darwin's theory of evolution. Darwin explained how God wasn't necessary for creation, and very rapidly, his theory was accepted as scientific fact. Today, the vast majority of Western elites no longer believe in God or the spiritual world. "Nature" has replaced Creation. All that exists is physical matter in a purposeless universe.

This Enlightenment rebellion against God had a particularly profound effect in France. The famous French philosopher Rousseau (1712–1778), who rejected the Christian doctrine of original sin, laid the ideological foundation for the French Revolution—a political and theological revolution.

The French Revolutionaries succeeded in overthrowing not only the monarchy but also an increasingly corrupt Catholic Church authority. It culminated in 1793 at a ceremony held in the most revered Catholic cathedral in France, Notre Dame, where a literal statue of the "goddess of reason" was erected before the altar. The symbolism couldn't be more explicit. Enlightened human reason had replaced God.

Today, France is one of the world's most secular countries. Ideas have consequences, and among other profound consequences, the Enlightenment rebellion against God significantly affected how people thought about art and beauty.

Artist and Art Historian Robert Florzak explains:

> Beginning in the late nineteenth-century France, a group dubbed The Impressionists rebelled against the . . . classical standards of beauty [rooted in Christian ideas and principles]. Whatever their intentions, the new modernists sowed the seeds of aesthetic relativism—the "beauty is in the eye of the beholder" mentality. Today, everybody loves the Impressionists. And, as with most revolutions, the first generation or so produced work of genuine merit. Monet, Renoir, and Degas still maintained elements of disciplined design and execution, but with each new generation, standards declined *until there were no standards. All that was left was personal expression.* (italics added)[22]

The Impressionist rebellion against the former "classical standards" of beauty rooted in God and Creation marked a turning point in Western art and creativity. These artistic revolutionaries threw out objective, transcendent standards for beauty but offered nothing to replace them beyond individual preference and personal expression.

The "classical standards" for beauty	The modern and postmodern rejection of classical standards
Begins with God	Rejects God and begins with man
Based on objective reality	Based on subjective personal expression
Inspires, uplifts, and deepens	Leads to hopelessness and despair
Constructive and transformational	Destructive and de-formational
The soul is edified	Damages the human spirit

How has this rejection of biblical standards of beauty played itself out over the past two centuries? Today, the EDEN Gallery, a global network of high-end art galleries, defines postmodern art this way: "Postmodernist artists have stretched the meaning of art to embrace the idea that 'anything can be art.'"[23] The idea that art isn't about beauty; it's about personal, individual expression is almost universally accepted. That expression can be hideous, but it is still "art."

Take the famous example of American artist Andres Serrano. In 1987, he unveiled his so-called work of art called "Piss Christ." It depicts a plastic crucifix submerged in a glass tank of the artist's urine. The National Endowment for the Arts sponsored his creative work, for which he won numerous awards.

Many objected, claiming, "There's nothing beautiful about this. It isn't art. It's hideous and blasphemous." But they were ridiculed and told they had no right to make such judgments. After all, "beauty is in the eye of the beholder."

According to Robert Florczak,

The profound, the inspiring, and the beautiful [have now been] replaced by the new, the different, and the ugly. . . . The former, classical standards, gave the world "The Birth of Venus" and "The Dying Gaul," while modern and postmodern standards have given us "The Holy Virgin Mary," fashioned with cow dung and pornographic images, and "Petra," the prize-winning sculpture of a policewoman squatting and urinating—complete with a puddle of synthetic urine.[24]

When we reject God, we not only lose objective truth and goodness, but we lose objective beauty as well. Much of today's creative expression is little more than open rebellion against God, the source of all beauty. As a result, it moves towards the hideous, repulsive, repellent, and grotesque.

This rebellion against classical standards has ripples that extend far beyond the fine arts. Today, they shape how we think about creativity in nearly every realm of human endeavor, from urban planning to architecture to literature, music, education, and beyond.

We see the bitter fruits everywhere. Many of our major cities, from Portland, Oregon, to Santiago, Chile, are now filled with graffiti, their streets littered with trash and even human excrement. Abandoned buildings with boarded-up windows line streets—a previous generation's magnificent architecture and urban design thoroughly despoiled. Darrow recalls walking through the dusty, dirty streets of the former Soviet Union, where the apartment buildings were "falling apart, dreary, and gray. They looked more like prison cells than homes."

When we reject God, beauty fades away, and we are left only with ugliness. That is a world in which no human being should ever want to live. The consequences of a world shorn of beauty are enormous and soul-destroying.

How has the evangelical church responded? Sadly, not by vigorously defending and preserving the classical standard of beauty and its magnificent legacy but mainly by ignoring it and dismissing beauty as an unimportant subject.

For more than a century, the Bible-believing church has suffered under a theology of disengagement and separation from the culture. This theology emerged as a reaction to the increasing secularization of the West, particularly in the United States. To its champions, the increasingly secular world is doomed to judgment and utter annihilation. Therefore, the church's mission is to evangelize, plant churches, and attempt to rescue people from what one Christian writer described as "The Late, Great Planet Earth."

According to this theology, the risen Jesus has authority in heaven and the church but nowhere else. Christian cultural engagement, or efforts to influence culture based on Christian principles, are frowned upon, including the creative work of Christians in the culture. The only work that has any real eternal significance is work in the church or the areas of missions and outreach as a "full-time Christian worker." Everyone else's work has little value beyond providing money to support these full-time Christian workers.

As the bible-believing church gave up its historic mission to be salt and light, creating and shaping culture based on biblical ideas and principles, those advocating non-Christian systems of belief found virtually no opposition to their efforts to shape the institutions of the culture in ways that aligned with their destructive beliefs.

While Christians lost their vision to influence culture, those advocating secular ideologies like Marxism and postmodernism did not. To their credit, they have successfully "discipled the nations" of the West, as evidenced by the fact that their core ideas and first principles are firmly ensconced in our most important cultural institutions.

As my friend Darrow says, "If the church doesn't disciple the nation, the nation will disciple the church." Someone is always actively shaping the culture. If it is not the church with true ideas rooted in the Bible, it will be others with false and destructive ideas, and when this happens, things become chaotic and fall apart.

When false beliefs are at the foundation of our cultural institutions, particularly our educational institutions, Christians are not immune from their influence. The church is not separate from the culture but is *in* the culture as teachers, farmers, business people, designers, artisans, architects, and artists. If the Bible has nothing to say about these areas of human endeavor, as this faulty theology implies, and if false modern and postmodern ideas and principles are at their foundation, it should come as no surprise that many Christians absorb them, and this is certainly true when it comes to beauty.

The evangelical church has largely lost the biblical truth about beauty. Instead, we've largely absorbed the false modern and postmodern ideas about beauty. Today, most Christians believe that beauty is entirely subjective, a matter of personal taste, and nothing more. They have lost any sense of beauty's objective, transcendent nature, or they simply ignore beauty or act like it doesn't matter. According to Darrow Miller,

> Many churches today view art as nothing more than decoration, or perhaps an enhancement for their worship or evangelism programs. They see it as a "church thing" and no more—nice to have, but not essential. . . . Perhaps they view art as frivolous, a waste of money, or worldly.[25]

Take, for example, our church buildings. With rare exceptions, evangelical and charismatic churches too often focus on the merely functional—the most space for the least money. We see far too many churches that look like warehouses. Many, in fact, are just that. The same applies to our worship music, which typically imitates popular standards in the culture with their increasingly low standards of excellence.

For Christian artists, designers, artisans, and other creatives, our theology of cultural separation and disengagement has left them feeling abandoned, believing falsely that their creative gifts and talents have little use outside of church worship services or as entertainment for other Christians.

Thankfully, this is changing, as a few courageous Christian filmmakers, artists, artisans, and musicians are recovering the rich biblical tradition of beauty. Incredible opportunities await those with the vision to create genuine beauty amid a world filled with the hideous and profane.

HOW SHOULD WE THEN LIVE?

As followers of Jesus, the source of all beauty, let's do what we can to recover a proper, biblical understanding of beauty. As Christ's ambassadors, our calling is to represent Him truthfully. We can't do that without showing forth His beauty in all of its radiant splendor. The world is hungry for beauty. After all, says Cynthia Pearl Maus:

> The universal love of beauty is one of the resources of human life that Christianity ought to pervade with its spirit and claim as its own. It is to this instinctive love of the beautiful that the artist makes his appeal and gets therefore, a wider hearing for the truth that is present in this universally loved form.[26]

Here are several ideas on how each of us can display the good, true, and beautiful.

Examine your thinking

Start with your own assumptions about beauty. Most of us have assumed that beauty is entirely subjective and not an objective, universal reality rooted in God's nature.

Another all-too-common assumption for evangelical Christians is that beauty isn't essential and has nothing to do with gospel proclamation. We know we are to speak the truth and reject lies. We know we are to do what is morally right or virtuous and reject what is sinful, immoral, and unjust. But do we know equally well that we are to create and celebrate beauty and reject the hideous, and that this is as important as the first two?

If these false assumptions describe your thinking, repentance is the first step. As we've said in previous chapters, repentance literally means "to change your mind." Change the way you think. Take your thoughts captive and make them obedient to Christ (2 Corinthians 10:5). Recognize and embrace the truth that beauty is as central to God's essence as truth, goodness, or moral perfection. Treating beauty as optional is to betray a profoundly faulty understanding of God. If our knowledge of God is defective, so too will be our witness of Him in the world. In fact, beauty may be the most potent and strategic gospel witness in this generation.

Beauty in everyday life

If beauty is a moral necessity, how can we bring more of it into our lives? Here are some simple ideas:

Bring order and beauty to your personal spaces. Beauty is associated with cleanliness and orderliness. Jordan Peterson famously taught young people that to bring order into their lives, they should start by "making their bed." That's good advice that applies to beauty as well. Create beauty in your personal spaces, such as your apartment, bedroom, or home, and start by getting things in order. Put things away, hang up your clothes, clean, and set your place in order. Make this a habit and part of your routine.

Beautify your outdoor spaces. Do you have a yard or garden overrun with weeds and plants that need trimming? Can you do some simple, inexpensive landscaping to bring beauty to your space? Work to transform your outdoor spaces, no matter how small, into something beautiful.

How about your own body? Do you have good personal hygiene habits? Are you caring for your body well? What improvements can you make here?

Cultivate inner beauty. Remember, too, that genuine beauty is both inner and outer. Are you cultivating the inner beauty the apostle Peter spoke of? This is a spirit of gentleness, humility, and genuine love for your family, friends, and neighbors.

Plant and display flowers. "One of the things I love about living in Switzerland," Darrow said, "is the celebration of beauty in the form of flower boxes on the windows."

> No matter how humble the farmhouse, color explodes in all the window boxes every spring. This custom serves no practical purpose. These plants can't be eaten. They are just beautiful. There is such a need for this understanding of beauty in all of our lives and the life of our communities.[27]

Darrow also recalls how Larry Ward, the founder of Food for the Hungry, used to say, "Food for the Hungry should be known as the relief and development organization that plants flowers in refugee camps."[28] We should plant flowers in places of displacement, drabness, poverty, suffering, and death because they point us to grace and to its divine Source. Pointing to the heavenly Father's care, Jesus said, "Consider the lilies, how they grow: they neither toil nor spin, yet I tell you, even Solomon in all his glory was not arrayed like one of these" (Luke 12:27, ESV).

So make it a regular practice to bring beauty into the "small places" of home, work, school, and neighborhood. God made us to create and welcome beauty into the fabric of our lives. Music is for our ears, painting for the eyes, meals for the eyes and palate, dance for the body, and sculpture for the eyes and touch. From the grand scale of a cityscape to the delicate flowers planted in a window box, let's infuse beauty into the places we touch. There is no such thing as too much beauty. God made our souls to delight in it, treasure it, rejoice in it, and share it with the world.

Care for God's beautiful creation

God's magnificent creation is a source of immense beauty, so we should care for it. But, sadly, this simple idea has become controversial in the church. Many Christians understandably react against environmentalists who often operate from neo-pagan and anti-human assumptions and worship "nature" as a god. Others react against the increasingly shrill cries about an impending "climate catastrophe." As a result, many of us simply choose to avoid the subject. But reacting against non-Christian ideologies or movements isn't helpful. Instead, let's recover a genuine ethic of creation rooted in some basic biblical principles that we all can agree on.

First, it is creation, not "nature" or "the environment." God's magnificent handiwork displays intricate artistry, design, order, and diversity. He created it both beautiful and bountiful. "The Lord God made all kinds of trees grow out of the ground—trees that were pleasing to the eye and good for food" (Genesis 2:9).

Second, God loves His creation. He is not indifferent to it. He declares that it is "very good" (Genesis 1:31). He rejoices in His creation (Psalm 104:31), and He cares for it (Psalm 104:10–18; 27–28). We should see it the same way God does.

Third, He created us in His image to have dominion over His creation (Genesis 1:26; 28) and to steward His creation. In Genesis 2:15, we read, "The Lord God took the man and put him in the Garden of Eden to work it and take care of it." To "care for" means to protect and preserve creation carefully and treat it like a magnificent work of art. To "work it" means that God invites us to join Him in His creative enterprise by expanding the garden. He gave us the ability to apply our creativity to His creation and develop ever more beautiful and productive innovations. In the words of Michael Novak:

> Humans are called to be co-creators with God, bringing forth the potentialities the Creator has hidden. Creation is full of secrets waiting to be discovered, riddles which human intelligence is expected by the Creator to unlock. The world did not spring from the hand of God as wealthy [or as beautiful] as humans might make it.[29]

Humans are not a blight upon creation, as Sir David Attenborough, the narrator of the documentary series *Life on Earth*, contends. He recently spewed that humans "are a plague on the earth" and "behind every threat [to wildlife] is the frightening explosion in human numbers."[30] This way of thinking about our fellow humans leads to catastrophic consequences. It isn't uncommon for powerful people to talk openly about their desire to reduce the global population by several billion to "save the environment."[31]

No, we are the crescendo of God's creative work and have a vital role in creation. People like Attenborough don't understand that God gave us the unique capacity to leave God's creation even more beautiful and productive than we found it. Now it is true that, as fallen rebels, we also destroy, despoil, pollute, and rape God's creation for selfish ends. Still, as redeemed children of God, we can recover our original task as wise stewards of creation, causing it to be "liberated from its bondage to decay" (Romans 8:21).

As Psalm 119:4 says, God's creation "speaks" to people everywhere about His existence, power, and goodness. We should allow it to speak and do our part to amplify His voice.

Here are a few simple ways. Pick up trash wherever you find it as you walk down the street. Bring beauty to your community by cleaning up trash in public spaces. Organize clean-up parties to paint over graffiti and clear the heaps of rubbish and refuse in your community.

Create genuine beauty

For those whose vocation involves creative work, including artisans, filmmakers, designers, musicians, chefs, photographers, writers, and artists, you have a vital role to play in God's Kingdom. In the stirring words of Landa Cope:

> Whether you are gifted in body, ear, or eye, your gift is a celebration of God and a part of the call of God on your life. . . . So, whether you are celebrating the use of your gift in the church's work to minister to Christians or to minister to the many who do not go to church, you are ministering Christ. . . . You don't have to justify your gift by doing religious material. . . . Your gift is justified because it is part of who God is and how He has made you. . . . The world needs your gift and the celebration of beauty and joy it brings. Do not hold back! Let's begin the new renaissance.[32]

In recent years, Christian artists and creators have earned a reputation (whether fairly or not) for inferior work that copies trends in pop culture and adds a "Christianizing" element, such as a gospel message or biblical themes. With a few exceptions, most leading writers, painters, novelists, musicians, composers, filmmakers, and architects are non-Christians. But we, of all people, should be producing works of the highest quality and most excellent beauty. The God we worship is the source of all beauty! We should make it our mission to honor Him in our creative work.

Instead of imitating pop culture with inferior quality, let's intentionally base our creative work on the objective, universal principles of beauty we discussed earlier. Continue to grow in discovering these principles and deepening your knowledge of them. Create genuine beauty that will stand out for its artistry and excellence, motivated by a deep desire to honor God and display His glory to a dying world. Just think about the kind of impact this would have on the culture.

Of all people, Christians have the greatest motivation to work for excellence. The apostle Paul instructs, "Whatever you do, work at it with all your heart, as working for the Lord, not for human masters" (Colossians 3:23), and "Whatever you do, do it all for the glory of God."

Pastors, equip and honor the artists, designers, and artisans in your congregation.

Because many evangelical churches operate from a theology of disengagement and separation from the culture, the message to Christians in the pews is that their work in the culture has little value. Music, film, art, and design are seen as worldly endeavors with little intrinsic importance. Christian creators, artists, designers, and artisans are relegated to second-class citizenship in church life. For their work to have any value, it must be done with spiritual or religious themes or employed inside the church, in worship or outreach.

This whole way of thinking about Christianity urgently needs to change. God calls people into various vocations. There are no second-class Christian vocations. Pastors' role is to equip their congregations to apply biblical principles to their vocations to honor Christ, serve their neighbors, and bless our nations.

The God we serve is the source of all beauty; therefore, the church should be a fountainhead of beauty in the culture. So pastors must envision, encourage, and equip the artisans, artists, and designers in their congregations to fulfill their calling. This kind of encouragement and training is more important than ever because, in our postmodern society, beauty communicates the truth about God in a way that reason, logic, and debate rarely do.

Make beauty central in communicating the gospel.

When God communicates with us, He does so using language and reason (logos), our moral conscience (ethos), and our feelings and emotions through beauty (pathos). The church has rightly focused on the proclamation of the truth, particularly the gospel message, using the helpful tools of Christian apologetics (logos). We've also communicated on issues of sin and morality (ethos). However, we've almost entirely neglected beauty (pathos) in our witness. This neglect is partly due to a pragmatic view of missions: Proclaim the gospel, save people, and plant churches. Anything else is a distraction.

But beauty is anything but a distraction when it comes to communicating truthfully about God. For people steeped in postmodern assumptions—who deny objective truth and objective morality, trying to reason about these subjects using words and logic has little impact. However, beauty speaks like a trumpet blast at the opening of a symphony. In the words of Bishop Robert Barron:

> I think the best way to evangelize . . . is to move from the beautiful then to the good then to the true. And to get that backward is often to evangelize very ineffectively."[33]

When Christians communicate the gospel in this order, they have the opportunity to quench the soul-thirst of many people with Christ's living water, offer a compelling preview of the heavenly banquet to come, and, in so doing, fulfill the Great Commission.

The power of beauty in communicating truth is an insight shared by the great Soviet dissident Aleksandr Solzhenitsyn. In 1970, he was awarded the Nobel Prize for Literature. In his acceptance speech, he drew attention to another great Russian author, Fyodor

Dostoevsky, and a profound but puzzling remark he once made about beauty:

> One day, Dostoevsky threw out the enigmatic remark: "Beauty will save the world." What sort of a statement is that? For a long time I considered it mere words. How could that be possible? When in bloodthirsty history did beauty ever save anyone from anything? Ennobled, uplifted, yes—but whom has it saved?
>
> . . . But those works of art which have scooped up the truth and presented it to us as a living force—they take hold of us, compel us, and nobody ever, not even in ages to come, will appear to refute them. So perhaps that ancient trinity of Truth, Goodness, and Beauty is not simply an empty, faded formula as we thought in the days of our self-confident, materialistic youth. If the tops of these three trees converge, as the scholars maintained, but the too blatant, too direct stems of Truth and Goodness are crushed, cut down, not allowed through— then perhaps the fantastic, unpredictable, unexpected stems of Beauty will push through and soar to that very same place, and in so doing will fulfill the work of all three. In that case, Dostoevsky's remark, "Beauty will save the world," was not a careless phrase but a prophecy. After all, he was granted to see much, a man of fantastic illumination.[34]

Beauty is truth, truth is beauty.

JOHN KEATS

CHAPTER 10

LOVE

And now these three remain: faith, hope and love.
But the greatest of these is love.

Beloved, let us love one another, for love is from God,
and whoever loves has been born of God and knows God
. . . because God is love.

LOVE

(1) A source of pleasure, joy, or delight. (2) A strong affection, often accompanied by romantic feelings and sexual attraction. (3) To value, cherish, or treasure. (4) Fidelity and devotion. Faithful commitment. (5) To seek the good of another, to give for his or her benefit, even at a significant personal cost.

LOVE REDEFINED

(1) A source of pleasure, joy, or delight. (2) A strong affection, often accompanied by romantic feelings and sexual attraction.

In his book, *The Rise of Christianity*,[1] social scientist Rodney Stark asks how a tiny group of 120 persecuted, rejected, oppressed, and reviled Christians (see Acts 1:14) could transform Rome from a pagan culture to a Christian empire in just three hundred years?

Stark discovered the answer: The radical new beliefs held by the Christians brought about a whole new vision of humanity. In pagan Rome, the gods certainly did not love the people who worshiped them. But the Christians believed in a God who, for the first time in human history, loved those who loved Him. Not only that, but He also required that those who loved Him love others and even love their enemies.

A second critical belief was that the Christian God was merciful and required His followers to show mercy. Mercy was almost unheard of in Roman paganism. Rome was well-known for its cruelty. Stark describes an emperor who sent gladiators into the Coliseum to kill each other so that his son could experience the shedding of blood to the death as a celebration of his coming into manhood.

A third critical belief was that culture should be stripped of ethnic and class segregation. In early Christian worship services, a nobleman and an enslaved person would come together to worship God as brothers. In Roman culture, this idea was completely absurd.

A fourth critical idea was that men should love their wives as they loved themselves. Everybody in the Roman world *knew* that men were superior to women. Roman men owned their wives and their children. They could kill their children without legal consequence because the children were mere property. But in this new Christian religion, you were to love your wife and children as you loved yourself.

Christians also rejected abortion and infanticide. Stark quotes a letter from a Roman soldier who had been recently married and was on the battlefront. He wrote home to his wife and said, "Darling, I miss you so much. I'm so glad you're pregnant." He said, "If it's a boy, take care of it and nurture it. If it's a girl, set it outside and let it die. Love, Your Husband."

That was typical. But in this new religion, all of life—whether disabled, whether an unborn baby, whether girl or boy, whether slave or nobleman—was sacred.

Finally, Christians loved people whether they were Christian or not, especially during times of sickness. Christians stressed love and charity as central duties of faith, seen most clearly during the epidemics that swept through the Roman world.

When someone in a home contracted the dreaded illness, other family members fled for their lives, leaving the sick alone. But Christians, rather than flee, drew near, caring tenderly and often contracting the illness as a result. They did this not only when their own became ill but also with people outside their community.

Why? Because the God they worshiped loved them, drew near to them, and gave Himself for them, even to the point of death. They were simply following His example.

They also seemingly had no fear of death because their Savior rose from the dead and promised that He would raise them from the grave as well.

Stark notes that a sick person's chances of survival improved significantly with minimal care. Not only this, but those who survived likely converted to the Christian faith. In a short time, many Roman citizens converted, abandoned their pagan beliefs, and embraced the beliefs, value system, and practices of the Christ-followers.

In AD 40, there were only one thousand believers in the Roman world. Stark estimates that by AD 300, the number was six million. Constantine legalized Christianity and paved the way for it to become the state religion in AD 381. The love shown by the Christians transformed the Roman world.

TRUTH ABOUT LOVE

The Supremacy of Love

Of all the words explored in this book, love is the most important because it is the vital center of God's character. The apostle John used the word *love* to describe the essence of God's nature.

> Beloved, let us love one another, for *love is from God*, and whoever loves has been born of God and knows God . . . because *God is love*. (1 John 4:7–8, ESV, italics added)

Jesus underscored the supremacy of love by elevating it to "the greatest commandment," our highest moral duty.

> Love the Lord your God with all your heart and with all your soul and with all your mind. This is the first and greatest commandment. (Matthew 22:37-38)

The apostle Paul reiterated Christ's words in Romans 13:8–10, declaring that "love is the fulfillment of the law." Paul penned the most important words ever written on the subject in his magnificent exposition in 1 Corinthians 13.

> If I speak in the tongues of men and of angels, but have not love, I am a noisy gong or a clanging cymbal. And if I have prophetic powers, and understand all mysteries and all knowledge, and if I have all faith, so as to remove mountains, but have not love, I am nothing. If I give away all I have, and if I deliver up my body to be burned, but have not love, I gain nothing. (1 Corinthians 13:1–3, ESV)

He concluded with these immortal words: "And now these three remain: faith, hope and love. *But the greatest of these is love*" (1 Corinthians 13:13, italics added).

Paul also places love first on his famous list of the "fruit of the Spirit" in Galatians 5:22–23, ESV:

> The fruit of the Spirit is love, joy, peace, patience, kindness, goodness, faithfulness, gentleness and self-control.

Again, we see the centrality of love in perhaps the most well-known Bible verse of all, John 3:16:

> For God so loved the world that he gave his one and only Son, that whoever believes in him shall not perish but have eternal life.

There is no more critical word—no more important concept—than love, so nothing could be more important than understanding it as clearly as possible.

What Is Love?

The word "love" can be challenging to define because we use it to describe our feelings about objects as varied as pizza, beautiful sunsets, a spouse, or God. To make sense of this, consider that when we say, "I love pizza," we use the word in a shallow but not necessarily false way. However, we are in much deeper waters when we speak about God's love for us, our love for our children, or what it means to love your enemies.

> **LOVE**
> (1) A source of pleasure, joy, or delight. (2) A strong affection, often accompanied by romantic feelings and sexual attraction. (3) To value, cherish, or treasure. (4) Fidelity and devotion. Faithful commitment. (5) To seek the good of another, to give for his or her benefit, even at a significant personal cost.

At the shallow end, love describes things we enjoy or delight in. As we move toward the deeper end, love describes our relationships with people we hold dear and long to be near. At the deepest end, love transcends personal desires and involves pursuing another person's highest good, even at a significant cost. This selflessness is what makes love so beautiful and powerful.

So, how do we begin to define such a deep, rich, and multi-layered word as love? It helps to understand that love, like a priceless diamond, has various facets. These facets can appear contradictory, but each is essential and overlapping, and together, they form a magnificent whole.

Let's look at each of these facets in order. But let's also remember that discarding any facet damages the richness of the concept. Also, remember that the aspects are not disconnected silos. They build on one another.

THE FIVE FACETS OF LOVE

1. We love what gives us pleasure, joy, and delight.
Noah Webster highlights this facet in the definition of love in his 1828 Dictionary of the American Language:

> To be pleased with; to regard with affection, on account of some qualities which excite pleasing sensations or desire of gratification . . . In short, *we love whatever gives us pleasure and delight.* (italics added)

Antonyms for this aspect of love include *despise*, *abhor*, and *loathe*.

We cannot understand love apart from emotions such as joy, happiness, and delight. We see their deep connection in Bible passages such as Zephaniah 3:17:

> [God] will take great delight in you;
> > in his love He will no longer rebuke you,
> > but will rejoice over you with singing.

Still, some will claim that genuine love has nothing to do with feelings or emotions. We often hear that "love is not a feeling but an act of the will." There is truth in this. At times love requires hard choices and sacrifices. But even then, joy will surely follow for actions done in love.

Consider that Jesus paid the ultimate price to redeem those He loved, even though we were His enemies (Romans 5:10). While there was no joy in those hours of painful suffering, joy followed:

> For the joy set before Him, [Jesus] endured the cross,
> scorning its shame, and sat down at the right hand of the
> throne of God. (Hebrews 12:2)

Our heavenly Father, who loves us supremely, wants us to experience "joy to the full" (John 15:11). Our well-intentioned attempts to separate love from emotions such as joy and delight damage the richness of the concept. They lower Christianity into something akin to Buddhism or Stoicism, which encourage adherents to deny and suppress their emotions.

If you think that a faithful Christian life is limited to joyless obedience and duty, you are missing out. Jesus proclaimed: "I have come that they may have life, and have it to the full" (John 10:10). Love is inseparable from joy and delight.

2. We love those for whom we feel deep affection.

A second universal aspect of love is affection. We love those for whom we feel deep affection or close attachment. We love people we long to be near, spend time with, and develop intimate relationships with. This facet of love describes the feelings of a parent for a child, among close friends, or in marriage.

Words that express the opposite of this aspect of love include not hatred but apathy and indifference.

The Hebrew word *yada*, translated into English as "to know," captures this aspect of love. Yada describes a close, warm affection rooted in a deep desire to know another person intimately. It is a face-to-face closeness that sometimes refers to sexual intimacy; for example, "Adam knew [*yada*] his wife Eve, and she conceived and bore Cain" (Genesis 4:1, ESV). An entire biblical book, the Song of Solomon, celebrates this aspect of love.

> Let him kiss me with the kisses of his mouth—for your
> love is more delightful than wine. (1:2)

You have captivated my heart, my sister, my bride; you have captivated my heart with one glance of your eyes. (4:9, ESV)

We should be deeply grateful that God created us with the capacity to experience strong feelings and emotions and feel intense joy, pleasure, affection, and delight in our loving relationships with others.

Yada is also used to describe God's love toward us. He desires to be known by us intimately, in a "face-to-face" way. This is how He revealed Himself to Moses (Exodus 33:11). It is also why He left His heavenly throne and came to earth in the person of Jesus. He longed to be near and reveal Himself to us. To hold us in His arms and wash our feet. To heal us. God loves you more deeply than you realize or could ever dream of.

3. We love what we value, cherish, and treasure.

The next facet of love concerns value and worth. We love that which we treasure. The opposite of this aspect of love is to treat others as insignificant or worthless.

Genuine love is based upon a God-ordained system of value and worth. The greater the value, the greater the priority of our love. God determines the relative value of people and things. He established this system of value at creation.

When our loves are rightly ordered, we flourish, but when they are disordered, things fall apart. Loving other people or things more than God is idolatry and is profoundly destructive. We'll explore this critical aspect of love in more detail later in the chapter.

4. We love that to which we are faithfully committed.

The next aspect of love is committed faithfulness. Antonyms for this aspect of love include disloyalty, betrayal, and unfaithfulness.

God's love expresses itself in His faithful commitment, even to those who reject and turn away from Him. As the apostle Paul said in 2 Timothy 2:13, ESV, even "if we are faithless, [God] remains faithful—for He cannot deny himself."

The biblical concept of covenant, an irrevocable promise of fidelity, is an essential characteristic of love. God expresses His love for His people in the Old and New Testaments in promises of unbreakable devotion or covenants.

> I have loved you with an everlasting love;
>> therefore I have continued my faithfulness to you.
> (Jeremiah 31:3, ESVB)

> [Nothing] in all creation, will be able to separate us from the
> love of God in Christ Jesus our Lord. (see Romans 8:35–39)

We also see this glorious facet of love beautifully expressed in the love that Ruth has for her mother-in-law, Naomi, whom she refuses to leave after tragedy befalls both women:

> Don't urge me to leave you or to turn back from you. Where
> you go I will go, and where you stay I will stay. Your people
> will be my people and your God my God. Where you die I
> will die, and there I will be buried. (Ruth 1:16–17)

A beautiful picture of this aspect of love is the promise of lifelong fidelity, "for better or worse . . . till death do us part," is the centerpiece of the traditional Christian marriage vow.

5. To love is to seek the good of another, even at a significant personal cost.

Now we delve into the final and most profound dimension of love. Theologian Wayne Grudem characterizes it as "self-giving for the benefit of others,"[2] a sentiment echoed by Bible teacher Paul David Tripp, who defines it as "willing self-sacrifice for the good of another that does not require reciprocation or that the person being loved is deserving."[3]

This love, called *agape* in the New Testament, is the pinnacle of love, and the highest form of *agape* is a willingness to sacrifice your own life for the sake of another. There is no greater love than this.

> Greater love has no one than this, that someone lay down his life for his friends. (John 15:13, ESV)

This selfless, self-sacrificing love is the cornerstone of biblical Christianity. It is not just a sentiment but a powerful force that has the potential to transform lives and communities.

Let's compare this aspect of love with its antonyms. Arrogant, self-absorbed narcissism stands as the antithesis of selfless love. The opposite of selfless, other-serving love is the dehumanization and exploitation of others for selfish gain.

Jesus highlighted *agape* in the story of the Good Samaritan, in which he defined "neighbor love" as other-focused, compassionate, sacrificial giving for the good of another, even a stranger or an enemy.

Jesus exemplified this kind of selfless love throughout His life. He actively sought out the blind, the lame, the sinner, and the diseased. He empathized with them, reached out to them, forgave them, and healed them. The pinnacle of His love was His sacrificial death on the cross. As the apostle John wrote:

> This is how we know what love is: Jesus Christ laid down his life for us." (1 John 3:16)

We are not just encouraged to do this but are *called* to emulate this selfless love.

Agape love is utterly foreign to our fallen world. It finds its source in God, as revealed in Scripture, and nowhere else. When we follow the example of Jesus and put this love into action, there is immense transformational power, as the opening illustration of this chapter highlights.

BIBLICAL WORDS FOR LOVE

In the New Testament, the most common Greek word translated into English as "love" is *agape*, which appears more than two hundred times. *Agape* love is a love of choice that requires faithfulness, commitment, and sacrifice without expecting anything in return. It describes Christ's sacrificial service for fallen people, most fully displayed through His atoning death on the cross. Here's one example found in 1 John 4:10:

> This is love [agape]: not that we loved God, but that he loved us and sent his Son as an atoning sacrifice for our sins.

In the Old Testament, the Hebrew word *hesed* is translated into English as "love" or "lovingkindness." It appears 246 times in the Hebrew Scriptures. We see it, for example, in Psalm 103:8, an oft-repeated description of God in the Old Testament.

> The Lord is compassionate and gracious, slow to anger, abounding in love [*hesed*].

Hesed is synonymous with goodness, kindness, faithfulness, mercy, and compassion. God's hesed is unchanging, consistent, steadfast, and unfailing. As the repeated refrain of Psalm 136 declares, "His love [*hesed*] endures forever."

God's love, as revealed in Scripture, is deeper and more profound than we can fully understand. Where human love is imperfect, God's love is perfect.

THE CHARACTERISTICS OF LOVE (1 CORINTHIANS 13)

What does *agape*, or the most profound form of love, look like in everyday terms? The apostle Paul paints a marvelous picture for us in 1 Corinthians 13:4–7.

> Love is patient, love is kind. It does not envy, it does not boast, it is not proud. It does not dishonor others, it is not self-seeking, it is not easily angered, it keeps no record of wrongs. Love does not delight in evil but rejoices with the truth. It always protects, always trusts, always hopes, always perseveres.

According to the great apostle, *agape* is characterized by faithfulness, commitment, and devotion. It is "patient" and "not easily angered." It isn't overly sensitive or quick to take offense but rather "keeps no record of wrongs." It shows grace and forgiveness and is always ready to reconcile.

It "always trusts." It is ready to extend trust and will work toward rebuilding it when violated. It is "always persevering," even through difficult times. It doesn't easily quit or give up on a relationship but "always hopes."

Love treats others with dignity and respect. It is "kind" and "does not dishonor others." It looks for the good in others and not just their faults and shortcomings. It "always protects" the worth, dignity, reputation, and God-given rights of others.

Agape love is not "proud," selfish, "self-seeking," or self-centered. It "does not envy" when good things or success come to others, nor does it "boast" over one's successes. Instead, it fixes its eyes on others and not on self. It sets itself to work for the good of others.

Genuine love is firmly rooted in truth, as revealed in God's Word and His creation. Love opposes lies and deceptions but "rejoices in the truth," including moral truth. It "does not delight in evil" but rejoices in what is just, upright, and morally good.

GOD IS THE SOURCE OF LOVE

Where does love come from? Not from the often-selfish character of the pagan gods, such as those from ancient Greece or Rome, or in the lives and teachings of the Buddha or Muhammad. It is entirely absent from the secular, materialistic worldview rooted in Darwinism and the "survival of the fittest." No, love finds its source in God and nowhere else. We would have no concept of it apart from Him.

God is not an impersonal power, force, idea, or philosophical "prime mover." He is a *person*. To love someone and be loved in return are characteristics of free, personal beings, which is what God is. Because God exists at the foundation of all things, the universe is ultimately personal, and love is the most elemental reality of all. Secularism is a lie. The most fundamental reality is not matter, energy, or the will to power—it is *love*.

We learn about love from God's written revelation and the living example of Jesus Christ. We see the centrality of love to God's character in His profound revelation of Himself to Moses on Mount Sinai. There, He proclaimed His Name, which revealed His essential character:

> Then the Lord came down in the cloud and stood there with him and proclaimed his name, the Lord. And he passed in front of Moses, proclaiming, "The Lord, the Lord, the compassionate and gracious God, slow to anger, *abounding in love* and faithfulness, *maintaining love to thousands*, and forgiving wickedness, rebellion and sin. (Exodus 34:5–6)

Note carefully the first words God uses to describe His character in Exodus 34:5–7: Compassion, grace, patience (slow to anger), and above all, love. *He abounds in love.* Love is the foundation of everything else.

This love, so central to God's character, existed before time and creation in the love between Father, Son, and Holy Spirit. Jesus spoke of this love in John 17:24:

> Father, I want those you have given me to be with me where I am, and to see my glory, the glory you have given me because *you loved me before the creation of the world.* (italics added)

We also see the love within the Trinity at Jesus's baptism in the Jordan River. As He emerged from the water, Jesus saw the heavens open, and the Spirit of God descended upon Him like a dove. He then heard a voice from heaven—the voice of the Father: "This is my Son, *whom I love*; with Him I am well pleased" (Matthew 3:16–17, italics added).

Hear the Father-heart of God. This is my beloved Son. I delight in Him. I treasure Him. He is of infinite worth to me.

In the same way, we hear the love of the Son for the Father expressed in His profound commitment to honor, glorify, and obey Him.

> The world [must] learn that *I love the Father* and do exactly what my Father has commanded me". (John 14:31, italics added)

Incredibly, God extends this joyous celebration of love between Father, Son, and Holy Spirit that existed from eternity past to you, me, and everyone else. Jesus said:

> As the Father has loved me, so have I loved you. Now remain in my love . . . I have told you this so that my joy may be in you and that your joy may be complete." (John 15:9–11)

As writer Alyssa Roat rightly notes, "God loves from an outpouring of who He is."[4] Some falsely believe God created human beings because He was lonely and needed someone to love. The truth is that, as the verses above illustrate, complete love and fullness of joy existed between the three persons of the Trinity before the creation of humanity. At creation, this love and joy overflowed to God's image-bearers so that we, in turn, could extend it to others.

Love is like a river whose source is God, but it flows outward, covering and filling our lives with God's boundless joy so that we, in turn, can overflow that same love and joy to others.

There is no more important truth than this. God loves you more than you could ever hope or fully realize. God, your Maker, treasures you and cares deeply about every part of your life. He delights in you and longs to be near you in a deep, personal, and eternal relationship. He views you as immensely valuable—so valuable that He was willing to lay down His life for you.

When you grasp this, it will transform you and become the bedrock of your identity.

Many find this unbelievable. They feel deeply unworthy of God's love, for they know they've done horrible, unspeakably shameful things. They've ignored and rejected God. They've lived only for self-gratification, disregarding what this lifestyle cost others. There is no way God could love them.

But amazingly, God loves us despite our rebellious hearts and sinful deeds.

God demonstrates his love for us in this: While we were still sinners, Christ died for us. (Romans 5:8)

While we were His enemies, God loved us and freely chose to pursue us. Paraphrasing John 3:16, God loved this sinful, fallen, corrupt, and evil world so much that He gave His one and only Son, that whoever believes in Him shall not perish, but have eternal life.

You may wonder, does God *really* love me? Look to the cross. The apostle John declares, "This is how we know what love is: Jesus Christ laid down his life for us" (1 John 3:16). Personalize this: This is how I know I am loved by God. Jesus Christ laid down His life for *me*.

This supreme sacrifice was not some emotionless duty, for that is not what love is. Jesus went to the cross because He *treasures* you and everyone else. He doesn't rejoice in our sinfulness and rebellion, to be sure, but is filled with great joy when we respond to His love by turning from our sins in humble repentance. Jesus said:

> There will be more rejoicing in heaven over one sinner who repents than over ninety-nine righteous persons who do not need to repent. (Luke 15:7)

A repentant sinner brings God great joy because, like the Prodigal Son, they have come home into the loving arms of their heavenly Father. The Bible truly is a love story of a God so filled with love for His rebellious children that He was willing to pay the ultimate price to reconcile with us and be near us forever.

CREATED TO LOVE

Just as love is central to God's character, it is also central to ours. As image-bearers of God, we are hard-wired for love. We all experience joy and delight in God's magnificent creation. We love to walk on a beach at sunset. We love to enjoy a delicious meal with family and friends. We love beautiful music. We also experience love in our most fundamental relationships: marriage, family, and close friends. Loving others and being loved by them is essential for human flourishing. Without love, human existence would be virtually impossible. Life would be empty and meaningless.

While love is part of human nature, the fall of humankind profoundly distorts how we love. We love money or power more than we love people made in God's image. We love ourselves more than others. In our fallen, selfish condition, we often practice the opposite of love. We break our promises, divorce our spouses, neglect our children, and seek our self-interest above the good of others. Conflict, hatred, apathy, indifference, betrayal, and unfaithfulness are far too common.

And yet, people worldwide, and for all times, have experienced love, imperfectly and incompletely. It is part of our *imago Dei*. It gives our lives meaning, purpose, and belonging. We long for the love of another, and we find joy and meaning in our lives by loving others.

In recent years, scientists have discovered how deep this hardwiring goes in new research into oxytocin, sometimes called the "love hormone." Oxytocin is a natural hormone vital to many human behaviors and social interactions. It is released during sexual intercourse and plays a crucial role in building bonds of trust and personal attachment between husband and wife. It is also released during breastfeeding and helps establish a close bond between mother and child.[5]

We are "fearfully and wonderfully made" (Psalm 139:14), down to the hormones God provided that help us love and be loved.

This human hardwiring for love makes complete sense from the vantage point of the biblical story of reality. It makes no sense, however, in the framework of the dominant worldview of the post-Christian West. This worldview denies God's existence and views human beings as purposeless accidents of the evolutionary process. Love is incompatible with this worldview.

In his book *Flesh and Machines*, Rodney Brooks, a professor emeritus at the Massachusetts Institute of Technology, writes that a human being is nothing but a machine—a "big bag of skin full of biomolecules" interacting by the laws of physics and chemistry. But he confesses that seeing people this way is difficult—it doesn't come naturally. He writes, "When I look at my children, I can *when I force myself* . . . see that they are machines" (italics added).

But does he treat them as if they are robots or machines? Of course not. He readily admits: "That is not how I treat them . . . I interact with them on an entirely different level." In other words, he loves them. Why? He has no answer, because the very concept of love doesn't fit into his worldview. He says, "I maintain two sets of inconsistent beliefs."[6]

Loving his children comes naturally to Dr. Brooks and all of us because we are made in God's image, even if we deny it. Reducing our children to biological machines is unnatural. We must "force" ourselves against all our instincts to do this because it is a lie. Nancy Pearcey says:

> We test [the truthfulness] of a worldview by taking it into the laboratory of ordinary life. Can it be lived out consistently in the real world without doing violence to human nature? Does life function the way the worldview says it should? Does it fit reality? Does it match what we know about the world?[7]

Regarding love, the biblical worldview passes the "real world" test with flying colors, whereas secular postmodernism fails.

GENUINE LOVE IS RIGHTLY ORDERED

The Bible has a great deal to say about loving relationships. At creation, God established four fundamental relationships common to all people: our relationships with God, ourselves, others, and creation.

FOUR FUNDAMENTAL RELATIONSHIPS, IN ORDER OF IMPORTANCE

1. With God
2. With ourselves
3. With others
4. With the material world (creation)

As Augustine of Hippo taught in the fourth century, there is a God-ordained order of priority to these relationships based on value or worth. Put simply, the greater the worth, the greater the priority to love.

God is at the pinnacle. He is supremely worthy of our love and devotion as the Holy, Almighty Creator of all. Next, in order of value, come God's image-bearers, including ourselves. All people, whether male or female, rich or poor, powerful or vulnerable, born or unborn, regardless of age or ethnicity, are precious to God.

As Jesus taught:

> "Love the Lord your God with all your heart and with all your soul and with all your mind." This is the first and greatest commandment. And the second is like it: "Love your neighbor as yourself." All the Law and the Prophets hang on these two commandments. (Matthew 22:37–40)

Last, in order of value, comes the stuff of the created world, including the physical environment, plants, animals, and things we create, like money, cars, homes, businesses, cities, and everything else.

Jesus underscored this system of value in Matthew 6:26, NLT:

> Look at the birds. They don't plant or harvest or store food in barns, for your heavenly Father feeds them. And aren't you far more valuable to him than they are?

God delights in His magnificent creation. He loves and cares for it, including the birds, but humans are "far more valuable."

Our relationships thrive when we understand and respect the God-established order and prioritize our love accordingly. However, when we neglect this order, things start to crumble. Disordered love is a hideous counterfeit. It morphs into destructive idolatry and becomes a source of evil.

Recall that Noah Webster defined love as the source of joy, pleasure, and delight. He also correctly acknowledged that we achieve this only when we love God above all else.

> If our hearts are right, we love God above all things as the source of all that is good, desirable, and excellent. In Him, we find our greatest joy.[8]

But our fallen hearts are not right. As the great Reformer John Calvin observed, "our hearts are perpetual idol factories." Our fallen hearts still love, but they reject God and replace Him with the "idols" of money, fame, sex, power, narcotics, hedonistic pleasures, or even our spouse or children. These idols may satisfy us momentarily, but ultimately, they will leave us empty, frustrated, and often depressed.

Why? Because they are not the ultimate source of all that is good. That role is reserved for the Creator alone. Placing them as our first love will inevitably lead to disappointment. They are incapable of satisfying our deepest needs. Only God can. To paraphrase Blaise Pascal,

> There is a God-shaped vacuum in the heart of every person which cannot be filled by any created thing, but only by God the Creator, made known through Jesus Christ.[9]

Filling this void with anything other than God's love only leads to misery, which is why the first of the Ten Commandments says, "You shall have no other gods before me" (Deuteronomy 5:7). When we put God first in our hearts, where only He belongs, then all our other relationships can flourish.

To love God above all else is to find fullness of life and joy in a way that nothing else can even approach. As Jesus said, "I have come that they may have life, and have it to the full" (John 10:10). David, Israel's great Old Testament king, understood this when he wrote,

> In your presence there is fullness of joy; at your right hand are pleasures forevermore." (Psalm 16:11)

LOVING GOD

Loving God above all else is a central message of the Bible. We see it expressed in Old Testament passages such as Deuteronomy 6:4–5:

> Hear, O Israel: The Lord our God, the Lord is One. Love the Lord your God with all your heart and with all your soul and with all your strength.

Jesus was bold and direct when teaching His followers to prioritize their love for Him:

> Anyone who loves their father or mother more than me is not worthy of me; anyone who loves their son or daughter more than me is not worthy of me. Whoever does not take up their cross and follow me is not worthy of me. (Matthew 10:37–38)

Scripture commands us to honor and care for our fathers and mothers and love our spouses and family members (for example, Deuteronomy 5:16; Ephesians 5:22–33, 6:1–4), but not more than God Himself.

Tragically, it is all too possible to be "religious" yet not know God personally. Jesus spoke of this in sobering terms in Matthew 7:22–23:

> . . . many will say to me, "Lord, Lord, did we not prophesy in your name, and cast out demons in your name, and do many mighty works in your name?" And then will I declare to them, "I never knew you."

When Jesus says, "I never knew you," He is speaking about knowing in personal and relational ways. He is saying, "I never had a relationship with you." This relationship must be the paramount relationship in your life. God must be first in our hearts.

Sadly, many so-called Christians think of God in impersonal, philosophical, or cultural terms as the source of "Judeo-Christian" civilization. They may value Christian morality or biblical principles. We can and should appreciate these things, but we dare not miss the most essential truth. God is not an abstract idea or a philosophical concept. He is a *person*, and we properly relate to Him personally, in love.

But how exactly do we love the invisible, all-powerful Creator of the universe? Surprisingly, we love God in ways similar to how we love any other person.

- By delighting in Him. His moral perfection, His love, grace, justice, and beauty
- By worshiping, praising, and adoring Him
- By prioritizing our relationship with Him above all other relationships and seeking His Kingdom and righteousness above all else (Matthew 6:33)
- By investing time in our relationship, talking to Him frequently, and listening to His voice in prayer and His written words in Scripture
- By turning our thoughts and affections towards Him often throughout the day
- By cherishing His every word in Scripture
- By delighting in obeying His commands (John 14:21)
- By loving others because they bear His image and likeness (1 John 4:20–21), particularly the weakest and most vulnerable
- By introducing others to Him and inviting them into a personal relationship with Him (2 Corinthians 5:20)

- By not being ashamed of Him or denying our love for Him (Matthew 10:32–33) but by publicly declaring our devotion and allegiance to Him and speaking up when His character is slandered or attacked

These are just a few of the ways that we love God.

LOVING PEOPLE

When rightly ordered, loving God is our highest priority, followed closely by "loving your neighbor" or fellow human beings. As Jesus taught:

> Love the Lord your God with all your heart and with all your soul and with all your mind. This is the first and greatest commandment. *And the second is like it: Love your neighbor as yourself.* (Matthew 22:35–40, italics added)

Significantly, Jesus said, "The second is like" or similar to, the first. How? In this all-important way. God created all people in His image and likeness. The apostle John explains it this way:

> Whoever claims to love God yet hates a brother or sister is a liar. For whoever does not love their brother and sister, whom they have seen, cannot love God, whom they have not seen. And he has given us this command: Anyone who loves God must also love their brother and sister. (1 John 4:20–21)

The Bible teaches that we are to love God first and people second, but how we *express* our love for God is by loving others made in His image. Loving God and loving our neighbor are so closely intertwined in Scripture that the apostle Paul could write in Galatians 5:14:

The entire law is fulfilled in keeping this one command: Love your neighbor as yourself.

But this raises some questions. Who, exactly, is my "neighbor," and how ought I to love him? Jesus answered both questions in the Parable of the Good Samaritan (Luke 10:25–37). In the parable, He tells of a man who was robbed, brutally beaten, and left to die on the side of a remote mountain road. Sometime later, Jewish religious leaders happened to pass but diverted their eyes and chose to ignore the bloody victim, presumably because they were fearful of being robbed themselves or too preoccupied with their own agendas.

Remarkably, the "neighbor" is the one who eventually came to the desperate man's aid, a despised Samaritan, someone from a non-Jewish tribal group. Jesus's point is that genuine love extends beyond our immediate family and ethnic group, even to those we consider "enemies." Our neighbors include anyone and everyone, but particularly those who are neglected and overlooked and who desperately need help.

How did the Good Samaritan love his neighbor?

- *He didn't divert his eyes.* He stopped, and he looked. This is where love begins: by not closing our eyes to the pain and suffering around us, but instead, choosing to see people in need around us—people often hidden from view and on the margins of society.
- *He had compassion.* Compassion literally means to suffer together with another person. It is a profound sympathy that leads to personal, costly action.
- *He was other-focused.* He had to postpone his plans or agenda and put the needs of others first.
- *It involved personal risk.* In stopping to help the man on a dangerous road, he risked his safety at the hands of potential nearby robbers.

- *His love was costly.* It cost him his time and money, which he could have otherwise used for his own needs or desires.
- *He loved unconditionally, with "no strings attached" or promise of payback.*

In short, the love demonstrated by the Good Samaritan crossed lines of ethnicity and hostility. It was compassionate, gracious, costly, sacrificial, unconditional, unreciprocated, and undeserved.

This is exactly how Jesus demonstrated His love for us. He saw our broken condition. It filled His great heart with compassion and moved Him to costly action on our behalf. He drew near to us in the incarnation, entering our suffering and ultimately taking upon Himself the punishment we deserved, all to reconcile us to God. In the powerful words of Isaiah 53:4–5:

> Surley he took up our pain
> and bore our suffering,
> yet we considered him punished by God,
> stricken by him, and afflicted.
> But he was pierced for our transgressions,
> he was crushed for our iniquities;
> the punishment that brought us peace was on him,
> and by his wounds we are healed.

And incredibly, as the apostle Paul tells us, He did all this while we were still His "enemies". (Romans 5:10)

> But God demonstrates his own love for us in this: While we were still sinners, Christ died for us. (Romans 5:8)

Love demands that we see our enemies as God does—as His precious image-bearers who are objects of His redeeming love—and treat them accordingly. Here is what Jesus taught:

You have heard that it was said, "Love your neighbor and hate your enemy." But I tell you, love your enemies and pray for those who persecute you, that you may be children of your Father in heaven. He causes his sun to rise on the evil and the good, and sends rain on the righteous and the unrighteous. If you love those who love you, what reward will you get? Are not even the tax collectors doing that? And if you greet only your own people, what are you doing more than others? Do not even pagans do that? Be perfect, therefore, as your heavenly Father is perfect. (Matthew 5:43–48)

We are never more Christlike than when we love our enemies, and this opens the door to experiencing God's pleasure like nothing else. There is no greater joy than hearing our heavenly Father say these words in response to our obedience: "Well done, good and faithful servant" (Matthew 25:23).

Loving enemies unleashes incredible transformational power—the power to overcome evil (Romans 12:21). When we witness such transformation or are privileged to play a role in it through our obedience, we experience intense joy.

In His famous novel, *Les Misérables*, Victor Hugo powerfully portrayed the power of love to transform. The main character, Jean Valjean, is finally released after spending nineteen years in prison at hard labor for stealing a loaf of bread to feed his starving family.

However, one dark evening, he finds himself pursued by the police for a parole violation. Residents of a small village repeatedly refuse the desperate Valjean shelter. Only the saintly bishop, Monseigneur Myriel, welcomes him. How does the criminal Valjean repay his host's hospitality? By stealing his costly silverware.

The following day, the police apprehend Valjean red-handed with the stolen silverware and bring him back to the bishop for positive identification. But at that moment, the bishop does something remarkable and unexpected. Instead of condemning Valjean and sending him back to prison, he shows mercy by telling the police that he gave the silverware to Valjean as a gift.

Valjean is stunned by such mercy. After the police depart, the bishop looks gravely into Valjean's trembling eyes and speaks these immortal words:

> Jean Valjean, my brother, you no longer belong to evil but to good. I buy your soul from you; I withdraw it from black thoughts and the spirit of perdition and give it to God.

The extravagant love the bishop shows to his "enemy" transforms Valjean. He gives himself wholly to God and lives a new life, loving others sacrificially in the same way he was loved. He eventually becomes a respected mayor of a small French village. In perhaps the novel's most famous line, Valjean speaks this powerful truth, "To love another person is to see the face of God."

Returning to the Parable of the Good Samaritan, Jesus ends it with a terse command: Now that you know who your neighbors are and how you are to love them, *"go and do likewise"* (Luke 10:37). This is not a suggestion or recommendation. It is a command at the heart of biblical Christianity.

Before He ascended to heaven, Jesus commanded His followers to "Go and make disciples of all nations . . . *teaching them to obey everything I have commanded you*" (Matthew 28:19–20, italics added). What did he command? To "go and do likewise." To "love one another" (John 13:34) as the Good Samaritan loved—as Jesus loved. This love is the hallmark of a faithful Christian (John 13:35). It is at the center of our mission to the world.

We demonstrate our love and devotion to Jesus, our supreme authority, by obeying His commands. As He said:

Whoever has my commands and keeps them is the one who loves me. (John 14:21)

In the same way, Jesus demonstrated His love for the Father through obedience to His commands, saying:

I love the Father and do exactly what my Father has commanded me. (John 14:31)

That obedience took Jesus to the cross for the sake of love. That obedience demands that we love others in the same way.

THE ORDER OF LOVE IN HUMAN RELATIONSHIPS

Love involves a personal relationship and direct engagement with those nearest us in marriage, family, church, workplace, and community. The farther removed, the less able we are to love. Today, through internet-based technologies, we can have relationships with people in virtually every corner of the world, yet as wonderful as these technologies can be, they are no substitute for the whole-person interaction that love requires.

Jesus, in His wisdom, understands our finite capacity as individuals. He doesn't expect us to love all eight billion people on earth equally. The great Russian novelist Fyodor Dostoevsky once said, "The more I love humanity in general, the less I love man in particular."[10] In other words, the more preoccupied you are with "the world," the less you will be with the real people nearest you daily.

In the Bible, a hierarchy in our human relationships establishes priority for our love. Given the vital, God-ordained significance of marriage, if you are married, the most significant relationship in your life, after your relationship with God, is with your spouse (see Ephesians 5:22, 25). Next, in order of priority, comes your relationship with your children (1 Timothy 3:4–5), followed by love for your parents (Deuteronomy 5:16) and other family members

(1 Timothy 5:8). Next, in order of priority, comes the love we share with our brothers and sisters in Christ, particularly those we interact with regularly in a local church (Galatians 5:13–14), and finally, our love for others, including friends, neighbors, foreigners, the needy, and even enemies.

Relationships thrive when human relationships are rightly ordered and love is correctly prioritized.

LOVE'S RELATIONSHIP TO FREEDOM, JUSTICE, AND TRUTH

We've only scratched the surface of the depths and richness of love, but something else needs to be said in contrast to popular understandings of love today. We need to understand the relationship between love and three other vital words: freedom, justice, and truth.

Love and freedom

Freedom is not just a component of love but is an integral part. Love, by its very nature, must be freely chosen. It cannot be imposed, programmed, or coerced. Without the element of choice, love loses its essence.

At the center of God's nature are love and freedom. Because God is free, no one compels Him to do anything against His will. He loves us because He chooses to. We see this throughout the Bible. God chooses people and loves them, not because they are particularly lovable or worthy of God's special attention, but simply because He chooses them.

> The Lord did not set His affection on you and choose you because you were more numerous than other peoples, for you were the fewest of all peoples. But it was because the Lord loved you and kept the oath he swore to your ancestors. (Deuteronomy 7:7–8)

God's love for His people in the Old and New Testaments is based on His free choice and is sealed with a promise or "oath" of fidelity. This is the biblical concept of covenant, or faithful, enduring love.

As God's image-bearers, we, too, can freely choose. We are not robots or machines. God made us free so that we could relate to Him and others in love. While someone may force us to do things against our will, love will never be one of those things. Unless it is given freely, it is not love. And, like God, we can seal our love with a promise, or covenant, of fidelity (see Malachi 2:14). So the biblical foundation of love is free choice and promised faithfulness.

Love and justice

Love and justice coexist in God's character and human relationships.

Earlier, we looked at God's Name, proclaimed to Moses on Mount Sinai in Exodus 34:5–7. God's Name conveys His essential character, and love is at the core, expressed in compassion, mercy, grace, and forgiveness. God "abounds in love." But justice is also central to God's character. God's Name continues with these words:

> Yet [God] does not leave the guilty unpunished; he punishes the children and their children for the sin of the parents to the third and fourth generation.

Because justice involves wrath, judgment, and punishment, love and justice may seem paradoxical, but they are not. Love *requires* justice. Here's why.

Evil and injustice, tragically, are all too familiar in our fallen world, and while God loves sinners, He hates the evil and injustice they commit, and cannot overlook it in His moral perfection, or brush it off as no big deal.

Injustice is intolerable to Him because it harms people He loves. It stirs His wrath and moves Him to action. He will defend the victims of injustice and uphold their cause (Psalm 140:12). He will bring every evil act into judgment and punish it accordingly (Ecclesiastes 12:14).

In our human roles of authority as husbands, parents, elders, teachers, or civil authorities, we are responsible for doing this, too. We seek justice when someone harms a person under our care and protection. To fail to do this is a failure to love.

If you are a husband and father, for example, and someone breaks into your house and threatens harm to your wife and children, "loving your enemy" doesn't require that you passively stand aside and let the attacker have his way. That would violate your sacred duty to love and protect your wife and children. It would also be a failure to love the attacker because it would enable him to continue in his evil ways without consequence, which, if left unchecked, would lead to his ultimate destruction.

It is not loving to allow a sinner to continue on his sinful path without consequences. We must never sacrifice justice, which God loves, or enable evil, which God hates, in the name of love.

But how do we reconcile justice with Jesus's command to love our enemies and "turn the other cheek"? (Matthew 5:38–48). Shouldn't we overlook offenses and be quick to forgive?

To answer this question, we have to make an essential distinction. Is the injustice committed against us personally or against someone under our authority, care, and protection? If we are the victim, loving our enemy means that we should be ready to "turn the other cheek" or "hand over our cloak" (or our silverware, as the bishop in *Les Misérables* did when he was robbed).

While seeking justice for wrongs committed against us isn't always prohibited, a proper response requires careful discernment. Still, we should never lash out in revenge or return evil for evil. Pastor

Anthony Esteves correctly says, "Vengeance and vindictiveness have no place in the Christian life."[11] Instead, we can trust God to right all wrongs on His perfect timetable.

However, when injustices are committed to those under our care and protection, we have a sacred responsibility to pursue justice. Jesus was not commanding us to passively accept injustices done to others.

The Bible also frequently discusses the relationship between love, discipline, and punishment. Our fallen, sinful nature enables all kinds of wrongdoing, ultimately harming us and others. Those in positions of authority express love by caring enough to attempt to correct it through discipline and punishment, not by ignoring wrongdoing and the harm it causes.

> The Lord disciplines the one he loves,
>   and he chastens everyone he accepts as his son.
> (Hebrews 12:6)

> Whoever spares the rod hates their children,
>   but the one who loves their children carefully
> disciplines them. (Proverbs 13:24)

Ultimately, God's love and justice reach their full expression in the cross of Jesus Christ. Justice, because sin and human evil stirred God's holy wrath. Punishment and payment for that evil were required for justice to prevail. Love, because Jesus took the punishment we deserved on Himself, and paid our penalty in His blood.

Love and truth

Truth and love are inseparable. As the apostle Paul said, "Love rejoices with the truth" (1 Corinthians 13:6). However, today, in our "post-truth" world,[12] love is scandalously separated from truth, not only in the fallen world but increasingly also in the church.

We are told, for example, that by refusing to affirm people's sinful choices or chosen sexual "identities," we are not "loving," while speaking truthfully will brand you a fearful, intolerant "hater."

Today, much of the evangelical world places a high value on niceness. To be nice is to be loving, but in practice, this "niceness" means not speaking out against false and destructive cultural trends and beliefs, particularly those held by powerful and influential people. People who think this way want nonbelievers to think well of them and presumably be more open to the gospel. But this is an illusion. Dividing truth from love will give you neither.

As followers of Jesus, we are called to be gentle, humble, and gracious. But we are also called to speak truthfully. Kelly Monroe Kullberg rightly says: "Biblical truth and wisdom are the highest love for human beings."[13] To be silent or passive in the face of destructive, even deadly, cultural lies is to fail in our duty to love our neighbors. This dereliction of our Christian duty borders on apostasy. According to Catholic Archbishop Charles Chaput:

> [Christians] don't need to publicly renounce their [faith] to be apostates. They simply need to be silent when their [faith] demands that they speak out; to be cowards when Jesus asks them to have courage; to "stand away" from the truth when they need to work for it and fight for it.[14]

We must speak the truth in love (Ephesians 4:15), with humility and gentleness—but speak it we must.

In the same way, genuine compassion requires discernment of truth. For example, not everyone who appears to be in need is genuinely needy. The apostle Paul teaches that providing charity to people who seem needy but are not enables harmful behaviors. Some are non-disabled yet unwilling to work to provide for themselves (2 Thessalonians 3:10–12). Some immediate family members are unwilling to care for them as they ought (1 Timothy 5:4; 8). Some struggle with addiction, and simply giving them handouts will only enable their addiction, and that is never loving, even though it may feel like it.

Genuine compassion is reserved for those truly in need, like the man robbed, beaten, and left to die in the Parable of the Good Samaritan. When a genuine need appears, the Christian must act. To ignore such people is to fail to love them.

THE POSITIVE CULTURAL CONSEQUENCES

What the Bible teaches about love is unique. Nothing like it exists in any other religion or ideology. There may be no more radical, revolutionary, and transforming teaching in history.

Try to imagine a relationship between two people in which love doesn't exist, where there is no concern for the well-being of the other and no grace, mercy, or forgiveness. That relationship would devolve into a bitter conflict with no possibility of reconciliation.

Extend that to a family, whole community, society, or nation. What would happen?

Imagine a world devoid of love. It would experience unending hatred, conflict, and violence—a living hell. Yet, we can rejoice that love does exist! It is the essence of God's character, predating creation itself. Despite our unworthiness, God has lavished His love upon us. In the fullness of time, God came to us in the person of Jesus Christ, demonstrating love in action. We can be forgiven, reconciled to God, and filled with the Holy Spirit through faith in Christ. As new creations, we are empowered to love others as Christ loved us, becoming catalysts of transformation in our relationships, families, communities, and beyond.

Love and its corollaries—mercy, grace, compassion, forgiveness, joy, and sacrificial service—are the glue that strengthens and holds human relationships together. When we understand and experience love at its deepest levels and put it into practice daily, it changes our lives, filling us with joy that changes those around us, and ultimately, that changes the world.

The most powerful force is love at its deepest levels—that willingly sacrifices itself for the benefit of others, even more so when the "other" is an enemy. All the money or military might in the world can't compare. When followers of Jesus sacrificially loved God and their neighbors in the plague-stricken Roman Empire, a power was unleashed that transformed the Roman world into a Christian "empire" in a few short generations.

That same power is still available today, but the post-Christian West is rejecting and abandoning God and, in doing so, is losing genuine love in both knowledge and practice. The consequences are seen in rising levels of distrust, conflict, growing tribalism, anxiety, and depression. Followers of Jesus have a powerful opportunity to demonstrate genuine love as the center of our mission to the world. That love will shine with a blinding light in the growing darkness and lead people to God.

But first, we must discern and reject the false, counterfeit love that has replaced genuine love in mainstream culture and, alarmingly, even in many of our churches.

REDEFINED LOVE

Genuine love is a deep, rich, multifaceted concept rooted in God's nature. It is so deep that there is no bottom to it. You could spend a lifetime plumbing the depths of love and only scratch the surface.

But what happens to love when a person, a society, or a culture abandons God? It becomes flat and one-dimensional. It loses its depth, richness, and power. Stripped of its essential qualities, it ceases to be genuine love and becomes a destructive counterfeit.

> ## LOVE REDEFINED
> (1) A source of pleasure, joy, or delight. (2) A strong affection, often accompanied by romantic feelings and sexual attraction.

Tragically, this is what is happening in the post-Christian, post-truth West, which has reduced love to personal affection and sexual desire.

Consider the viral hashtags #LoveWins and #LoveIsLove.

The Human Rights Campaign (HRC), the world's largest LGBTQ+ advocacy organization, created these hashtags in 2015 as part of a massive PR campaign to promote so-called "same-sex marriage."

An article titled "HRS's #LoveWins Hashtag Goes Viral" explains:

> The #LoveWins hashtag was the dominant message around the Supreme Court's marriage equality decision in June [2015]. HRC received overwhelming support and engagement from countless individual citizens, prominent celebrities such as Taylor Swift, political leaders like President Barack Obama and Hillary Clinton, and businesses such as Ben and Jerry's, who sent supportive messages about marriage equality to their millions of followers on social media. . . .
>
> #LoveWins was spoken on countless news outlets throughout the day as coverage of the decision played out. Everywhere people turned, whether it was the front page of a local paper, a national paper, the nightly news, or their Twitter or Facebook feed, #LoveWins appeared.[15]

The article concludes:

> #LoveWins defined not only the marriage equality victory, but the immense excitement and joyous emotions of a day and a decision that will go down in history.

When The Human Rights Campaign uses the word "love" in such a central way to brand its movement, people everywhere are influenced in how they understand love. And what is that understanding? That love is nothing more than intense feelings of romantic affection and sexual attraction. You see this understanding of love explicitly in the redefinition of marriage that appeared in Western dictionaries around this time:

> Marriage is a legally recognized, romantic caregiving relationship between consenting adults who intend to live together as sexual and domestic partners.[16]

Boiled down to its essence, the HRC's position is that same-sex couples have a legal right to marry because #LoveWins," with "love" understood to be a sexual relationship "between two consenting adults" based upon intense feelings of romantic affection.

Since 2015, the "two consenting adults" aspect of this definition has been under scrutiny, with groups now pushing for the normalization of polyamory, or three or more consenting adults, while others even openly challenging why "adult" is necessary.

Unmoored from the Bible, words such as marriage and love become whatever influential people and their interest groups like the HRC want them to be, as long as they can impose that definition on the rest of us. When defined subjectively, "love" is used to justify any form of sexual desire while demanding others affirm their sinful choices and actions, no matter how evil or destructive.

What's missing from this stripped-down, counterfeit version of "love"? Only the most profound aspects.

- Truth is gone. Genuine love "rejoices in the truth" (1 Corinthians 13:6), but counterfeit love rejects truth, including the truth about sex and marriage. Sexual intimacy is indeed an essential aspect of love, but only sex between a husband and wife, male and female, in marriage, as God intends.

- Fidelity, or covenant faithfulness, is also gone. The new definition of marriage, based on the counterfeit definition of love, completely erases this vital aspect, which, tragically, was stripped from Western understandings of love long before the same-sex marriage movement began in the 1980s. California first legalized no-fault divorce in 1969; by 2010, every state had followed suit. The implied understanding of love is intense feelings of romantic affection stripped of fidelity or "till death do us part."

Tragically, this false feelings-based understanding of love has become firmly rooted in the church, as well as the broader culture, where divorce rates are nearly identical. Christian men and women routinely explain their decision to divorce by saying, "I just don't love him (or her) anymore," meaning I don't *feel* the same romance or emotional thrill in our relationship.

Because counterfeit love rejects God, it also rejects the God-ordained order of love, twisting love into a destructive idolatry. The love of money, pleasure, power, or fame replaces God at the top of the hierarchy.

Disordered love is a hideous, narcissistic, emotion-driven, hedonistic counterfeit. It promises happiness, but that promise is a mirage. No amount of illicit sex, money, power, or fame can satisfy our deepest human needs. Idolizing these false gods leaves people empty, broken, and ultimately destroyed. As the apostle Paul taught, "Whoever sows to please their flesh, from the flesh will reap destruction" (Galatians 6:8a).

Real love, however, promises life to the full (John 10:10), eternal life (Galatians 6:8b), and fullness of joy (John 15:11). This joy comes only when we love God above all and paradoxically when we "deny ourselves" and place the needs of others ahead of our own. As Jesus taught:

> If anyone would come after me, let him deny himself and take up his cross and follow me. For whoever would save his life will lose it, but whoever loses his life for my sake will find it. For what will it profit a man if he gains the whole world and forfeits his soul? Or what shall a man give in return for his soul? (Matthew 16:24–26, ESV)

And finally, gone is the most profound aspect of love, *agape*, or sacrificial service for the good of another. With agape stripped away, so are its corollaries: grace, mercy, compassion, and forgiveness.

Where *agape* is radically other-centered, false love is fundamentally self-centered. Where agape is based on choice regardless of feelings, false love is based entirely on feelings and emotions.

With the abandonment of God, darkness has been descending on the Western world. The self-centered narcissism and decadence of counterfeit love are one result. Another is the re-emergence of atheist ideologies such as Marxism in its most recent iteration, cultural Marxism, or "critical theories," which is now the dominant worldview in shaping the institutions of the post-Christian West. Just take a look at the sorry state of our universities.

Where genuine love is quick to forgive and "keeps no record of wrongs," this toxic ideology replaces truth with power and gratitude with grievance. In this culture, there is no "love your neighbors," much less "love your enemies." There is no grace. No forgiveness. No mercy. Only a never-ending struggle for power and domination. If left unchecked in its headlong drive to replace Christianity at the heart of the West, it will destroy us.

The only hope of avoiding this fate is for the church of Jesus Christ to show the world "the more excellent way" of genuine love. That means followers of Jesus must rebuild cultures in our homes, offices, neighborhoods, and communities based on genuine love. To do that, we must understand what authentic love is and how it differs from counterfeit love and put it into practice daily.

HOW SHOULD WE THEN LIVE?

Genuine love must to be taught by faithful pastors and Christian teachers and applied in the daily lives and relationships of all followers of Christ. We should all grow in our knowledge and practice of love, including its various facets, particularly *agape*, the most profound aspect of love.

Christians must also clearly understand the counterfeit definition of love now dominant in the culture. This counterfeit is also deeply rooted in our churches. A few critical errors need to be urgently addressed to recover a genuine understanding and practice of love in our churches.

Confusion about love and emotions

As noted earlier, the counterfeit definition reduces love to powerful emotions of romantic affection and sexual desire. It is self-centered and narcissistic. This counterfeit is tragically entrenched in the church, particularly when it comes to male-female relationships and marriage. This emotions-driven understanding of love is commonly used as a justification for divorce, but it is a lie.

Genuine love is not emotions-driven. It is driven by our will, choice, and agency, *regardless of our feelings*. We choose to love, even when we don't feel like it. We don't allow emotions to drive us because emotions are unsteady. They come and go. If our love were based entirely on feelings, it would be inconsistent and conditional, but that is not the nature of love. Genuine love is firm, consistent, faithful, and unconditional. It forgives and keeps no record of wrongs. It seeks to reconcile and rebuild trust.

Because feelings and emotions are so powerful, loving this way is extremely challenging. We can't do it in our strength alone. We need God to help and strengthen us, trusting He will be more than happy to supply us with the power necessary to exercise genuine love.

To choose to love someone who has harmed us deeply when emotions such as anger, bitterness, resentment, and vengefulness are so strong that we feel helpless against their power is nothing short of a miracle.

But when such miracles occur, the watching world is confronted with God's reality and power, a combination that changes things. The miracle of loving our enemies is a brilliant light shining in the dark. It has the power to transform lives and cultures, and that is precisely what our calling is.

So, free will and choice drive genuine love and not feelings, but today, many Christians overreact by claiming that love has *nothing* to do with feelings or emotions. This is false. Feelings such as joy and delight are central to love. To separate love from our emotions does irreparable damage to the concept. The proper balance is understanding that feelings and emotions are central to love but cannot *drive* love. Our free choice is the engine that drives the train, and the feelings and emotions must follow, as they inevitably will.

Mistaking love for "niceness" or "winsomeness"

Equating love with niceness is perhaps the most widespread and destructive confusion about love in our churches. It is false at several different levels.

The basic idea is that Christians should be kind, gentle, and respectful, which is true, but the idea goes beyond this. Being kind, gentle, and respectful toward others means we must *affirm* their beliefs and behaviors, even if they are false and destructive.

When challenged, advocates of this winsome approach to love will respond that Jesus loved and affirmed sinners. Yes, He did, *but He didn't affirm their sin.* Jesus told them what they were doing was sinful and called them to repent (see John 8:1–11). He spoke truthfully about sin and, at the same time, loved sinful people.

Separating truth from love destroys love. As the apostle Paul says, we must "speak the truth in love" (Ephesians 4:15) and avoid the temptation to divide them.

The false understanding of love as "niceness" separates truth from love for fear of being seen as harsh or offensive, which, advocates claim, will harm our gospel witness.

However, this way of thinking not only redefines love as "niceness" but turns it into a utilitarian means to the end of evangelism. Evangelism is essential, but it is not the highest end. Love is. Love is the highest calling and duty of every Christian. What if the people we evangelize are not open to the gospel or refuse our invitation to attend church? Does that excuse us from loving them?

The evangelical church has taken something essential—evangelism—and made it something ultimate, and this is the source of many of its problems. Evangelism is a means to a larger end. Evangelism is about converting people into Christ-followers, who must be carefully discipled to love as He loved. *That* is the end.

Author and cultural commentator John Daniel Davidson addressed this problem with great clarity:

> Many Christian leaders have accepted this false notion that "winsomeness" and "being nice" are the best ways to win people over to the faith and not to speak clearly about moral truth. It is a great mistake because the loving thing to do is to tell the truth. If you love someone, you must tell the truth because you don't want them to persist in the lie that harms and damages them.

When it comes to an issue like transgenderism, the loving thing for Christian leaders to do is not to pretend that this is normal or healthy but it is to tell the truth about transgender ideology—to save people who might be ensnared in it and help those who are ensnared to get out. A willingness to tell the truth has been sorely lacking from our Christian leaders across the denominations in the United States. This has to change. We have to grow a spine, and our leaders have to get some backbone and be willing to speak the truth—truth about men and women, the unborn, about how society should be structured, about marriage, about children, and speak it clearly and unapologetically, in love, without caveats. That is loving. That is the way to love people as Christ loved them. That is also the way to win souls and convert a nation, not to apologize for the truth.[17]

As we conclude, reflect on your understanding and practice of love. Here are several questions to consider.

Are your loves rightly ordered? Do you have other "gods" (or idols) you are devoted to more than God? Do you love things, like wealth, more than people? Are you like the "rich young man" described in Matthew 19:16–22? He loved God but was unwilling to put God first in His heart, ahead of his great wealth. When Jesus asked him to "sell [his] possessions and give to the poor," he was unwilling to make such a sacrifice.

And make no mistake: Sacrifice is indeed required if we love something or someone more than God. This kind of sacrifice is excruciating when we focus on what we are giving up. It is much easier, however, when we focus on what we gain, namely the eternal and abundant, joy-filled life God intended for us. What we gain is so valuable that, by comparison, we lose nothing and gain everything.

Here's how Jesus taught us to think about this trade-off:

> The kingdom of heaven is like treasure hidden in a field.
> When a man found it, he hid it again, and then in his joy
> went and sold all he had and bought that field.
>
> Again, the kingdom of heaven is like a merchant
> looking for fine pearls. When he found one of great value,
> he went away and sold everything he had and bought it.
> (Matthew 13:44–46)

Or, in the words of pastor John Piper:

> Deny yourself the short, unsatisfying pleasures of the
> world so that you can have fullness of joy and pleasures
> forevermore at God's right hand.[18]

What do you need to "sell" or give up to rightly order God and His Kingdom at the pinnacle of your love and devotion? And remember, just because something is of lesser value does not mean it has no value and doesn't deserve our love. Take, for example, God's magnificent creation. It is of lesser value than God or people made in His image, but it still has immense worth and fully deserves our love, care, and respect.

The proper order of love applies to our human relationships as well. Reflect on your relationships with your spouse and children (if you are married), coworkers, neighbors, friends, fellow Christians, others in your community, and even enemies.

If you are married, do you prioritize love for your spouse and then your children before other relationships? Do you prioritize love for your brothers and sisters in Christ before those outside the Body of Christ?

Beyond this, are you actively loving others in your community, particularly those hurting, broken, and neglected? Are you making time in your busy life to stop and "see" these people around you and not simply pass by them preoccupied with your agenda and priorities? What practical actions can you take to "suffer together with them"? Are you prepared to get your hands dirty, minister to their needs, and heal their wounds, even if they are your enemies? Even if it means significant personal cost?[19]

Love is a river

John, the beloved apostle, shortly before he passed from this world, penned these immortal words that capture the essence of life and human existence:

> Dear friends, let us love one another, for love comes from God. Everyone who loves has been born of God and knows God. Whoever does not love does not know God, because God is love. This is how God showed his love among us: He sent his one and only Son into the world that we might live through him. This is love: not that we loved God, but that he loved us and sent his Son as an atoning sacrifice for our sins. Dear friends, since God so loved us, we also ought to love one another. No one has ever seen God; but if we love one another, God lives in us and his love is made complete in us. (1 John 4:7–12)

Love is at the center of everything. It is central to God's character and the joyous dance of love between Father, Son, and Holy Spirit. It's at the center of our lives. God made us know His love and find our highest value and purpose in it. But love is like a river. Its source is God, and it flows into our lives and transforms us, and we, in turn, are to overflow that love to those around us so that they too may join in the dance and, in this way, fill the world with the love of God.

This truth is almost too beautiful to believe, but it *is* true. As we end this book, may you and I always remember that our highest purpose is found both in knowing the love of God and spreading it to others. In the powerful words of Tim Mackie and Jon Collins of the BibleProject:

> Christian faith involves trusting that at the center of the universe is a Being overflowing with love for His world. This means that the purpose of human existence is to receive this love, which has come to us in Jesus, and then give it back to others, creating an ecosystem of other-focused, self-giving love.[20]

ACKNOWLEDGMENTS

This book is dedicated to my dear friend and mentor, Darrow L. Miller.

To my beloved wife, Kimberly, and my wonderful children, Kaila, Jenna, Luke, Isaac, and Annelise, who spent many hours helping me refine the contents of this book and provided so much support, feedback, and inspiration, thank you from the bottom of my heart.

To my long-time friend, partner in ministry, and mentor, Darrow Miller, who lit a spark in my mind many years ago by saying, "If you want to transform culture, you begin by transforming language," I've learned so much from you about the power of words, and your passion for God's Word and the Living Word, Jesus Christ, has deeply inspired me. Thank you for your faithful friendship, support, and love. This book would not have been possible without you.

To my dear friends and co-workers at the Disciple Nations Alliance, Dwight Vogt, Luke Allen, Tim Williams, Bob Moffitt, Chloe Carson, Shawn Carson, John Bottimore, Jon Taylor, Eric Dalrymple, Blake Williams, Gary Paisley, and Bob Evans, without your help, support, ideas, discussions, and critiques over many long years, I would never have completed this book. Your partnership in ministry means the world to me. Thank you.

I'd also like to thank the many people who supported this project—too many to mention you all—but a special thanks to Karsten and Bonnie Solheim, Clay Howerton, Howard and Roberta Ahmanson, George and Bev Tingom, Carolyn Beckett, Rick Salyer, Tim and Pam Manthei, John and Kim Bottimore, Damon and

Amanda Rich, Bob and Judy Merwin, Jon and Mary Young, Greg and Kathy Carson, Bob and Judy Moffitt, Mark Houghton, and John Seger. I'm deeply grateful for your generous support for this project.

To the incredibly talented and professional wordsmith Stan Guthrie, thank you for putting your special touch on this book. I appreciate your patience over the years it took to bring this book to life. And to Tim Beals, president of Credo House Publishing, it has been a joy to work with you and the other wonderful people on your team. Thank you.

To Jesus, the lover of my soul, my King, and my redeemer. Thank you forever, thank you.

Soli Deo Gloria.

ABOUT THE AUTHOR

Scott David Allen is president of the Disciple Nations Alliance. He is a frequent teacher on topics ranging from Christianity and culture to worldview, family, biblical justice, and poverty. He has authored and co-authored numerous books, including his bestselling book *Why Social Justice Is Not Biblical Justice: An Urgent Appeal to Fellow Christians in a Time of Social Crisis.*

Before serving as president of the Disciple Nations Alliance, Scott served for nineteen years with the Christian poverty alleviation organization Food for the Hungry.

He has traveled extensively in Africa, Asia, and Latin America, equipping Christian leaders to embrace a biblical worldview and to live it out personally and publicly in faithfulness to Christ's command to make disciples of all nations.

He and his wife, Kimberly, live in Bend, Oregon. Scott is the proud father of five children and has three grandchildren.

ENDNOTES

INTRODUCTION

1   https://www.dailysignal.com/2015/04/21/what-you-need-to-know-about-gay-marriage-and-the-supreme-court/

2   Cahill, Thomas, *The Gifts of the Jews: How a Tribe of Desert Nomads Changed the Way Everyone Thinks and Feels.* Anchor Books/Nan A Talese (August 17, 1999), n.p.

3   John Milton, AZQuotes.com, Retrieved February 22, 2024, from AZQuotes.com Web site: https://www.azquotes.com/quote/1373492.

4   John Stonestreet, "The Court's Attack on Language," LightSource, August 24, 2015, https://www.lightsource.com/devotionals/breakpoint/the-courts-attack-on-language-11740334.html.

5   Kevin DeYoung, "Thinking Theologically About Racial Tensions: Life Together in the Church," The Gospel Coalition, July 29, 2020, https://www.thegospelcoalition.org/blogs/kevin-deyoung/thinking-theologically-about-racial-tensions-life-together-in-the-church/.

6   Robert Wilken, as quoted by Rod Dreher in "Critics of the Benedict Option," The American conservative, July 8, 2015, https://www.theamericanconservative.com/critics-of-the-benedict-option/.

7   In this book, I start from a conviction that the Bible is God's absolute, objective truth for all people for all times. The statement of faith from the church I attend, Eastmont Church in Bend, Oregon, expresses my conviction well: "The Bible is without error in concept or detail in the original writings. It is breathed out in its entirety by God, divinely preserved, and, therefore, trustworthy. We believe the Holy Spirit superintended human authors so that, through their individual personalities and literary styles, they composed and recorded God's Word. It is God's written revelation, complete in the 66 books of the Old and New Testaments. It is the supreme authority in all matters to which it speaks and is sufficient for life, conduct, and practice, understandable by every believer. We believe Scripture must be understood through the literal, contextual, grammatical, and historical method of interpretation, and applied under the guidance of the Holy Spirit." If you don't share this conviction but are open to honestly exploring the truthfulness of the Bible, I recommend this book as a place to start that exploration: *Scripture and Truth* by D.A. Carson (Editor), John D. Woodbridge (Editor), Baker Academic (September 1, 1992).

8   "An Unlikely Convert: An Interview with Rosaria Butterfield," *Tabletalk*, March 25, 2015, https://www.ligonier.org/learn/articles/unlikely-convert/.

9   Matt Smethurst, "20 Quotes from Rosaria Butterfield's New Book on Sexual Identity," The Gospel Coalition, July 7, 2015, http://www.thegospelcoalition. org/article/20-quotes-from-rosaria-butterfields-new-book-on-sexual-identity.

CHAPTER 1

1   The second part of this definition is adapted from Delgado and Stefancic, *Critical Race Theory: An Introduction*, 2001, 104. This quote is from the book's second edition and, after criticism, was removed in subsequent editions.

2   For a column leading off with this example, see Stan Guthrie, "Telling the Truth in a Post-Truth Culture," BreakPoint, http://www.breakpoint.org/2018/04/ telling-the-truth-in-a-post-truth-culture/.

3   Jackie Strause, "Golden Globes: Oprah Calls for Day When Women Never Have to Say 'Me Too' Again," *The Hollywood Reporter*, January 7, 2018, https:// www.hollywoodreporter.com/news/oprah-winfrey-golden-globes-2018-speech-1072351.

4   Quoted in Conor Friedersdorf, "The Difference Between Speaking 'Your Truth' and 'The Truth,'" *The Atlantic*, January 8, 2018, https://www.theatlantic.com/ politics/archive/2018/01/the-power-and-perils-of-speaking-your-truth/549968/.

5   The actual quote is, "Against [empiricism], which halts at [observable] phenomena—'There are only facts'—I would say, no, facts is precisely what there is not, only interpretations. We cannot establish any fact 'in itself': perhaps it is folly to want to do such a thing." In "Nietzsche on the Impossibility of Truth," http://neamathisi.com/new-learning/chapter-7-knowledge-and-learning/ nietzsche-on-the-impossibility-of-truth.

6   "The Correspondence Theory of Truth," *Stanford Encyclopedia of Philosophy*, May 10, 2002 (revised May 28, 2015).

7   Charles J. Chaput, "The Splendor of Truth in 2017," *First Things*, October 2017, https://www.firstthings.com/article/2017/10/the-splendor-of-truth-in-2017.

8   Nancy Pearcey, *Love Thy Body: Answering Hard Questions about Life and Sexuality* (Grand Rapids: Baker Books, 2018), https://books. google.com/books?id=OGAyDwAAQBAJ&pg=PT21&lpg=PT21&dq=Each+ part+of+an+organ+is+exquisitely+adapted+to+the+others,+and+all+interact+ in+a+coordinated,+goal-directed+fashion+to+achieve+the+purpose+ of+the+whole&source=bl&ots=uk21vxhCWB&sig=Btr_b8aubRuGjgN3I AhC558Ty3c&hl=en&sa=X&ved=0ahUKEwjgipSGhaTaAhXxY98KHd3n BLkQ6AEIKTAA#v=onepage&q=Each%20part%20of%20an%20organ%20 is%20exquisitely%20adapted%20to%20the%20others%2C%20and%20all%20 interact%20in%20a%20coordinated%2C%20goal-directed%20fashion%20 to%20achieve%20the%20purpose%20of%20the%20whole&f=false.

9   Pearcey, *Love Thy Body*, 22.

10   See, for example, "Famous Scientists Who Believed in God," http://www. godandscience.org/apologetics/sciencefaith.html.

11   *NAS Exhaustive Concordance,* 571. *emeth,* http://biblehub.com/hebrew/571.htm.

12   Quoted in Stephen Hand, "The Great Liberal Death Wish Malcom Muggeridge," In the Alternative blog, June 11, 2017, https://stephenhand2012.wordpress.com/2017/06/11/the-great-liberal-death-wish-malcolm-muggeridge/.

13   Pearcey, *Love Thy Body,* 20.

14   The articles and books, both popular and academic, supporting the accuracy and reliability of the Bible are numerous. One resource on the popular side is Robert Velarde, "How Do We Know the Bible Is True?," Focus on the Family, https://www.focusonthefamily.com/faith/the-study-of-god/how-do-we-know-the-bible-is-true/how-do-we-know-bible-is-true. See also the documentary "The God Who Speaks," at www.thegodwhospeaks.org.

15   Gregory Koukl, *The Story of Reality: How the World Began, How It Ends, and Everything Important that Happens in Between* (Grand Rapids: Zondervan Publishing House, 2017), 112.

16   C. S. Lewis, *Mere Christianity* (New York: Harper Collins, 2001), 51–52.

17   https://www.transparency.org/files/content/tool/1997_CPI_EN.pdf; https://www.transparency.org/news/feature/corruption_perceptions_index_2017.

18   Ravi Zacharias, *Zacharias 2 in 1—Deliver Us from Evil & Jesus Among Other Gods* (Nashville: Thomas Nelson, 2009), 84.

19   Harvard University, "History," https://www.harvard.edu/about-harvard/harvard-glance/history.

20   "Veritas" has not always been the school's public motto. "*Veritas,* which is Latin for 'truth,' was adopted as Harvard's motto in 1643, but did not see the light of day for almost two centuries. Instead, in 1650, the Harvard Corporation chose *In Christi Gloriam,* a Latin phrase meaning 'For the glory of Christ.'
      Veritas eventually was discovered in old college records by Harvard President Josiah Quincy III, and re-emerged in 1836 when it appeared on a banner celebrating the College's 200th anniversary. The word briefly lived on in the Harvard seal from 1843 to 1847, when it was booted off in favor of *Christo et Ecclesiae,* or 'For Christ in the Church.'
      "In time, *Veritas* would become the one word most closely associated with Harvard. But it took an 1880 poem by writer and Professor of Medicine Oliver Wendell Holmes to revive it for good. The poem urged Harvard to 'let thine earliest symbol be thy last.' If ubiquity is any measure, Holmes' poetic wish came true. *Veritas* was Harvard's oldest idea for a motto and, after centuries of neglect, is here to stay." See "Seal of Approval," https://news.harvard.edu/gazette/story/2015/05/seal-of-approval/.

21   Thomas Jefferson to William Roscoe, quoted in "Follow Truth," Thomas Jefferson Foundation, December 27, 1820, https://www.monticello.org/site/jefferson/follow-truth-quotation.

22   Sinan Aral, "How Lies Spread Online," *The New York Times,* March 8, 2018, https://www.nytimes.com/2018/03/08/opinion/sunday/truth-lies-spread-online.html.

23   See the beginning of this chapter.

24   For more on Mars Hill Audio, go to https://mha-members.org/.

25   Quoted in "The Selfie Craze Case," April 16, 2014, https://diarysheets.wordpress.com/2014/04/16/the-selfie-craze-case/.

26   Allan Bloom, *The Closing of the American Mind* (New York: Simon and Schuster, 1987), 25.

27   Card. Joseph Ratzinger, "Pro Eligendo Romano Pontifice," Vatican Basilica, April 18, 2005, http://www.vatican.va/gpII/documents/homily-pro-eligendo-pontifice_20050418_en.html.

28   Quoted in Dominique Mosbergen, "Stephen Hawking Says 'There Is No God,' Confirms He's An Atheist," *Huffington Post,* September 25, 2014, https://www.huffingtonpost.com/2014/09/25/stephen-hawking-atheist_n_5882860.html.

29   William B. Provine, "Darwinism: Science or Naturalistic Philosophy?" in a debate with Phillip E. Johnson, April 30, 1994, quoted in "God Questions—a dialogue," Carl Stecher and Peter S. Williams, bethinking.org, https://www.bethinking.org/does-god-exist/god-questions-a-dialogue/4-problem-of-evil.

30   See, for example, "the fact/value distinction," Rochester Institute of Technology Philosophy Department, https://www.rit.edu/cla/philosophy/quine/fact_value.html.

31   Eric Metaxas and Roberto Rivera, "Enlightenment Now? The Feel-Good Philosophy of Scientism," BreakPoint, April 13, 2018, https://www.breakpoint.org/breakpoint-enlightenment-now/.

32   Quoted in "A letter worth receiving . . .", The Fellowship of St. Barnabas, June 11, 2016, http://www.stbarnabasabq.org/a-letter-worth-receiving/.

33   See Hebrews 11:3 and 1:3a.

34   Jordan Peterson, "Jordan Peterson: Postmodernism: How and why it must be fought," 2017 Manning Centre Conference, February 25, Ottawa, Manitoba, https://www.youtube.com/watch?v=Cf2nqmQIfxc&vl=en.

35   Nancy Pearcey, *Finding Truth: 5 Principles for Unmasking Atheism, Secularism, and Other God Substitutes* (Colorado Springs: David C. Cook, 2015), 82-83.

36   Jeremy Rifkin, *Algen: A New Word—A New World* (New York: Viking, 1983), 244, quoted in D.A. Carson, *Christ and Culture Revisited* (Grand Rapids: Wm. B. Eerdmans Publishing Co., 2008), 89.

37   "Exploring Gender Identity: Can a 5'9, White Guy Be a 6'5, Chinese Woman?," Family Policy Institute of Washington, n.d., https://www.youtube.com/watch?v=xfO1veFs6Ho.

38   John Zmirak, "Planned Parenthood and the Gift of Death," *The Stream,* August 26, 2015, https://stream.org/planned-parenthood-gift-death/.

39   Amy B. Wang, "'Post-truth' named 2016 word of the year by Oxford Dictionaries," *Washington Post,* November 16, 2016, https://www.washingtonpost.com/news/the-fix/wp/2016/11/16/post-truth-named-2016-word-of-the-year-by-oxford-dictionaries/?utm_term=.c3eee5f38a90.

40   Aral, *op. cit.*

41   Richard Pérez-Peña, "Studies Find More Students Cheating, With High Achievers No Exception," *The New York Times,* September 7, 2012, https://www. nytimes.com/2012/09/08/education/studies-show-more-students-cheat-even-high-achievers.html.

42   Pearcey, *Finding Truth*, 120.

43   Peterson, "Jordan Peterson: Postmodernism: How and why it must be fought," *op. cit.*

44   Os Guinness, *Impossible People: Christian Courage and the Struggle for the Soul of Civilization* (Downers Grove: IVP Books, 2016), 201.

45   See, for example, the author's seven-part blog series on narratives, "What's Wrong With a Story?," starting June 27, 2016, http://darrowmillerandfriends. com/2016/06/27/story-destructive-power-of-narrative/.

46   See, for example, Christopher Booker, "Climate change: this is the worst scientific scandal of our generation," *The Telegraph*, November 28, 2009, https:// www.telegraph.co.uk/comment/columnists/christopherbooker/6679082/ Climate-change-this-is-the-worst-scientific-scandal-of-our-generation.html.

47   Matthew Harrington, "Survey: People's Trust Has Declined in Business, Media, Government, and NGOs," *Harvard Business Review*, January 16, 2017, https:// hbr.org/2017/01/survey-peoples-trust-has-declined-in-business-media-government-and-ngos.

48   Quoted in "1984 Philosophical Viewpoints Quotes," https://www.shmoop.com/ study-guides/1984/philosophical-viewpoints-quotes.html.

49   "metanoia," Merriam-Webster online dictionary, https://www.merriam-webster.com/dictionary/metanoia.

50   Lesslie Newbigin, *Truth to Tell: The Gospel as Public Truth* (Osterhaven Lecture), (Grand Rapids: Wm. B. Eerdmans Publishing Co., 1991), quoted in "The Gospel as public truth—it must govern every facet of human life . . . ," The Humanitas Forum on Christianity and Culture, November 11, 2014, http://humanitas. org/?p=3159.

51   Pearcey, *Finding Truth*, 51.

52   Quoted in Amy K. Hall, "Finding Truth: Why Worldviews Commit Suicide," Stand to Reason, https://www.str.org/w/finding-truth-why-worldviews-commit-suicide?p_l_back_url=%2Fsearch%3Fq%3Dfinding%2Btruth%253A%2B why%2Bworldviews%2Bcommit%2Bsuicide.

53   Archbishop Charles Chaput, "The priests we need," October 6, 2016, CatholicPhilly.com, http://catholicphilly.com/2016/10/homilies-speeches/the-priests-we-need/.

54   "A Call to Repentance & Renewal: An Open Letter to Christian pastors, leaders and believers who assist the anti-Christian Progressive political movement in America," American Association of Evangelicals, September 27, 2016, http:// americanevangelicals.com/.

55   Newbigin, *Truth to Tell, op. cit.*

56   Francis Schaeffer, *The Great Evangelical Disaster* (Wheaton: Crossway Books, 1984), 37.

57   Michael Novak, "Truth and Freedom," *First Things*, January 2, 2009, https://www.firstthings.com/web-exclusives/2009/01/truth-and-freedom.

58   J.I. Packer, *"Fundamentalism" and the Word of God* (Grand Rapids: Eerdmans Publishing Co., 1958), 34.

59   Alexander Solzhenitsyn, "Nobel Lecture," The Alexander Solzhenitsyn Center, https://www.solzhenitsyncenter.org/nobel-lecture.

60   "Living in truth," *The Economist*, December 31, 2011, https://www.economist.com/node/21542169.

61   Václav Havel, "The Power of the Powerless," http://www.vaclavhavel.cz/showtrans.php?cat=eseje&val=2_aj_eseje.html&typ=HTML.

62   Aleksandr Solzhenitsyn, 1970 Nobel Prize acceptance speech, quoted in Os Guinness, "Differences Make a Difference," from *Time for Truth: Living Free in a World of Lies, Hype & Spin*, http://www.issuesetcarchive.org/articles/bissar20.htm.

CHAPTER 2

1   Not her real name. Some details in this story have been changed for the sake of privacy.

2   A popular translation. Here is another: "You stir us so that praising you may bring us joy, because you have made us and draw us to yourself, and our heart is unquiet until it rests in you," Maria Boulding, translator, Augustine, *Confessions*, 1.1 (New York: New City Press, 1997), 14.

3   Dallas Willard, *Renovation of the Heart: Putting on the Character of Christ* (Colorado Springs: NavPress, 2012 edition), 144.

4   James K. A. Smith, *Letters to a Young Calvinist: An Invitation to the Reformed Tradition* (Grand Rapids: Brazos Press, 2010), 109.

5   Aleksandr Solzhenitsyn, *The Gulag Archipelago: An Experiment in Literary Investigation* (Volume One) (New York: Basic Books, 1997), 168.

6   Malcolm Muggeridge, *Something Beautiful for God* (New York: Ballantine Books edition, 1971), 15.

7   Rodney Stark, *The Rise of Christianity: How the Obscure, Marginal Jesus Movement Became the Dominant Religious Force in the Western World in a Few Centuries* (San Francisco: HarperSanFrancisco, 1997), 82.

8   Personal interview with the author.

9   See Darrow L. Miller with Stan Guthrie, *Nurturing the Nations: Reclaiming the Dignity of Women in Building Healthy Cultures* (Downers Grove: InterVarsity Press, 2012).

10   Wesley J. Smith, *A Rat Is a Pig Is a Dog Is a Boy: The Human Cost of the Animal Rights Movement* (New York: Encounter Books, 2010).

11 Reuters, quoted in "Zoo in Copenhagen Exhibits New Primates (Fully Clothed)," *The New York Times*, August 29, 1996, https://www.nytimes.com/1996/08/29/world/zoo-in-copenhagen-exhibits-new-primates-fully-clothed.html.

12 Vishal Mangalwadi, *The Book that Made Your World* (Nashville: Thomas Nelson, 2011), 75.

13 Nancy Pearcey, "Liberal Elites Are Killing Martin Luther King, Jr.'s Vision," CNS News, January 17, 2018, https://www.cnsnews.com/commentary/nancy-pearcey/liberal-elites-are-killing-martin-luther-king-jrs-vision.

14 "Martin Luther King, Jr.'s 'I Have a Dream' Speech," http://www.ushistory.org/documents/i-have-a-dream.htm, accessed March 7, 2018.

15 Universal Declaration of Human Rights, http://www.un.org/en/universal-declaration-human-rights/, accessed March 7, 2018.

16 See, for example, Max Stackhouse, "Sources of Basic Human Rights Ideas: A Christian Perspective," Pew Research Center, January 27, 2003, http://www.pewforum.org/2003/01/27/sources-of-basic-human-rights-ideas-a-christian-perspective/, accessed March 9, 2018.

17 Nelson Mandela, "The Mandel[a] Visit; Excerpts From Mandela Speech to Joint Meeting of Congress," *The New York Times*, June 27, 1990, https://www.nytimes.com/1990/06/27/world/the-mandel-visit-excerpts-from-mandela-speech-to-joint-meeting-of-congress.html?searchResultPosition=4, accessed March 7, 2018.

18 Rod Dreher, "Democracy Is Dying; Persecution Is Coming," *The American Conservative*, June 26, 2015, http://www.theamericanconservative.com/dreher/democracy-is-dying-persecution-is-coming/comment-page-5/.

19 Michael J. Sandel, *Democracy's Discontent: America in Search of a Public Philosophy* (Cambridge: Harvard University Press, 1996), 13, 14.

20 Carl R. Trueman, "A Medieval Perspective on Modern Identity Politics," *First Things*, January 2, 2015, https://www.firstthings.com/blogs/firstthoughts/2015/01/modern-identity-politics-a-medieval-perspective.

21 Nancy Pearcey, *Love Thy Body*, 210.

22 BBC The Social, https://www.youtube.com/watch?v=udI-Go8KK2Q.

23 Michael Novak, "Lose the Story, Lose the Culture," *National Review*, July 2, 2016, https://www.nationalreview.com/2016/07/religious-liberty-america-threatened-secularism/.

24 Nancy Pearcey, *Finding Truth* (Colorado Springs: David C. Cook, 2015), 118.

25 Jordan Peterson, "On Claiming Belief in God: Commentary and Discussion with Dennis Prager," *The Jordan B. Peterson Podcast*, July 7, 2019, https://podcasts.apple.com/ca/podcast/on-claiming-belief-in-god-commentary-discussion-with/id1184022695?i=1000443831568

26 Quoted in "Supreme Court's Response to the Question: When Does Life Begin?" United States Conference of Catholic Bishops, http://www.usccb.org/issues-and-action/human-life-and-dignity/abortion/supreme-courts-response-to-the-question-when-does-life-begin.cfm.

27   Quoted in Michael Egnor, "A (New) Argument for Abortion," *Evolution News and Science Today*, May 12, 2017, https://evolutionnews.org/2017/05/a-new-argument-for-abortion/.

28   See Center for Medical Progress, http://www.centerformedicalprogress.org/cmp/investigative-footage/.

29   Mary Elizabeth Williams, "So what if abortion ends life?" *Salon*, January 23, 2013, https://www.salon.com/2013/01/23/so_what_if_abortion_ends_life/.

30   Pearcey, *Love Thy Body*, 18-19.

31   Alexandra DeSanctis, "Little-Known Facts about *Roe v. Wade*," *National Review*, January 23, 2017, https://www.nationalreview.com/2017/01/roe-v-wade-abortion-supreme-court-harry-blackmun-trimesters-federal-law-state-laws/.

32   Eric Metaxas and Roberto Rivera, "Eugenics and Its Victims," BreakPoint, November 17, 2017, https://www.breakpoint.org/breakpoint-eugenics-and-its-victims/.

33   David J. Galton and Clare J. Galton, "Francis Galton: and eugenics today," *Journal of Medical Ethics*, 1998;24:99—105, http://jme.bmj.com/content/medethics/24/2/99.full.pdf.

34   Francis Galton, *Hereditary Genius*, 1869, http://galton.org/books/hereditary-genius/.

35   Alana Varley, "Margaret Sanger: More Eugenic Than Fellow Eugenicists," CareNet, January 16, 2018, https://www.care-net.org/abundant-life-blog/margaret-sanger-unintelligent-people-are-a-drain-on-society-0-0-0-0.

36   Lutz Kaelber, "Eugenics: Compulsory Sterilization in 50 American States," a presentation at the 2012 Social Science History Association, https://www.uvm.edu/~lkaelber/eugenics/.

37   "Forced Sterilizations," Jewish Virtual Library, https://www.jewishvirtuallibrary.org/nazi-persecution-of-the-mentally-and-physically-disabled.

38   Pearcey, *Love Thy Body*, 84.

39   David Satter, "100 Years of Communism—and 100 Million Dead: The Bolshevik plague that began in Russia was the greatest catastrophe in human history," *The Wall Street Journal*, November 6, 2017, https://www.wsj.com/articles/100-years-of-communismand-100-million-dead-1510011810.

40   Eric Metaxas and Anne Morse, "Too Few Women," BreakPoint, May 11, 2018, https://breakpoint.org/breakpoint-too-few-women/

41   Bill McMorris, "Taxpayers Still Funding Planned Parenthood," *Washington Free Beacon*, March 30, 2018, http://freebeacon.com/issues/taxpayers-still-funding-planned-parenthood/.

42   Sally C. Curtin, M.A., Margaret Warner, Ph.D., and Holly Hedegaard, M.D., M.S.P.H., "Increase in Suicide in the United States, 1999–2014," Centers for Disease Control and Prevention, April 2016, https://www.cdc.gov/nchs/products/databriefs/db241.htm.

43   Marc A. Thiessen, "Babies with Down syndrome have a right to life," March 11, 2018, Washington Post Writers Group, http://www.richmond.com/opinion/

their-opinion/guest-columnists/marc-a-thiessen-column-babies-with-down-syndrome-have-a/article_8451dd98-a730-5572-a38f-2f268261bb8b.html.

44   John Gray, *Straw Dogs: Thoughts on Humans and Other Animals* (London: Granta Books, 2002), 151.

45   Colin Fernandez, "Want to save the planet? Don't have children! Study finds bringing new life into the world is the most destructive thing you can do to the environment," *Daily Mail*, July 11, 2017, http://www.dailymail.co.uk/news/article-4687400/Study-Want-save-planet-Don-t-children.html.

46   Bill Chappell, "U.S. Births Dip To 30-Year Low; Fertility Rate Sinks Further Below Replacement Level," National Public Radio, May 17, 2018, https://www.npr.org/sections/thetwo-way/2018/05/17/611898421/u-s-births-falls-to-30-year-low-sending-fertility-rate-to-a-record-low.

47   "Lowest Birth Rates In The World By Country," *World Atlas*, https://www.worldatlas.com/articles/countries-with-the-lowest-birth-rates-in-the-world.html.

48   Lee Silver, *Remaking Eden: Cloning and Beyond in a Brave New World* (New York: Avon Books, 1998).

49   Ray Kurzweil, *The Singularity Is Near: When Humans Transcend Biology* (New York: Viking Penguin, 2005).

50   Mortimer J. Adler, *The Difference of Man and the Difference It Makes* (New York: Fordham University Press, 1967), 264.

51   Muggeridge, 29.

52   Muggeridge, 29.

53   Rodney Stark, "The Rise of Christianity: A Sociologist Reconsiders History," Frontline, https://www.pbs.org/wgbh/pages/frontline/shows/religion/why/starktheology.html.

54   Ryan T. Anderson, "Calling and Witness, Holiness and Truth," *First Things*, July 14, 2013, https://www.firstthings.com/web-exclusives/2013/07/calling-and-witness-holiness-and-truth.

55   Pearcey, *Love Thy Body*, 64.

56   Pearcey, *Love Thy Body*, 93-94.

57   Nancy Flanders, "Pro-life clinics outnumber abortion facilities 2,700 to 739," Live Action, December 1, 2017, https://www.liveaction.org/news/pro-life-pregnancy-centers-outnumber-abortion-clinics-across-country/.

58   Anderson, *op. cit.*

59   Anderson, "*op. cit.*

60   Pearcey, *Love Thy Body*, 260.

CHAPTER 3

1   Michael Hobbes, "Together Alone: The Epidemic of Gay Loneliness," *Huffington Post*, March 2, 2017, https://highline.huffingtonpost.com/articles/en/gay-loneliness/.

2   Pearcey, *Love Thy Body*, 35.

3   Pearcey, *Love Thy Body*, 35.

4   Todd Wilson, *Mere Sexuality: Rediscovering the Christian Vision of Sexuality* (Grand Rapids: Zondervan, 2017), 69.

5   Glenn Stanton, comments provided to the author, June 20, 2018.

6   Simon Chan, "Why We Call God 'Father,'" *Christianity Today*, August 13, 2013, https://www.christianitytoday.com/ct/2013/july-august/why-we-call-god-father.html.

7   Stanton, *op. cit.*

8   Stanton, *op. cit.*

9   See Deuteronomy 22:5: "A woman shall not wear a man's garment, nor shall a man put on a woman's cloak, for whoever does these things is an abomination to the Lord your God."

10   Wilson, 35.

11   Wilson, 70-71.

12   Elisabeth Elliot, *The Mark of a Man: Following Christ's Example of Masculinity* (Grand Rapids: Fleming H. Revell, 1981), 26.

13   Paula Johnson "His and hers . . . healthcare," TED Talk, December 2013, https://www.ted.com/talks/paula_johnson_his_and_hers_healthcare/transcript?language=en.

14   Bruce Goldman, "Two minds: The cognitive differences between men and women," *Stanford Medicine*, Spring 2017, https://stanmed.stanford.edu/2017spring/how-mens-and-womens-brains-are-different.html.

15   Wilson, 74.

16   Wilson, 73.

17   Pearcey, *Love Thy Body*, 29.

18   Wilson, 101–102.

19   Ryan Anderson, "Why Marriage Matters Most," The Heritage Foundation, July 10, 2013, https://www.heritage.org/marriage-and-family/commentary/why-marriage-matters-most.

20   Kevin DeYoung, *What Does the Bible Really Teach about Homosexuality?* (Wheaton: Crossway, 2015), 74.

21   Wilson, 100-101.

22   Timothy Keller with Kathy Keller, *The Meaning of Marriage: Facing the Complexities of Commitment with the Wisdom of God* (New York: Penguin Books, 2013), 257.

23   Pearcey, *Love Thy Body*, 217.

24   Wilson, 30.

25   G. K. Chesterton, *G. K.'s Weekly*, January 29, 1928.

26   John Stonestreet, "Redefining Marriage Redefines Parenthood," BreakPoint, April 15, 2015, http://www.breakpoint.org/2015/04/redefining-marriage-redefines-parenthood-2/.

27   Pearcey, *Love Thy Body*, 188.

28   Dennis Prager, "Judaism's Sexual Revolution: Why Judaism (and then Christianity) Rejected Homosexuality," OrthopraxyToday.org, http://www.orthodoxytoday.org/articles2/PragerHomosexuality.php, reprinted from *Crisis* 11, no. 8 (September 1993).

29   Pearcey, *Love Thy Body*, 189.

30   Rod Dreher, "Sex After Christianity: Gay marriage is not just a social revolution but a cosmological one," *The American Conservative*, April 11, 2013, http://www.theamericanconservative.com/articles/sex-after-christianity/.

31   Alex Morris, "Tales from the Millennials' Sexual Revolution," *Rolling Stone*, March 31, 2014, https://www.rollingstone.com/feature/millennial-sexual-revolution-relationships-marriage.

32   Pearcey, *Love Thy Body*, 28.

33   Wilson, 49.

34   Stanton (*op. cit.*) writes, "Masturbation, like pornography, is incomplete because it doesn't involve the communion of two self-giving people, one to another. It's sex for one and isn't God's ideal for us; it's merely taking from one's self and doesn't mirror the nature of the Trinity. No member of the Trinity turns in on Himself in any manner. Their relational expression is always to the others. Remember, God said it was not good for man (or woman) to be alone, and in sexualized form, that's what masturbation is."

35   See, for example, Wayne Jackson, "Sexual Promiscuity — A National Plague," *Christian Courier*, https://christiancourier.com/articles/sexual-promiscuity-a-national-plague.

36   Pearcey, *Love Thy Body*, 119.

37   Pearcey, *Love Thy Body*, 118-119.

38   Laura Sessions Stepp, *Unhooked: How Young Women Pursue Sex, Delay Love and Lose at Both*, (New York: Riverhead Books, 2008) 243.

39   Anne Malone, "What the Hook-up Culture Has Done to Women," *Crisis Magazine*, June 14, 2016, https://www.crisismagazine.com/2016/hook-culture-done-women.

40   Stanton, *op. cit.*

41   "Porn Sites Get More Visitors Each Month Than Netflix, Amazon And Twitter Combined," *The Huffington Post*, December 6, 2017, https://www.huffingtonpost.com/2013/05/03/internet-porn-stats_n_3187682.html.

42   Chris Morris, "Porn business optimistic despite piracy, condom battles," CNBC, January 20, 2015, https://www.cnbc.com/2015/01/14/porn-business-optimistic-despite-piracy-condom-battles.html.

43   Carolyn C. Ross, "Overexposed and Under-Prepared: The Effects of Early Exposure to Sexual Content," *Psychology Today*, August 13, 2012, https://www.psychologytoday.com/us/blog/real-healing/201208/overexposed-and-under-prepared-the-effects-of-early-exposure-to-sexual.

44   Belinda Luscombe, "Porn and the Threat to Virility," *TIME*, May 31, 2016, http://time.com/4277510/porn-and-the-threat-to-virility/.

45   Jennifer Fulwiler, "Why My Support for Abortion Was Based on Love . . . and Lies," *National Catholic Register*, January 23, 2013, http://www.ncregister.com/blog/jennifer-fulwiler/the-enemy-of-sex.

46   Pearcey, *Love Thy Body*, 195-196.

47   U.S. LGBT Identification Steady at 7.2%, The Gallup Organization, https://news.gallup.com/poll/470708/lgbt-identification-steady.aspx

48   Pearcey, *Love Thy Body*, 202.

49   See, for example, https://www.genderbread.org/.

50   Pearcey, *Love Thy Body*, 212.

51   Christopher F. Rufo, "Radical Gender Lessons for Young Children: Evanston–Skokie's school district adopts a curriculum that teaches pre-K through third-grade students to "break the binary" of gender," *The City Journal*, April 21, 2022, https://www.city-journal.org/article/radical-gender-lessons-for-young-children

52   Eugene Volokh, "You can be fined for not calling people 'ze' or 'hir,' if that's the pronoun they demand that you use," *The Washington Post*, May 17, 2016, https://www.washingtonpost.com/search/?query=you+can+be+fined.

53   "In California, parents may lose custody of the child if they resist gender transition," CNBCTV18.com
Sept   9,   2023,   https://www.cnbctv18.com/world/california-passes-bill-incorporating-gender-affirmation-in-child-custody-cases-explained-17758741.htm.

54   Melissa Moschella, "The Rights of Children: Biology Matters," *Public Discourse*, February 20, 2014, http://www.thepublicdiscourse.com/2014/02/11620/.

55   Mary Eberstadt, The Zealous Faith of Secularism, *First Things*, January 2018, https://www.firstthings.com/article/2018/01/the-zealous-faith-of-secularism.

56   Andy Kroll, "Meet the Megadonor Behind the LGBTQ Rights Movement," *Rolling Stone*, June 23, 2017, https://www.rollingstone.com/politics/features/meet-tim-gill-megadonor-behind-lgbtq-rights-movement-wins-w489213.

57   Associated Press, "Mozilla CEO resignation raises free-speech issues," *USA Today*, April 4, 2014, https://www.usatoday.com/story/news/nation/2014/04/04/mozilla-ceo-resignation-free-speech/7328759/.

58   CBS News, "Apple CEO rips 'religious freedom' legislation," March 30, 2015, https://www.cbsnews.com/news/apple-ceo-tim-cook-says-indiana-religious-freedom-law-is-dangerous/.

59   Wilson, 38.

60   Morgan Lee, "Here's How 770 Pastors Describe Their Struggle with Porn," *Christianity Today*, January 26, 2016, https://www.christianitytoday.com/2016/01/how-pastors-struggle-porn-phenomenon-josh-mcdowell-barna/.

61   Rosaria Butterfield, "Love Your Neighbor Enough to Speak Truth: A Response to Jen Hatmaker," The Gospel Coalition, October 31, 2016, https://www.thegospelcoalition.org/article/love-your-neighbor-enough-to-speak-truth/.

62   John Stonestreet, "Same-Sex Marriage and the Evangelical Church: A Symposium," BreakPoint, January 22, 2015, http://www.breakpoint. org/2015/01/sex-marriage-evangelical-church-symposium/.

63   *Masterpiece Cakeshop v. Colorado Civil Rights Commission*, Wikipedia, https:// en.wikipedia.org/wiki/Masterpiece_Cakeshop_v._Colorado_Civil_Rights_ Commission.

64   April 28, 2018. The event was hosted by a group called "Phoenix Catholic" and it was held at St. Mary's High School in Phoenix. Here's the link to a video: https://www.youtube.com/watch?v=5b9f0X_HBDA

65   Pearcey, *Love Thy Body*, 81.

CHAPTER 4

1   This definition is based on one provided by Ryan Anderson in "Why Marriage Matters Most," The Heritage Foundation, July 10, 2013, https://www.heritage. org/marriage-and-family/commentary/why-marriage-matters-most.

2   Mary Eberstadt, "The Zealous Faith of Secularism," *First Things*, January 2018, https://www.firstthings.com/article/2018/01/the-zealous-faith-of-secularism.

3   Karl Stern, *The Flight from Woman* (New York: Farrar, Straus and Giroux, The Noonday Press: 1965), 274.

4   Nathanael Blake, "3 Years of Experience Have Only Proved Obergefell was a Mistake," *The Federalist*, June 28, 2018, http://thefederalist.com/2018/06/28/3-years-experience-proved-obergefell-big-mistake/.

5   J.I. Packer, *Concise Theology: A Guide to Historic Christian Beliefs* (Wheaton: Tyndale House / Foundation for Reformation, 1993), 233.

6   Chris and Lisa Cree, "Contracts vs. Covenants—Why the Difference Matters," https://newcreeations.org/contracts-vs-covenants-why-the-difference-matters/.

7   John Piper, *This Momentary Marriage: A Parable of Permanence* (Wheaton: Crossway Books, 2009), 25.

8   Piper, *This Momentary Marriage*, 17.

9   Ryan T. Anderson, *Truth Overruled: The Future of Marriage and Religious Freedom* (Washington, D.C.: Regnery Publishing, 2015), 25.

10   David Blankenhorn, "Protecting marriage to protect children," *Los Angeles Times*, September 19, 2008, http://www.latimes.com/la-oe-blankenhorn19-2008sep19-story.html#.

11   See, for example, Larry Gelten, "'Cheap sex' is making men give up on marriage," *New York Post*, September 2, 2017, https://nypost.com/2017/09/02/cheap-sex-is-making-men-give-up-on-marriage/.

12   *Marriage and the Public Good: Ten Principles*, The Witherspoon Institute, Princeton, N.J., August 2008, http://winst.org/wp-content/uploads/WI_ Marriage_and_the_Public_Good.pdf.

13   W. Bradford Wilcox and Nicholas H. Wolfinger, "Hey Guys, Put a Ring on It," *National Review*, February 9, 2017, https://www.nationalreview.com/2017/02/ marriage-benefits-men-financial-health-sex-divorce-caveat/.

14   William A. Galston, "The Poverty Cure: Get Married," *The Wall Street Journal*, October 27, 2015, https://www.wsj.com/articles/the-poverty-cure-get-married-1445986205?mg=id-wsj.

15   Anderson, *Truth Overruled*, 26.

16   Ryan T. Anderson, "Redefine Marriage, Make Government Bigger," The Heritage Foundation, April 16, 2013, https://www.heritage.org/marriage-and-family/commentary/redefine-marriage-make-government-bigger.

17   Robert Rector, "Marriage: America's Greatest Weapon Against Child Poverty," The Heritage Foundation, September 12, 2012, https://www.heritage.org/marriage-and-family/commentary/redefine-marriage-make-government-bigger.

18   W. Bradford Wilcox, "Reconcilable Differences: What Social Sciences Show about the Complementarity of the Sexes in Parenting," *Touchstone*, November 2005, 32, 36.

19   *Manhattan Declaration: A Call of Christian Conscience*, November 20, 2009, http://www.manhattandeclaration.org/.

20   Blake, "3 Years of Experience," *op cit*.

21   "How Many Abortions per Year in the World 2024," World Population Review, https://worldpopulationreview.com/economics/how-many-abortions-per-year-in-the-world.

22   "Premarital Sex Is Nearly Universal Among Americans, And Has Been For Decades," Guttmacher Institute, December 19, 2006, https://www.guttmacher.org/news-release/2006/premarital-sex-nearly-universal-among-americans-and-has-been-decades.

23   Katherine Kersten, "The risks of cohabitation," Center of the American Experiment, April 4, 2011, https://www.americanexperiment.org/article/the-risks-of-cohabitation/.

24   Bella DePaulo, "What Is the Divorce Rate, Really?," *Psychology Today*, February 2, 2017, https://www.psychologytoday.com/us/blog/living-single/201702/what-is-the-divorce-rate-really.

25   Anderson, *Truth Overruled*, 48.

26   Riki Wilchins, "We'll Win the Bathroom Battle When the Binary Burns," *The Advocate*, April 29, 2016, https://www.advocate.com/commentary/2016/4/29/well-win-bathroom-battle-when-binary-burns.

27   Ed Whelan, "Justice Alito's Dissent in SSM Case," *National Review*, June 26, 2015, https://www.nationalreview.com/bench-memos/justice-alitos-dissent-ssm-case-ed-whelan/.

28   Anderson, *Truth Overruled*, 41.

29   "Beyond Same-Sex Marriage: A New Strategic Vision for All Our Families & Relationships," August 8, 2006, https://mronline.org/2006/08/08/beyond-same-sex-marriage-a-new-strategic-vision-for-all-our-families-relationships/.

30   Robert P. George, "What Few Deny Gay Marriage Will Do," *First Things*, April 16, 2013, https://www.firstthings.com/blogs/firstthoughts/2013/04/what-few-deny-gay-marriage-will-do

31   Sean McDowell and John Stonestreet, *Same-Sex Marriage: A Thoughtful Approach to God's Design for Marriage* (Grand Rapids: Baker Books, 2014), 15.

32   "Unmarried Childbearing," Centers for Disease Control and Prevention, https://www.cdc.gov/nchs/fastats/unmarried-childbearing.htm.

33   "Births to Unmarried Women," Child Trends, https://www.childtrends.org/indicators/births-to-unmarried-women.

34   Anderson, *Truth Overruled*, 31.

35   Isabel V. Sawhill, "Families at Risk," in *Setting National Priorities: The 2000 Election and Beyond*, ed. Henry J. Aaron and Robert D. Reischauer (Washington: Brookings Institution Press, 1999), 97, 108.

36   Benjamin Scafidi, *The Taxpayer Costs of Divorce and Unwed Childbearing First-Ever Estimates for the Nation and All Fifty States*, Institute for American Values, et al., http://americanvalues.org/catalog/pdfs/COFF.pdf.

37   Aaron Kheriaty, "Dying of Despair," *First Things*, August 2017, https://www.firstthings.com/article/2017/08/dying-of-despair.

38   Anderson, *Truth Overruled*, 52.

39   Peter Epps, "Vital Distinctions," Hang Together Blog, May 4, 2015, http://www.hangtogetherblog.com/2015/05/04/vital-distinctions/.

40   Pascal-Emmanuel Gobry, "America's birth rate is now a national emergency," *The Week*, August 12, 2016, http://theweek.com/articles/642303/americas-birth-rate-now-national-emergency.

41   According to one estimate, raising just one child to the age of 18—excluding any subsequent college education—costs $233,610, See Aimee Picchi, "Raising a child costs $233,610. Are you financially prepared to be a parent?," *USAToday*, February 26, 2018, https://www.usatoday.com/story/money/personalfinance/2018/02/26/raising-child-costs-233-610-you-financially-prepared-parent/357243002/.

42   David Brooks, "The Year of Domesticity," *The New York Times*, January 1, 2006, https://www.nytimes.com/2006/01/01/opinion/the-year-of-domesticity.html.

43   McDowell and Stonestreet, *Same-Sex Marriage*, 101.

44   Ed Stetzer, "Marriage, Divorce, and the Church: What do the stats say, and can marriage be happy?," *Christianity Today*, February 14, 2014, https://www.christianitytoday.com/edstetzer/2014/february/marriage-divorce-and-body-of-christ-what-do-stats-say-and-c.html.

45   Wilson, *Mere Sexuality*, 79.

46   McDowell and Stonestreet, *Same-Sex Marriage,* https://www.familylife.com/articles/topics/marriage/archived-content/miscellaneous/5-things-we-can-do-to-build-up-marriage/.

47   John Stonestreet and Roberto Rivera, "Children Aren't Optional," BreakPoint, July 19, 2018, http://www.breakpoint.org/2018/07/breakpoint-children-arent-optional/?utm_source=Colson+Center+Master+List&utm_campaign=12df4bbff9-EMAIL_CAMPAIGN_BP+Daily_COPY_01&utm_medium=email&utm_term=0_84bd2dc76d-12df4bbff9-6668569.

48   McDowell and Stonestreet, *Same-Sex Marriage*, 131.

49   McDowell and Stonestreet, *Same-Sex Marriage*, 100.

50   George M. Marsden, *Jonathan Edwards: A Life* (New Haven: Yale University Press, 2003), 500-501.

51   Ed Stetzer, "3 Low Cost/High Impact Family Traditions: A guest post by Kimberly Thornbury," The Exchange, November 6, 2014, https://www.christianitytoday.com/edstetzer/2014/november/3-low-costhigh-impact-family-traditions.html.

CHAPTER 5

1   https://www.lexico.com/en/definition/freedom

2   Lily4Congress, https://www.lilytangwilliams.com/.

3   https://blog.acton.org/archives/100574-the-logic-of-the-soul-6-quotes-from-whittaker-chambers-letter-to-my-children.html

4   Amy Green, "The Purging of Liberty," The Foundation for American Christian Education, May 18, 2022, https://face.net/the-purging-of-liberty/.

5   Hunter Baker, "Habermas on Christianity, Europe, and Human Rights," June 3, 2009, Acton Institute, https://blog.acton.org/archives/10604-habermas-on-christianity-europe-and-human-rights.html.

6   See full quote at Provine, W.B., "Darwinism: Science or Naturalistic Philosophy? The Debate at Stanford University," William B. Provine (Cornell University) and Phillip E. Johnson (University of California, Berkeley), videorecording © 1994 Regents of the University of California. See also "Evolution = atheism, no purpose," Dr William B. Provine, Professor of Biological Sciences, Cornell University, Creation.com, https://creation.com/wm-provine-evolution-=-atheism-no-purpose.

7   Hillary Mayell, "India's 'Untouchables' Face Violence, Discrimination," *National Geographic*, June 2, 2003, https://www.nationalgeographic.com/pages/article/indias-untouchables-face-violence-discrimination.

8   Rod Dreher, "The Threats In Tucker's Brain," April 5, 2022, The American Conservative, https://www.theamericanconservative.com/dreher/tucker-carlson-brain-liberalism-postliberalism-christianity/.

9   Quoted in Dennis Prager, "Cahill's Gift," Catholic Education Resource Center, https://www.catholiceducation.org/en/culture/catholic-contributions/cahill-s-gift.html.

10   John Piper, "A Reason to Be Vaccinated: Freedom," October 19, 2021, Desiring God, https://www.desiringgod.org/articles/a-reason-to-be-vaccinated-freedom.

11   "Extract from Thomas Jefferson to Roger C. Weightman," https://tjrs.monticello.org/letter/443.

12   Graham Shearer, "Calvinism and Liberty," *Mere Orthodoxy*, May 11, 2022, https://mereorthodoxy.com/calvinism-and-liberty/.

13   Brad Littlejohn, "Ahmari among the Protestants," American Reformer, https://americanreformer.org/2022/02/ahmari-among-the-protestants/.

14 Cecil B. DeMille, "The Ten Commandments and You," Brigham Young University, May 31, 1957, https://speeches.byu.edu/talks/cecil-b-demille/ten-commandments-and-you/.

15 Robert Barron, "The Law That Sets You Free," *Word on Fire*, March 28, 2023, https://www.wordonfire.org/videos/the-story-for-all-seasons/the-law-that-sets-you-free/.

16 The marriage of political authority and religious authority is also manifest in orthodox Islam. Only biblical Christianity allows for a separation of church and state as institutions. For more on this, read *This Book Changed Everything: The Bible's Amazing Impact on Our World* (Vol. 1) by Vishal Mangalwadi, particularly Chapter 7: Bloodshed for Tolerance.

17 Quoted in Samuel L. Blumenfeld, "The Founding Fathers on Religion and Morality," Chalcedon, December 1, 1997, https://chalcedon.edu/magazine/the-founding-fathers-on-religion-and-morality.

18 Laura Ingalls Wilder, *Little Town on the Prairie* (New York: HarperCollins, 1969), 76..

19 https://www.lexico.com/en/definition/freedom.

20 Quoted in Cornell Law School, Legal Information Institute, https://www.law.cornell.edu/supct/html/91-744.ZO.html.

21 Insert endnote.

22 Christopher Rufo, "My interview with IM-1776 on political activism in the digital age," https://christopherrufo.com/winning/.

23 Rufo, "My interview."

24 Paul Kingsnorth, "The Cross and the Machine," *First Things*, June 2021, https://www.firstthings.com/article/2021/06/the-cross-and-the-machine

25 "Jordan Peterson, Vishal Mangalwadi, and the Power of the Bible to Transform Culture," *Ideas Have Consequences*, Disciple Nations Alliance podcast, https://podcasts.apple.com/us/podcast/jordan-peterson-vishal-mangalwadi-and-the-power-of/id1601740314?i=1000567330760.

26 Mark T. Mitchell, "Plutocratic Socialism and War on the Middle Class," The American Conservative, September 9, 2022, https://www.theamericanconservative.com/plutocratic-socialism-and-war-on-the-middle-class/.

27 Mitchell, *op. cit.*

28 Rod Dreher, "The Threats in Tucker's Brain," April 5, 2022, *The American Conservative*, https://www.theamericanconservative.com/dreher/tucker-carlson-brain-liberalism-postliberalism-christianity/.

29 Stiles J. Watson, Chalcedon Foundation, "Biblical Self-Government," September 18, 2007, https://chalcedon.edu/resources/articles/biblical-self-government.

30 Ronald Reagan, Freedom Speech, https://www.reagan.com/ronald-reagan-freedom-speech.

31 Katy Faust, "I'm Not A Powerful Person, But I Still Plan To Help Save America," The Federalist, February 5, 2021, https://thefederalist.com/2021/02/05/im-not-a-powerful-person-but-i-still-plan-to-help-save-america/.

32 Faust, *op. cit.*

33   "Martin Niemoller: 'First They Came For . . . ,'" Holocaust Encyclopedia, https:// encyclopedia.ushmm.org/content/en/article/martin-niemoeller-first-they-came-for-the-socialists.

34   https://www.thesocialdilemma.com/.

35   Faust, *op. cit.*

CHAPTER 6

1   This historically Protestant conviction differs from Roman Catholicism which places church officials in positions of sole authority to interpret the Bible. The Roman Catholic hierarchy of authority moves from the Bible to church officials, and then to the laity. The Reformers rejected this. Their hierarchy of authority moved from the Bible to all Christians. This is why they worked to put the Bible directly into the hands of everyday people, by translating the Scriptures into common languages, enabling everyone to access directly the instructions and commands of God, through His Word, in an unmediated way.

2   This is an online publication taken from the book J.I. Packer, *Concise Theology: A Guide to Historic Christian Belief,* Carol Stream, IL: Tyndale House Publishers, 2001, https://www.monergism.com/thethreshold/sdg/Trinity.html

3   This quote is taken from the title of Francis Schaeffer's book *No Little People,* Wheaton, IL: Crossway, 1st Edition, 2003.

4   From the screenplay of the Peter Jackson 2001 film adaptation of J.R.R. Tolkien's novel *The Lord of the Rings: The Fellowship of the Ring.* The quote was taken from this webpage: https://www.quotes.net/mquote/56488.

5   I'm indebted to Everett Piper, former president of Oklahoma Wesleyan University for these insights.

6   An excellent summary of *critical theory* is available from *The Stanford Encyclopedia of Philosophy*, https://plato.stanford.edu/entries/critical-theory/.

7   Gloria Steinem, *Revolution from Within: A Book of Self-Esteem* (2012), 259. https://libquotes.com/gloria-steinem/quote/lbg2a6f .

8   Jory Micah, "The Rise of Evangelical Feminism," *Relevant*, March 29, 2016, https://relevantmagazine.com/faith/rise-evangelical-feminism/.

CHAPTER 7

1   This chapter was developed into its own book: Scott D. Allen, *Why Social Justice Is Not Biblical Justice: An Urgent Appeal to Fellow Christians in a Time of Social Crisis* (Grand Rapids: Credo House Publishing, 2020).

2   Matthew Bunson, "The State of the Union: 'Let Us Build a Culture That Cherishes Innocent Life," *National Catholic Register*, February 6, 2019, http://www.ncregister.com/blog/mbunson/the-state-of-the-union-let-us-build-a-culture-that-cherishes-innocent-life.

3   ABC News Politics Twitter feed, February 5, 2019, https://twitter.com/ABCPolitics/status/1092997836252209157.

4   "Reproductive Justice," SisterSong, https://www.sistersong.net/reproductive-justice.

5   Allyson Hunter, "Study Shows the Leading Cause of Death Is Abortion," Texas Right to Life, August 3, 2018, https://www.texasrighttolife.com/study-shows-the-leading-cause-of-death-is-abortion/.

6   Jason L. Riley, "Let's Talk about the Black Abortion Rate," *The Wall Street Journal*, July 10, 2018, https://www.wsj.com/articles/lets-talk-about-the-black-abortion-rate-1531263697.

7   Ryan Scott Bomberger, "The Democrat Party: Not Enough African-Americans Aborted," The Radiance Foundation, February 1, 2019, http://www.theradiancefoundation.org/blackhistorymonth/.

8   http://webstersdictionary1828.com/.

9   Webster's 1828 Dictionary: "Justice: The virtue which consists in giving to everyone what is his due; practical conformity to the laws and to principles of rectitude in the dealings of men with each other; honesty; integrity in commerce or mutual intercourse. Justice is distributive or commutative. Distributive justice belongs to magistrates or rulers, and consists in distributing to every man that right or equity which the laws and the principles of equity require; or in deciding controversies according to the laws and to principles of equity. Commutative justice consists in fair dealing in trade and mutual intercourse between man and man."

10   Gregory Koukl, *The Story of Reality* (Grand Rapids: Zondervan Publishing House, 2017), 76.

11   As discussed in R. C. Sproul's "Which Laws Apply?" Ligonier Ministries, https://www.ligonier.org/learn/articles/which-laws-apply/.

12   Ken Wytsma, *Pursuing Justice* (Nashville: Thomas Nelson, 2013), 89.

13   "Natural Law," New Advent, http://www.newadvent.org/cathen/09076a.htm.

14   As quoted in Wytsma, 95.

15   Kevin DeYoung, "Is Social Justice a Gospel Issue?" The Gospel Coalition, September 11, 2018, https://www.thegospelcoalition.org/blogs/kevin-deyoung/social-justice-gospel-issue/.

16   Tim Keller, "What Is Biblical Justice?" *Relevant,* August 23, 2012, https://relevantmagazine.com/god/practical-faith/what-biblical-justice.

17   http://www.ushistory.org/declaration/document/.

18   See, for example, Deuteronomy 6:4–5; Mark 12:30–31.

19   Koukl, 97.

20   Paraphrased from Koukl, 154.

21   https://www.transparency.org/research/cpi/overview.

22   For more information on this topic, see "The Elements of Due Process," Legal Information Institute, https://www.law.cornell.edu/constitution-conan/amendment-14/section-1/the-elements-of-due-process.

23   Noah Rothman quoted in Graham Hillard, "The Social-Justice Movement's Unjust Crusade," *National Review,* March 25, 2019, https://www.nationalreview.com/magazine/2019/03/25/the-social-justice-movements-unjust-crusade/.

24   See Paul Austin Murphy, "Antonio Gramsci: Take Over the Institutions!" *American Thinker,* April 26, 2014, https://www.americanthinker.com/articles/2014/04/antonio_gramsci_take_over_the_institutions.html.

25   Quoted in Al Mohler, "Why Religion, If Not Based in Truth, Is Grounded in Nothing More Than Moral Aspirations," *The Briefing,* December 19, 2018, https://albertmohler.com/2018/12/19/briefing-12-19-18/.

26   Justin Taylor, "Aleksandr Solzhenitsyn: 'Bless You, Prison!'" The Gospel Coalition, October 14, 2011, https://www.thegospelcoalition.org/blogs/justin-taylor/aleksandr-solzhenitsyn-bless-you-prison/.

27   Timothy B. Lee, "Google Fired James Damore for a Controversial Gender Memo—Now He's Suing," *Ars Technica,* January 9, 2018, https://arstechnica.com/tech-policy/2018/01/lawsuit-goes-after-alleged-anti-conservative-bias-at-google/.

28   John Stonestreet, "Good Families Are Unfair?" *BreakPoint,* The Colson Center for Christian Worldview, May 20, 2015, https://www.christianheadlines.com/columnists/breakpoint/good-families-are-unfair.html.

29   Stonestreet, "Good Families Are Unfair?"

30   Rebecca Klar, "Pressley: Democrats Don't Need 'Any More Black Faces That Don't Want to Be a Black Voice,'" *The Hill,* July 14, 2019, https://thehill.com/homenews/house/453007-pressley-democrats-need-any-more-black-voices-that-dont-want-to-be-a-black.

31   Wilson, "I Was the Mob Until the Mob Came for Me," *Quillette,* July 14, 2018, https://quillette.com/2018/07/14/i-was-the-mob-until-the-mob-came-for-me/.

32   As quoted in an interview by Tim Stafford in "Mere Mission," *Christianity Today,* January 5, 2007, https://www.christianitytoday.com/ct/2007/january/22.38.html.

33   See John R.W. Stott, *Issues Facing Christians Today* (Basingstoke: Marshalls, 1984).

34   John Stonestreet and David Carlson, "'Emanuel': The Untold Story of the Charleston Shooting," *BreakPoint,* June 12, 2019, http://www.breakpoint.org/breakpoint-emanuel/.

35   Nancy Pearcey, *Total Truth: Liberating Christianity from Its Cultural Captivity* (Wheaton, Crossway, 2008), 58.

CHAPTER 8

1   "BreakPoint: The Dogma of Senators Feinstein and Franken—No Place for Faith in Public Life," September 13, 2017, https://www.patheos.com/blogs/e2medianetwork/2017/09/breakpoint-dogma-senators-feinstein-franken-no-place-faith-public-life-2/.

2   Eric Metaxas, *Letter To The American Church,* 2022, Salem Books, 69-70.

3   "10 Key Bible Verses on Faith," Crossway, March 26, 2020, https://www.crossway.org/articles/10-key-bible-verses-on-faith/

4   "10 Key Bible Verses on Faith," *op. cit.*

5   To get started, see John Piper, "Nine Ways to Know That the Gospel of Christ Is True," Desiring God, November 23, 1999, https://www.desiringgod.org/articles/nine-ways-to-know-that-the-gospel-of-christ-is-true.

6   Jeffrey M. Jones, "Confidence in U.S. Institutions Down; Average at New Low," Gallup, July 5, 2022, https://news.gallup.com/poll/394283/confidence-institutions-down-average-new-low.aspx.

7   See Clint Woods, "The Collision of Faith and Sport," Lipscomb University, November 4, 2023, https://lipscombsports.com/news/2023/11/5/spiritual-formation-the-collision-of-faith-and-sport

8   Bertrand Russell, "Will Religious Faith Cure Our Troubles?" *Human Society in Ethics and Politics.* Archived from the original on 2020-11-12. Retrieved 16 August 2009.

9   See Stan Guthrie, "Telling the Truth in a Post-Truth Culture," BreakPoint, April 5, 2018, https://breakpoint.org/telling-the-truth-in-a-post-truth-culture/.

10   Richard Dawkins, "The Blind Watchmaker: Why the Evidence Reveals a Universe Without Design," 1987, http://hyperphysics.phy-astr.gsu.edu/Nave-html/Faithpathh/dawkins.html.

11   Eric Metaxas, "Science Increasingly Makes the Case for God," *The Wall Street Journal,* December 25, 2014, https://www.wsj.com/articles/eric-metaxas-science-increasingly-makes-the-case-for-god-1419544568.

12   Phillip E. Johnson, "The Unraveling of Scientific Materialism," *First Things,* November 1997, https://www.firstthings.com/article/1997/11/the-unraveling-of-scientific-materialism.

13   See https://www.azlyrics.com/lyrics/whitneyhouston/whenyoubelieve.html.

14   Here are some excellent mostly contemporary Christian apologetics resources: https://godwords.org/my-list-of-apologetics-ministries/.

CHAPTER 9

1   Os Guinness, *The Call: Finding and Fulfilling the Central Purpose of Your Life* (Word Publishing, 1988), 194-5.

2   Elizabeth Lev, *How Catholic Art Saved the Faith: The Triumph of Beauty and Truth in Counter Reformation,* Art - 2019.

3   Quoted in K.C. Cole, *Sympathetic Vibrations: Reflections on Physics as a Way of Life* (New York: William Morrow & Co., 1985).

4   I am indebted to Darrow Miller for this and many other insights about beauty in this chapter, which are based on his outstanding book (with Stan Guthrie), *A Call for Balladeers: Pursuing Art and Beauty for the Discipling of Nations* (Act International Publishing, 2022), 107-108. Used with permission.

5   J. R. R. Tolkien, *On Fairy-Stories*, eds. Verlyn Flieger and Douglas A. Anderson (London: HarperCollins, 2014), 47-55.

6   M. Thomas Seaman, *Becoming True Worshipers: Experience More of God's Presence Through Deeper Worship* (Lulu Publishing, 2018), 106.

7   Some describe our modern and postmodern worldview as neo-Gnostic. According to Merriam-Webster, ancient gnosticism was "the thought and practice especially of various cults of late pre-Christian and early Christian centuries distinguished by the conviction that matter is evil and that emancipation comes through gnosis" (https://www.merriam-webster.com/dictionary/gnosticism).

8   This quotation of Urs von Balthaser is taken from a YouTube video by Robert Barron titled "Bishop Barron on Evangelizing Through Beauty," https://www.youtube.com/watch?v=bBMOwZFpZX0

9   Thomas Dubay, Goodreads, https://www.goodreads.com/quotes/6445316-we-human-beings-are-moved-by-music-as-no-other.

10   Thomas Dubay, *The Evidential Power of Beauty*, Ignatius Press, September 3, 2009, Kindle, 163.

11   Jerry Root and Stan Guthrie, *The Sacrament of Evangelism* (Chicago: Moody Publishers, 2011), 194-195.

12   Richard M. Reinsch, "Two faiths: The witness of Whittaker Chambers," https://www.acton.org/two-faiths-witness-whittaker-chambers

13   David Taylor, "A Holy Longing: Beauty is the hard-to-define essence that draws people to the gospel," *Christianity Today*, October 2008, http://www.christianitytoday.com/ct/2008/october/17.39.html.

14   J. R. R. Tolkien, *Tree and Leaf*, (London: Unwin Books, 1964), 61–62

15   J. R. R. Tolkien, *Tree and Leaf*, 61–62.

16   James Clear, "Best-Selling Books of All-Time," https://jamesclear.com/best-books/best-selling.

17   C. S. Lewis, quoted by Chuck Colson and Nancy Pearcey in *How Now Shall We Live?* (Wheaton, IL: Tyndale House Publishers, Inc., 1999), 449

18   R. C. Sproul, "The Calling to Excellence," *Tabletalk*, July 2023, https://tabletalkmagazine.com/posts/the-calling-to-excellence-2021–01/,

19   Robert Florzak, "Why Is Modern Art So Bad?" PragerU, September 1, 2014, https://www.prageru.com/video/why-is-modern-art-so-bad

20   Robert Florzak, "Why Is Modern Art So Bad?"

21   https://www.goodreads.com/quotes/1194450-beauty-is-no-quality-in-things-themselves-it-exists-merely

22   Florczak, "Why Is Modern Art So Bad?"

23   This quote is taken from the EDEN Gallery website. See this page: https://www.eden-gallery.com/news/postmodern-art-definition#:~:text=Using%20these%20new%20forms%2C%20postmodernist,challenged%20what%20came%20before%20it.

24   Florczak, "Why Is Modern Art So Bad?"

25   *A Call for Balladeers*, 28-29.

26   Cynthia Pearl Maus, Christ and the Fine Arts: An Anthology of Pictures, Poetry, Music, and Stories Centering in the Life of Christ (New York and London: Harper & Brothers Publishers, 1938).

27   This quote is from Darrow Miller, *A Call for Balladeers: Pursuing Art and Beauty for the Discipling of Nations* (Edmonton, WA: YWAM Publishing) 2022, p. 157.

28   This quote is from Darrow Miller, *A Call for Balladeers: Pursuing Art and Beauty for the Discipling of Nations* (Edmonton, WA: YWAM Publishing) 2022, p. 157.

29   Quoted in By Bradley J. Birzer, "Remembering Michael Novak's Democratic Capitalism," The Imaginative Conservative, September 27, 2021, https://theimaginativeconservative.org/2021/09/remembering-michael-novak-spirit-democratic-capitalism-bradley-birzer.html.

30   Tom Hennigan, *Caring About Creation for the Right Reasons*, Answers in Genesis, https://answersingenesis.org/environmental-science/stewardship/caring-about-creation-right-reasons/.

31   See, for example, this clip of Jane Goodall speaking at the World Economic Forum in 2020: https://twitter.com/wideawake_media/status/1690305655532302336?s=20.

32   Landa Cope, "Calling Christian Artists to Reach a World Desperate for Beauty," Darrow Miller and Friends, November 7, 2011, http://darrowmillerandfriends.com/2011/11/07/calling-christian-artists-to-reach-a-world-desperate-for-beauty/ (excerpted from The World is Desperate for Beauty).

33   Bishop Robert Barron from this video: https://youtu.be/bBMOwZFpZX0?si=JHj4Q266W_zdan7y

34   Aleksandr Solzhenitsyn, "Nobel Lecture," The Aleksandr Solzhenitsyn Center, https://www.solzhenitsyncenter.org/nobel-lecture.

CHAPTER 10

1   For a full discussion of this topic, see Rodney Stark, *The Rise of Christianity: How the Obscure, Marginal Jesus Movement Became the Dominant Religious Force in the Western World in a Few Centuries* (HarperSanFrancisco, 1997).

2   Wayne Grudem, *Systematic Theology: An Introduction to Biblical Doctrine*, 2nd Edition (Grand Rapids: Zondervan Academic), 237.

3   Paul Tripp, "24 Ways to Love in 2024," Wednesday Word: A Weekly Devotional with Paul Tripp, February 14, 2024, https://www.paultripp.com/wednesdays-word/posts/24-ways-to-love-in-2024.

4   Alyssa Roat, "What is Agape Love? Bible Meaning and Examples," Christianity.com, April 17, 2024, https://www.christianity.com/wiki/christian-terms/what-does-agape-love-really-mean-in-the-bible.html.

5   "Oxytocin," Cleveland Clinic, https://my.clevelandclinic.org/health/articles/22618-oxytocin.

6   Nancy Pearcey, *Finding Truth: 5 Principles for Unmasking Atheism, Secularism, and Other God Substitutes* (Colorado Springs: David C. Cook, 2015), 164

7   Pearcey, 143.

8   Noah Webster, "Love," 1828 *Dictionary*, https://webstersdictionary1828.com/Dictionary/love.

9   For the original passage and wording, see Nick Nowalk, "Pascal's God-Shaped Hole," *ichthus*, May 2, 2011, https://harvardichthus.org/2011/05/pascal_hole/.

10   *The Brothers Karamazov*, "Chapter 4—A Lady of Little Faith," https://ccel.org/d/dostoevsky/karamozov/htm/book02/chapter04.html.

11   Anthony Esteves, "Love Your Enemy," Calvary Advisor, https://www.calvaryadvisor.org/love-your-enemy.

12   See Allson Flood, "'Post-truth' named word of the year by Oxford Dictionaries," *The Guardian,* November 15, 2015, https://www.theguardian.com/books/2016/nov/15/post-truth-named-word-of-the-year-by-oxford-dictionaries.

13   This quote from Kelly Kullberg can be found in this book review on this webpage: http://pneumareview.com/owen-strachan-the-colson-way-reviewed-by-kelly-monroe-kullberg/#google_vignette

14   Archbishop Charles Chaput, "Archbishop Chaput's Weekly Column: A New Kind Of Sacrament," Archdiocese of Philadelphia, June 10, 2019, https://archphila.org/archbishop-chaputs-weekly-column-a-new-kind-of-sacrament/.

15   "HRC'S #LOVEWINS HASHTAG GOES VIRAL; CELEBRATES MARRIAGE EQUALITY VICTORY," Human Rights Campaign, https://shortyawards.com/8th/hrcs-lovewins-hashtag-goes-viral-celebrates-marriage-equality-victory.

16   Microsoft's embedded dictionary.

17   "Author John Daniel Davidson says paganism in America is on the rise," *The Tucker Carlson Podcast,* April 30, 2024, https://tuckercarlson.com/listen/]

18   John Piper, "Joy Changes Everything: An Invitation to Christian Hedonism," Champion Forest Baptist Church | Houston, November 12, 2017, https://www.desiringgod.org/messages/joy-changes-everything.

19   I recommend two outstanding practical resources developed by my colleague Bob Moffitt, president of the Harvest Foundation, to help churches and individuals put love into practice: Seed Projects and Disciplines of Love. These free resources are available on the Harvest website: https://harvestfoundation.org/curriculum/materials/.

20   "Agape-Love," BibleProject, December 21, 2017, https://bibleproject.com/explore/video/agape-love/

INDEX

S

CONTINUE YOUR JOURNEY

Q 10wordsbook.org

BIBLE STUDY

This study guide is designed for small group Bible study and is built around a ten-part short video series and thoughtful discussion questions.

PODCAST

Join Scott on the *Ideas Have Consequences* podcast as he discusses each of the ten words from the book. The podcast is a great way to introduce people to the book and study guide.

ABOUT THE DISCIPLE NATIONS ALLIANCE

disciplenations.org

Nations, communities, families, and people are broken and crying out for hope, healing, and restoration. God blessed His people, the Church, to be His ambassadors in reconciling and restoring the broken nations of this world.

Our vision at the Disciple Nations Alliance is to see blessed nations profoundly shaped by biblical truth in ways that lead to freedom, justice, and human flourishing.

Learn how you can join the movement at *disciplenations.org*.

Disciple Nations Alliance